Spiritualism in the
American Civil War

ALSO BY R. GREGORY LANDE

*Psychological Consequences
of the American Civil War* (McFarland, 2017)

Spiritualism in the American Civil War

R. Gregory Lande

McFarland & Company, Inc., Publishers
Jefferson, North Carolina

LIBRARY OF CONGRESS CATALOGUING-IN-PUBLICATION DATA

Names: Lande, R. Gregory, author.
Title: Spiritualism in the American Civil War / R. Gregory Lande.
Description: Jefferson, North Carolina : McFarland & Company, Inc., Publishers, 2020. | Includes bibliographical references and index.
Identifiers: LCCN 2020026899 | ISBN 9781476682235 (paperback : acid free paper) ∞
ISBN 9781476640181 (ebook)
Subjects: LCSH: Spiritualism—United States—History—19th century | United States—History—Civil War, 1861-1865—Psychological aspects.
Classification: LCC BF1242.U6 L36 2020 | DDC 133.9073/09034—dc23
LC record available at https://lccn.loc.gov/2020026899

BRITISH LIBRARY CATALOGUING DATA ARE AVAILABLE

ISBN (print) 978-1-4766-8223-5
ISBN (ebook) 978-1-4766-4018-1

© 2020 R. Gregory Lande. All rights reserved

No part of this book may be reproduced or transmitted in any form or by any means, electronic or mechanical, including photocopying or recording, or by any information storage and retrieval system, without permission in writing from the publisher.

Front cover image: "The dying soldiers" circa 1870 engraving (Library of Congress)

Printed in the United States of America

McFarland & Company, Inc., Publishers
  Box 611, Jefferson, North Carolina 28640
  www.mcfarlandpub.com

Historical research supplied the framework
for *Spiritualism in the American Civil War*,
but the foundation was built by two others.
Brenda Lande, my wife, provided support
and encouragement, and cast a critical eye
when proofreading the manuscript.
Our son Galen Lande is a fountainhead
of creativity and technical prowess,
an everlasting source of inspiration
that kept this project moving forward.

Table of Contents

Preface   1

ONE—Antebellum Spiritualism   5

TWO—Science, Religion and Mysticism   26

THREE—Spiritualism During the Civil War   43

FOUR—Doctrine, Dilemmas and Doubts   66

FIVE—Assassination, Resurrection and Exploitation   92

SIX—Spreading the Faith   124

SEVEN—Phantoms of War   136

EIGHT—Pathos, Politics and Presumptions   167

Chapter Notes   193

Bibliography   205

Index   217

Preface

A Civil War soldier's silence was unsettling. For family and friends left behind at home, the letters from loved ones made up one of the few connections spanning the geographic gulf, an emotional bridge tenuously dependent on rickety mail service. When letters failed to inform, the next best source of information was newspapers, describing distant battles and perfunctorily citing casualties. Scanning the list might reveal a soldier's fate: perhaps killed in battle, injured, or taken prisoner. In most cases the reader's interest was unfulfilled, leaving the emotional emptiness intact. In some cases a fellow soldier or a government communiqué brought news of a loved one's fate.

When soldiers died on the battlefield, enmity and the exigencies of war often extracted a terrible toll, not the least of which was stripping the last trappings of humanity from the soldiers as their nameless, shattered corpses littered the area. As word of the carnage reached distant cities the resulting anguish fed further calls for retribution, fanning the flames of hatred that would burn for decades.

The Rebel rout of Union forces at the First Battle of Bull Run provided some of the first fuel that provoked scorching recriminations in Washington, as angry politicians brought forth soldiers denouncing a long list of the enemy's inhumanities. In a harbinger of the atrocities to come, a young soldier testified before members of the U.S. Senate that "the dead laid upon the field unburied for five days." Another witness bitterly recalled how Union soldiers "were buried in many cases naked, with their faces downward; they were left to decay in the open air; their bones were carried off as trophies."[1] Northern newspapers seized on these stories of battlefield atrocities and flagrantly denounced the adversary with lurid depictions of battlefield desecration.

As might be imagined, the Confederates' description of the Manassas battlefield differed in tone, accusing Union officials of minimizing their losses as part of a ham-fisted, shameless cover-up. "The actual loss of the

Preface

"The outrages upon the dead will revive the recollections of the cruelties to which savage tribes subject their prisoners. They were buried in many cases naked, with their faces downward. They were left to decay in the open air, *their bones being carried off as trophies*, sometimes, as the testimony proves, to be used as personal adornments, *and one witness deliberately avers that the head of one of our most gallant officers was cut off by a Secessionist, to be turned into a drinking-cup on the occasion of his marriage.*

" Monstrous as this revelation may appear to be, your Committee have been informed that during the last two weeks the skull of a Union soldier has been exhibited in the office of the Sergeant-at-Arms of the House of Representatives which had been converted to such a purpose, and which had been found on the person of one of the rebel prisoners taken in a recent conflict."—*Report of the Congressional Committee on the Conduct of the War.*

THE REBEL LADY'S BOUDOIR.

LADY (reads)—" *My dearest wife, I hope you have received all the little relics I have sent you from time to time. I am about to add something to your collection which I feel sure will please you—a baby-rattle for our little pet, made out of the ribs of a Yankee drummer-boy.*" &c., &c.

The outrages on the dead (*Frank Leslie's Illustrated Newspaper*, May 17, 1862).

enemy will never be known, it may now only be conjectured. Their abandoned dead, as they were buried by our people where they fell, were not enumerated, but many parts of the field were thick with their corpses, as but few battle-fields have ever been."[2]

The first battles of the Civil War started a trend that continued in the following years, with fallen soldiers hastily buried in shallow graves, an ignominious end that consigned countless corpses to an everlasting anonymity and left families futilely waiting for closure.[3] Filling the void for some was Spiritualism, which supposedly not only brought together lost loved ones, erasing the timeless boundary separating the living from the dead, but also promised a glorious eternal reunion in the afterlife.

Driven by desperation and dysphoria, an untold number of Americans sought the services of psychic mediums both during and after the war. An estimate of the number of spiritualists is at best guesswork, but one observer notably claimed nine million believers in 1861, a figure that supposedly grew to 11 million by 1867.[4] America's population in 1867 was slightly more than 36 million, suggesting that nearly one-third claimed spiritualism as their religion.[5] Less dramatic numbers, but still unrealistic, placed the number of spiritualists at the outset of the Civil War somewhere between one and five million, an accounting that included even the faintest interest, such as attendance at an entertaining lecture or séance.[6]

A more accurate head count during the waning phase of the religion's growth in the late nineteenth century came from spiritualists reporting "334 organizations, with 30 regular church edifices, not including halls, pavilions, and other places owned or occupied by them. There are 45,030 members."[7] While the real numbers will never be known, Spiritualism's influence on society is less debatable, an outsized impact spread by newspapers and magazines of the day chronicling its controversies and curiosities.

Spiritualism in the American Civil War pieces together Spiritualism's disparate historical threads, weaving a dark cloak behind which it hid exploitation and deceit. American Spiritualism's ascendancy and ancestry are, in major part, direct descendants from animal magnetism. The therapeutic use of magnets can be traced to ancient times, but their rediscovery and medical application in the eighteenth century was a watershed event showering seedlings that would later sprout animal magnetism, mesmerism, patent medicines, and Spiritualism: all covered by a dense thicket of controversy limiting the growth of legitimate medical magnetism.

For the author, the journey writing this book began with a simple but sobering assessment. Human emotions transcend time, and the loss of a loved one provoked anguish then no different from now. What differed was the sizeable segment of Civil War-era Americans who questioned death's imponderability and particularly its inevitability by shunning established philosophy, religion, and science for Spiritualism's soothing sophisms.

Clearly, America's Civil War created seismic shifts, an earth-shattering social tumult upending long cherished traditions. As wrenching as it was, by itself this disruption was not enough to shake people's faith. Newspapers and other publications increasingly informed the public about various scientific discoveries such as electricity and magnetism, mysterious forces hijacked by peddlers in pretense, an assorted group that included patent medicine makers, traveling medicine men, and stage-struck spiritualists. Patent medicines bottled belief behind labels touting cures from an electric or magnetic medicine, while savvy spiritualists sought sanctuary from suspicion by likening their faith to those same invisible forces.

My premise relies on mostly primary source materials, period newspaper stories that capture the flavor and facts of the time, along with other periodicals and books. In deciding which materials to choose, I relied on my experience as a psychiatrist, with curiosity my chief guide. This also required a different analysis, as for example in looking at patent medicine labels and not their contents for clues suggesting what ills the makers hoped to ease. In many cases it was not a physical disorder but a thinly and more acceptably disguised emotional problem, no doubt triggered at times by a person's painful mourning.

Historical research proceeds brick by brick as it builds a solid foundation, and the contributions of modern historians helped me construct this book. From this country's very beginning, skepticism of authority that clearly extended to religious dogmatism helped shape our national character. Christopher Grasso emphasized this point in *Skepticism and American Faith: From the Revolution to the Civil War* when noting that widespread religious doubt and derision provided an opening for Spiritualism.[8]

If social skepticism was the soil, then the American Civil War provided the fertilizer that spurred Spiritualism's growth. Bridget Bennett's *Transatlantic Spiritualism and Nineteenth-Century American Literature* makes a compelling case that Spiritualism's European migration to America grew in response to the Civil War's massive trauma and the human need to mourn.[9]

Often lost in casual analyses of Spiritualism was its role championing unpopular political positions of the time such as gender and racial equality, with the latter stance expressed by Spiritualism's staunch antislavery advocacy. Robert K. Nelson's chapter in *Apocalypse and the Millennium in the American Civil War Era* dwells in detail on abolition and Spiritualism, which the *Spiritualism in the American Civil War* also covers, albeit from the pages and perspectives of Spiritualism's most prominent Civil War-era periodicals.[10]

Cathy Gutierrez makes a cogent argument comparing the dynamism of Spiritualism's social influence to the European renaissance in *Plato's Ghost: Spiritualism in the American Renaissance.*[11] As an upstart faith, Spiritualism upended traditional religions by dispensing with gilded cathedrals, richly clothed clerics, and ceremonial rituals. But the faith's real sin was challenging the authority of established religions by offering an alternative pathway to salvation. Spiritualism was a fully decentralized faith that shunned pastors and priests, placing the believers in a direct line with their deity. There was no hell in the theology of Spiritualism, with the afterlife devoted to progressively repairing the spirit's imperfections. Spiritualism also soothed the emotional wounds of the Civil War with its core claim that the living could communicate with the dead. This book adds to that narrative as voiced by the phantoms of war.

ONE

Antebellum Spiritualism

American Spiritualism was born in Hydesville, New York. As would later be told, Michael Weekman was ending a long day and preparing for a night's sleep when a loud knock at his door interrupted his routine. Weekman opened the door and much to his surprise found no one waiting. After he closed the door the rapping grew louder and ever more insistent, but when he opened the door a second time the now-puzzled man again saw no one. After a few more rounds of rapping revealed no visitors, Weekman apparently gave no further thought to the mystery, although he did vacate the property shortly thereafter.

The little house in Hydesville did not stay vacant. Soon after Weekman's departure John D. Fox occupied the house, in December 1847. It seems unlikely that the former occupant of the house would have discussed the mysterious rappings with the Fox family, but soon after the newcomers arrived the manifestations began again.

Roughly three months after moving into the Hydesville house and after everyone had gone to bed, a series of loud knocking sounds awakened the family. As might be imagined, the noises scared the Foxes' two girls, Catherine, the younger one, and her sister Margaret, who was three years older. As the initial shock wore off, the family's curiosity overcame their fear, after which a room-by-room search for the source of the sound proved unproductive. The baffled but no longer frightened family could do no more. For the next several nights the rappings continued. After a succession of sleepless nights the exhausted family finally sought refuge in an early night's slumber, hoping their fatigue would deaden their reaction.

Once again the Fox family awakened to a boisterous cacophony of ever-louder rappings that Catherine and Margaret playfully mimicked. Years later, Mrs. Fox recalled that her children made "a similar noise by snapping their fingers. The youngest girl is about twelve years old; she is the one who made her hand go. As fast as she made the noise with her hands or fingers, the sound was followed up in the room. It did not sound any different at that time; only it made the same number of noises that the girl did. When she, stopped, the sound itself stopped for a short time.... The other girl, who is in her fifteenth year, then spoke in sport, and said, 'Now do just as I do. Count one; two, three, four,' &c, striking one hand in the other at the same time. The blows which she made were repeated as before. It appeared to answer her by repeating every blow that she made."[1]

The primitive communication intrigued Mrs. Fox, who ventured to ask whether the knocking emanated from the spirit world. Two raps answered the question affirmatively and encouraged Mrs. Fox to probe further. A series of questions followed from which Mrs. Fox learned that her interlocutor was an unhappy ghost, the spirit of a 31-year-old man murdered and buried in the basement.

The Fox family, seeking confirmation or celebrity, or perhaps both, shared the mystery with their neighbors. A small, hastily assembled group of curious neighbors soon made their way to the Fox family house and, after being quickly initiated into the spirit's preferred means of communication, started asking all sorts of questions. Much to their astonishment, the rappings correctly responded to their queries, many of which required intimate knowledge of the interrogator's life.

It was soon discovered that the spirit was more loquacious when an interviewer slowly spelled out each letter of the alphabet. The spirit signaled its selection by rapping when the chosen letter was pronounced. It was a slow and tedious process, much like tapping out the characters on a typewriter with one finger, but for the patient interviewer the spirit's response was worth it.

At first, the rapping was attributed to a restless spirit, the ethereal remnants of a murdered man buried in the basement of the small house. That explanation failed after the young girls' parents sent their children to Rochester, New York. Catherine moved in with Leah, an older married sister, while Margaret moved in with her brother David. The rappings moved along with the girls to Rochester, leaving behind any thoughts of a haunted Hydesville house as the sole source of the mysterious manifestations.

Leah, Catherine, and Margaret reluctantly accepted the notoriety that accompanied their roles as the phantoms' favorites and once again bowed to the dictates of the spirits when they took their show on the road, courting curiosity and controversy along the way.

Their first public appearance took place before a large audience at Corinthian Hall in Rochester, New York, on November 14, 1849. A committee of leading citizens agreed to monitor the affair in an effort to detect deception. Eliab W. Capron hosted the affair and began with

Mrs. Fish and the Misses Fox, the original mediums of the mysterious noises at Rochester Western, New York (Library of Congress, Prints and Photographs Division, Washington, D.C.).

a methodically detailed history of spiritual manifestations. As the event unfolded, mysterious rappings periodically filled the auditorium and seemingly signaled the spirits' approval of the night's event.

An excited audience greeted Catherine and Margaret's second public appearance in Rochester. Loud jeers and voices of disbelief followed the first committee's statement finding no fraud. Appeasing the crowd required the election of a second investigating committee, which the Fox sisters readily assented to. The hastily assembled group included a politician and a physician, who collectively tested every conceivable configuration, only to find the rappings emanating from windows, doors, and furniture all remotely located from the women. Suspecting ventriloquism, the physician tested that theory with a stethoscope but once again was left baffled. The second committee reported that "the sounds were heard, and their thorough investigation had conclusively shown them to be produced neither by machinery nor ventriloquism": a verdict that once again failed to squelch disbelief.

The Fox sisters complacently agreed to a third committee composed of avowed skeptics hostile to Spiritualism. Added to the usual ensemble were a group of women who disrobed the Fox sisters in a vain attempt to detect any trickery. After this ignominious debriefing, the female inquisitors testified that when the Fox sisters "were standing on pillows, with a handkerchief tied around the bottom of their dresses, tight to the ankles, we all heard the rappings on the wall and floor distinctly."

It was a raucous crowd that gathered at Rochester's Corinthian Hall for the third committee's report. Given the hooligans' previous behavior, and cognizant of their conclusions, the Fox sisters and the committee expected trouble. Tension was palpable as the committee delivered its report, and it soon exploded as ruffians appeared ready to rush the stage. Alert police urged everyone on the stage to leave, which was a prudent bit of advice they all accepted.

Eliab Capron, the emcee for the sisters' public debut in Rochester, encouraged Catherine to travel east and stay with his family. Catherine agreed and was soon conducting séances in Albany, New York, where she conjured up more than just rappings from the unearthly dwellers. Guests heard spirit music that wafted over the circle, others experienced the warm caress of unseen hands, and even the heaviest furniture moved to and fro as if weightless. Catherine's séances were greeted "with delight by bereaved mourners, to whom conclusive evidences of the presence and watchful guardianship of beloved spirit friends was clearly proven."[2]

The Fox sisters expanded their travels with a trip to Troy, New York, just north of the state's capitol, where a succession of exhibitions left the city marveling at the women's spiritual skills. With word of their marvelous manifestations spreading, it was only natural that their next performance in New York City was eagerly anticipated. Like royalty holding court, the women rented rooms at a fashionable downtown hotel and warmly welcomed visits from reporters, intellectuals, and politicians.

Among the first to visit the ladies were two newspaper reporters who described their hosts as "the eldest ... is about twenty-five years old, and has a pleasing and intelligent countenance. Her two sisters ... are of the ages of fourteen and eighteen. Their eyes and hair are dark, and their complexions of a transparent paleness."

Almost immediately following their entrance a raucous round of rappings regaled the reporters. After this gleeful greeting, one of the reporters launched a series of pointed inquiries about a long-deceased family member and received in return accurate answers. The second reporter's quest for similar information about a dead relative was far less successful and produced mostly embarrassing inaccuracies. Despite the incongruities experienced by the two reporters, they both agreed that there was no evidence of trickery, leaving the baffled pair to conclude that the performance was "a curious and puzzling affair."[3]

Other critics were less forgiving. What some of these cynics found objectionable was the $1 entrance fee the trio of women charged for their town hall displays. According to Leah, Horace Greeley of the *New York Tribune* had suggested that the women charge $5, a fee the newspaper editor considered sufficient to keep troublemakers at bay. Leah objected to what she considered an exorbitant charge, and after consulting the spirits she settled on the less lofty $1 admission.[4]

If Leah thought her financial benevolence would quell murmurs of discontent, she was mistaken. An astute reporter bluntly questioned "who in his senses can believe that those girls are commissioned from on High to stand between the living and the dead ... and have the exclusive privilege of opening to us, on payment of money, the gates of the spirit land?"[5]

Paradoxically, controversy helped the Fox sisters fill their venues. Learned men of high civic stature were not dissuaded, and they listened with rapt attention as the spirits rapped eloquent. Their attendance boosted the women's credibility, creating through their presence yet another essential partnership between the deceivers and the deceived.

A fawning magazine editorial in the popular *Home Journal* may have swayed some skeptics with a serendipitous observation. While seated at a séance next to one of the Fox sisters, the reporter casually rested his arm on his neighbor's chair. What happened next startled the reporter, as a thunderous rapping shook his neighbor's chair and left his undisturbed: a seemingly inexplicable sensation, sandwiched as he was between the two. Like a flat stone skipping across a placid lake, the reporter leaped over a multitude of rational explanations, including deception, by conjecturing that "if these knocking answers to questions are made (as many insist) by electric detonations, and if disembodied spirits are still moving, consciously, among us, and have thus found an agent, at last, electricity, by which they can communicate with the world they left, it must soon, in the progressive nature of things, ripen to an intercourse between this and the spirit-world."[6]

Just a few years after the Fox sisters captivated the country, another young girl joined the movement. Cora Hatch was born near Cuba, New York, in 1840, in the same general area of western New York that would become the epicenter of American Spiritualism.[7] Cora's father was open to the new belief after having attended a séance at the fledgling Hopedale utopian community. As events unfolded, it became clear that Cora's mother was also receptive.

Cora's transformation occurred when she was eleven years old. While sitting in a grove of trees near her house the impressionable little girl was quietly writing on a small chalkboard when she fell asleep. Upon awakening, Cora was surprised by a message on the chalkboard and asked for her mother's help in deciphering it. A close examination of the message and the signature convinced Cora's mother that the author was her dead other daughter.

Bewildered and upset, Cora's mother set the chalkboard aside, hoping to give the matter no further thought. A few days later the little girl lapsed into another dreamy, unconscious state during which Cora's mother anxiously handed the chalkboard to her stuporous daughter, who began writing furiously. The little scriber's messages were from various members of the family, all dearly departed, but through Cora's penmanship they proclaimed, "we are not dead."

Whatever disquiet accompanied the newest revelation soon dissipated. Cora's parents broadcast the spirit communications throughout their small community, and in short order curious neighbors came from near and far to see the young girl. As might be imagined, they sought answers to life's mysteries, in particular hoping to connect with a lost loved one. Cora obliged their requests and amazed her visitors with communiqués from the dead.

A benevolent ghost soon took charge of Cora, acting as a gatekeeper, holding back zealous spirits from overwhelming the frail girl. The spirit guide replaced the chalkboard by controlling Cora's voice, establishing a verbal channel with the denizens of the afterlife.

At a time when physicians still clung to antiquated practices, Cora called on the wise ones from the spirit world to help her heal the hurts that doctors could not. For several years she labored to relieve the sufferings of those who sought her care. Under the influence of her spirit guide, Cora prepared prescriptions, applied poultices, and even performed minor surgery. Satisfied customers kept the young girl busy, but her destiny was the stage and not the bedside: a platform bringing the wisdom of the spirit world to larger audiences.

From the outset, when speaking to local crowds or packed lyceums, Cora enchanted her audiences with equal measures of charm, clairvoyance, and intellect. Her lack of formal education was taken by many as credible evidence of unseen forces directing the girl's words. "Her eloquence and thoughts were far beyond anything that was taught in any of the schools or colleges, or in any branch of science in those days. Many remarkable prophecies were given by her when a child." Just before the War Between the States engulfed America, Cora Hatch was speaking to packed gatherings, attracting scoffers, supporters, and scientists all eager to hear words of wisdom from a "fair and slender girl, on whose flowing ringlets seventeen summers sit with light and easy grace."[8]

A typical night's entertainment began with a public challenge. Cora's manager solicited from the spectators volunteers who would draft metaphysical questions for the young medium. In most cases learned men, distinguished by their reputations in religion, science, or politics, were the audience's choice.

In response to the abstruse questions, often selected in an attempt to discredit the girl, Cora would seemingly enter an enchanted, introspective state of reverie, as if receiving messages from beyond. She would then rise from her chair and eruditely answer the questions. Cora's command of language and scholarly extemporaneous discussions fascinated the audience, no doubt convincing some skeptics that she was indeed channeling the wisdom of the spirit world.

Cora left her audiences bewildered. For some, preaching the gospel of Spiritualism was heretical, while others embraced the religion. Secular assessments ran the gamut from marveling at an uneducated girl's acumen to derisive accusations of fraud. In the latter group was a cocky, self-assured man who was certain he could trap the young girl. What followed was a humiliating lesson brought about by the seventeen-year-old girl.

Isaiah Rynders was a prominent member of the Bowery Boys, a group of young men eager for excitement and spoiling for fights, and Cora's lectures offered the man an opportunity for both. Rynders rose from the

Portrait of Cora L. V. Hatch (Gurney & Son).

audience and challenged the girl to explain the physical laws governing a gyroscope. Before the young medium could answer the question, Rynders sought to handicap her trial by posing additional questions focusing on the origins of plants, animals, and, with victorious fanfare, the human life of Jesus. Cora outmaneuvered her pretentious opponent by avoiding the gyroscope question and instead delivered an enigmatic discourse on the bonus questions. It was a shrewd strategy that left Rynders outwitted but "very agreeably disappointed."[9]

As Rynders later admitted, he came to Cora's show expecting and planning to expose a fraud. In the span of less than an hour, Cora completely changed Rynders's opinion, leaving the chastened skeptic effusively praising her pious presentation. Cynical commentators attributed the man's sudden conversion to "a pair of bright eyes, a pretty face, [and] a shower of glossy ringlets."[10]

Every now and then, Cora met her match. Her husband and stage manager drew curious crowds by promoting his wife's psychic prowess which he contended came from powers harnessing the wisdom of the spirit world. Spectators expected, and Cora's credibility required, that she unravel the most perplexing problems a skeptical audience could devise.

At a stop in Lynn, Massachusetts, in 1857, a citizens committee submitted a novel question for Cora's consideration. The committee settled on a mathematical problem for which the solution required a comprehensive knowledge of advanced geometry. Without a moment's hesitation the inspired spiritualist launched a seemingly rational monologue, purportedly clarifying classic mathematical principles. The high-brow-sounding sophistry probably would have sufficed were it not for several mathematicians in attendance who challenged the medium and demanded that she solve the problem. Cora could not, but she promised to consult the spirits again in one month's time and assuage her protagonists, an outcome that never materialized.[11]

In an effort to bring the musings of Cora to the masses, her husband compiled a collection of her speeches and published the trove in 1858 in a thick volume under her name, titled *Discourses on Religion, Morals, Philosophy and Metaphysics*. Among the many subjects in the book were topics on "the sources of human knowledge, modern spiritualism, spiritual communications, the religion of life" and a short discussion debating the merits of phrenology.[12]

Phrenology was a controversial practice, divining a person's character through a careful study of their cranium. A phrenologist claimed the ability to accurately detect a person's intellectual, moral, religious, vocational, criminal, and psychological propensities based on observations and calculations of a person's skull.[13]

Cora's endorsement of phrenology came from spirits who exclaimed that "we may venture to say that this science, as such, will become the most ready means of understanding man, of understanding the Universe, that has ever been devised by human intelligence."[14]

The seesaw assessment of the upstart faith continued, but a trend toward accepting the spiritual manifestations as genuine gradually gained ground. Opposing the drift was the *New York Herald*, one of the city's established and well-thought-of newspapers, which derisively dismissed the "mysterious Rochester rappings" as delusional or even worse as a humbug. Even so, the *Herald* begrudgingly acknowledged that another "unnamed" newspaper editor wholeheartedly supported the spiritual insurgency and, in a sign of his fervor, was launching the *Spiritual and Moral Instructor*.[15]

The "unnamed" editor of the *Spiritual and Moral Instructor* earning the *New York Herald*'s special rebuke was Isaiah S. Hyatt, a young impressionable man in his early twenties. By June 1851 Hyatt, "in pursuance of spiritual direction," began his duties in Auburn, New York, publishing the divine words of mediums Mrs. E.A. Benedict and the Rev. J.L. Scott as received from the world beyond. Five months later the two mediums left Auburn, peremptorily halting the publication in preparation for a move to Mountain Cove, Virginia.

Before the temporary lull in publication, the semimonthly newspaper was attracting regional attention, including from bemused skeptics. While believers accepted Benedict and Scott's rambling revelations as divine, cynics concluded that "Mr. Scott seems always foggy, frequently bewildered, and at times maudlin." In spite of the criticism, the growing numbers of spiritualists ensured a reliable, faithful audience for the *Spiritual and Moral Instructor*.[16]

Roughly a year before Hyatt took the helm of the fledgling *Spiritual and Moral Instructor*, upward of 100 mediums were communicating with the dead in Auburn, responding to a growing demand for their services. Mediums often published their success stories, but the strange story of a man named Baham seemed to suggest that Spiritualism had a dark side.[17]

Baham wantonly killed an itinerant peddler, and after a short trial a jury sentenced the man to death. A young female clairvoyant learned of the looming hanging and promised to reveal the mysteries surrounding the ethereal transition from life to death. Unfortunately for her, it did not go as she planned.

From the gallows Baham cursed and condemned his fellow citizens, vainly pleading innocence while darkly demanding vengeance. The impressionable young woman watched and listened with rapt attention before collapsing insensibly to the ground at the same moment the man began his eternal journey.

From that moment forward, the woman's life changed for the worse. An imperceptible power possessed the woman, supposedly representing the disembodied murderer. Baham's death did nothing to cool his hot head, and through the young medium he gave voice to dreadful denunciations directed toward those he held responsible for his hanging.

The girl progressively fell under the spell and dominion of Baham, even ceding control of her physical movements to the spiteful spirit. For some inexplicable reason Baham turned against his only portal to mortals, tormenting the young girl as she helplessly flailed and thrashed, seizure-like, under his malevolent influence. Finally, as Baham were reaching out from the grave with invisible, strangling hands, the young girl struggled to breathe. Her agony was impervious to the ministrations of family and doctors, and the throngs of visitors surely thought the girl's 36-hour ordeal would end in death.

As the girl teetered on the precipice, hovering precariously between life and death, another young female rapping medium acting under the guidance of benevolent spirits rescued her. After the rapping medium arrived she took hold of the possessed girl's hands, and while appealing to her spirit guides, serenity descended on the scene with Baham's banishment.

Spiritualists in Auburn began coalescing around an "Apostolic Movement," through the principle influences of Mrs. Ann Benedict, a psychic medium, and James L. Scott, a Baptist preacher. The Rev. Thomas L. Harris received a summons from the spirit world instructing him to depart his New York City congregation and join the fledgling group in Auburn, thereby completing the triumvirate that would develop a nascent apostolic community.

The Apostolic Movement seemed destined to sweep aside all religious competitors in Auburn as it accumulated hundreds of followers, including many of the city's leading figures. Harris and Scott spread their message through a newspaper devoted to the *Disclosures from the Interior and Superior Care for Mortals*. The publication's content supposedly came from the Apostle Paul, who after centuries of silence started rapping messages through Ann Benedict. Occasionally a rambunctious, roaming spirit would hijack the séance, betraying its presence through ribald rappings. Harris and Scott would push back, politely but firmly insisting the spirit cede the psychic to the Apostle Paul.

Scott interpreted a dream as a command to vacate Auburn in 1850 and settle the Apostolic Movement elsewhere. Further directions obtained through spirit rappings were sufficiently detailed for Scott, Benedict, and other pioneers to set their sights south. After a short discussion the spirits rapped their satisfaction with Mountain Cove, Virginia, and the little troupe immediately started buying land.

A few months later, as winter descended, nearly a hundred people populated the new community. Benedict apparently lost favor with the spirits and Scott quickly moved to replace her as the community's medium, insisting that divine intervention motivated the change. Few ripples accompanied the initial change in leadership, but rumblings of discontent soon followed.

Acting in accordance with what he claimed were spiritual commandments, Scott demanded that his faithful followers relinquish all property and possessions with an angelic appeal, "Come, then, to the mountain with thy substance. Give it to the Lord." Shortly after this declaration several members of the fledgling community took their belongings and left, leaving behind doubts and difficulties.

Scott and Harris tried to quell the growing mutiny through intimidation, but sensing that was not enough they sought spiritual authority. With their kingdom crumbling toward the end of 1852, the determined duo borrowed a page from the Biblical Book of Revelation and threatened the weak-kneed with plagues, famine, and fire. It was a ham-fisted effort that drove a deeper wedge between the few remaining members of the Apostolic Movement and their putative leaders.[18]

Members of established religions cast a wary eye on the rise of the Mountain Cove rappers and could not ignore their small but steadily growing influence. Spiritualism was an existential threat, and while traditional preachers probably applauded the internecine conflicts plaguing the fledgling Apostolic Movement, they could not abide Scott's self-anointed ascension as God's emissary.

Preaching to the faithful on October 31, 1852, the Rev. Joseph Twitchell addressed a Presbyterian congregation on the spiritual manifestations bewitching the nation. After briefly condemning spirit-guided rappings, writings, levitations, and clairvoyants as false prophets, Twitchell turned his attention to the Mountain Cove cult and its provocative leader.[19]

Twitchell scoffed at Scott's brand of spiritualism, ridiculing his claim that among all mortals on earth he alone was chosen as God's messenger. To prove his point, Twitchell extracted passages from the Mountain Cove Community's newspaper, the *Spiritual and Moral Instructor*, which carefully chronicled Scott's heavenly communions.

Among the small band of believers at Mountain Cove, Scott's divine revelations published in the *Spiritual and Moral Instructor* were the gospel truth. Twitchell believed otherwise and pointed to pomposities such as "Hear this and believe.... God thy Redeemer ... who hath the keys of death and hell addresseth you through one of your number." Twitchell denounced Scott's supposedly heaven sent proclamations and urged his Presbyterian audience to reject the wiles of Spiritualism.

Isaiah Hyatt was the editor of the *Spiritual and Moral Instructor* and among the growing group of disillusioned devotees chafing at Scott's pretentiousness and mounting despotism. The young editor of the newspaper grew increasingly disenchanted after noticing "many discrepancies and fallacious teachings ... forcing upon me the conclusion that the controlling power ... in no case was entitled to absolute confidence."[20]

The enlightened editor abruptly left Mountain Cove, leaving his readers in the lurch and provoking suspicion. In an effort to dispel the rumors and set the record straight, Hyatt wrote an impassioned account of his disappointment with Mountain Cove's spiritual leader and, mistakenly believing it would be published, sent his story to the *Spiritual and Moral Instructor*. Not surprisingly, James Scott, who was the subject of Hyatt's scorn, ignored the article, but the erstwhile editor prevailed when the *Spiritual Telegraph* published his report.

Conflicts about leadership and property ownership took their toll on Mountain Cove.[21] As a harbinger of the community's demise, the last issue of the *Mountain Cove Journal*, the successor to the *Spiritual and Moral Instructor*, posted a small advertisement in 1853 addressed "TO PRINTERS—the PRESS on which this paper is now printed is offered for sale very low, $100 cash."[22]

Scott cultivated controversy, while his partner, the Rev. Thomas Harris, remained more pragmatic. After leaving the failed Mountain Cove Community, Harris traveled the country spreading his spiritual visions and attracting small groups of converts. In 1875, more than two decades after his Virginia retreat, he founded the Fountain Grove Community in California, roughly 60 miles north of San Francisco.[23]

Even before the failed Mountain Cove experiment, Harris's magnetic personality was attracting attention. In the early 1850s Horace Greeley and his wife regularly attended Harris's Independent Church, providing further fodder favoring insinuations that the famous editor was a follower of Spiritualism. Greeley contributed to those suspicions with numerous articles he published in his influential *New York Tribune*.

When the Fox sisters made their debut in New York City in the summer of 1850, Greeley was among the women's audience. According to observers at the meeting, Greeley was not particularly impressed with the sisters' rappings, but his wife, distressed and despondent with the death of a son, insisted on another meeting. Greeley granted his grieving wife's request and invited the Fox sisters to spend a week in his home. Their acquiescence quickly captured the interest of Greeley's social circle, many of whom were intrigued by the novelty of the mystical séances.[24]

Even though Greeley supposedly placed no faith in Spiritualism, his recollection of an encounter with a psychic seemed to suggest at least some ambivalence. The newspaper editor recalled an unusual meeting a few days after the Fox sisters took up residence in his home. While he was languidly reading a book, Greeley's reverie was disturbed when a woman and her husband rather unceremoniously entered his house. He soon discovered that the intrepid pair was searching for the Fox sisters. After that awkward meeting, Mrs. Freeman introduced herself as a sensitive psychic medium and then promptly entered a trance state. After she made contact with the other world, Greeley professed that "what she reported as of or from those spirits might be ever so true or false for aught I know."[25]

Greeley quietly watched the impromptu performance and then demurely asked the entranced woman if he could speak with the spirits. Taking his hand in hers, Mrs. Freeman signaled her acquiescence, prompting Greeley to inquire whether "you see any brothers and sisters of mine in the spirit-world?" After a moment's hesitation Mrs. Freeman supposedly made contact with a young child named Horace.

A stone-faced and skeptical Greeley asked Mrs. Freeman to find other relatives. Once again the enterprising medium fell silent as she quietly searched the spirit world as requested. With an exclamation, Mrs. Freeman found another denizen of the dark but struggled to get the name right, beginning with Anna, then Almira, and finally in exhaustion simply settled on a name beginning with the letter A. Greeley's suspicions suffered a blow when he later admitted that Arminda, his two-year-old sister, had died decades earlier. Aside from his wife no one knew of the young girl's untimely demise, leaving the nonplussed newspaper editor struggling for an explanation.

Roughly six months later, the *New York Daily Tribune* continued fanning the fascination with the Fox sisters. An anonymous letter to the editor set forth a series of marvelous manifestations the writer witnessed and offered as proof of the sisters' sincerity. In one example, a family summoned a dead brother known for his musical inclinations, and with the Fox sisters' assistance he began rapping a popular tune of the time, prompting the attendees to merrily sing along. Even more convincing was the family's wish for the dearly departed to rap his favorite tune, a request summarily honored, leaving the room's mortals crying with disbelief.[26]

In another example, a man in poor health met with Leah Fox, desperately seeking conversation with his dead wife. Leah made the connection and his spirit wife painstakingly sent a message, with raps indicating a specific letter in the alphabet. It was a laborious means of communication, but the man was surely rewarded when his wife revealed "I have been with you, dear husband, in sickness and health; but you are unconscious of my presence. I know your infirmities and sympathize with you."

Skeptics unsurprisingly scoffed at the Rochester rappers and their mushrooming mimics. For every cynic a supporter seemed ready to oppose their distrust. The simplicity of the rappings was an obvious attack point, countered by enthusiastic defenders of the faith claiming that the "rappings are not simple sounds, but variations of sound transmitting various forms and degrees of intelligence ... a person may converse with a departed friend through one medium, obtain his signal, and know his friend by the same signal through any number of media."

Greeley eventually concluded "that any demonstration of spiritual existence outside of and after the death of the body, is contrary to nature and universal experience" and offered instead that "we know too little of Nature to decide ... that an occurrence is miraculous, or even unnatural, merely because it has no parallel within our knowledge." Greeley's even-handed response neither ratified nor refuted Spiritualism and paradoxically probably added a measure of credibility.

After leaving Greeley's home, the Fox sisters launched a road show that would take them to cities across the nation. A typical stop was in Detroit, Michigan, where the women rented a large three-story house for the exclusive purpose of enthralling the local citizens with their mysterious rappings. During their months in Detroit a nonstop retinue of the city's elite visited with the Fox sisters for the nominal admission price of $1.[27]

Not everyone fell for the Fox sisters' frenzy, but opponents faced an uphill struggle overcoming the basic allure of Spiritualism, which promised meetings with lost loved ones. Among the endless examples was a husband "whose love and ambition had been centered upon his wife, and who found the severest sting of death to be his parting with her, would not be entirely separated ... he would maintain a rapport relation to her spiritsoul." Of course, a medium was necessary to facilitate these communications, and with the demand from the grief-stricken growing rapidly, the Fox sisters soon had competition.[28]

Even more extraordinary than the propagation of psychics was the proliferation of their powers. The arduous task of pointing at the alphabet while a rapping spirit signaled the letter soon gave way to writing mediums who served as scribes for the spirits. This was an important development for loquacious and sagacious spirits, who could author volumes unfettered by restrictive rapping. The rapid evolution of mediums' powers soon produced enchanted speakers giving voice to the spirits and a dizzying array of physical manifestations such as spirits tipping tables, playing musical instruments, and making physical contact with their mortal counterparts.

No one harnessed spiritual powers and prowess quite like Daniel Dunglas Home. Home was born in Scotland in 1833 to a family that purportedly prophesized calamities through a spiritual "second sight." Daniel was nine years old when he came to America and at the time was spare in stature, weak and sickly, melancholic by nature, and preferred solitude to society.[29]

Daniel's first home in America was in Greeneville, Connecticut, a quiet community with nearby woods that afforded the young boy endless opportunities to commune with nature. While other boys were of the rough-and-tumble sort, Daniel was a sensitive soul soothed by his rural ramblings. As might be imagined, these were mostly solitary excursions, although an older boy named Edwin soon became a constant companion as the lonely, self-ostracized pair bonded in friendship.

A defining moment in Home's transition to becoming a trance medium grew out of one of these woodland walks. Both boys were voracious and impressionable readers, and an eerie ghost story about a cruel death that separated a romancing couple set their imaginations ablaze. Before they died the fictional couple promised each other that should one of them die prematurely, the other would forge a reunion from beyond the grave. With a solemn sincerity the deeply determined boys took a page from that story and pledged a similar vow.

Shortly after that declaration, Daniel and his family moved to Troy, New York, in what was surely a painful parting. Daniel's despondent departure was soon softened with a most remarkable vision. Daniel was just going to sleep and marveling at a brilliant moon when suddenly the room grew dark and a bright orb slowly materialized, revealing Edwin. His ghostly reincarnation reminded Daniel of the death pact the boys had made. A few days later Daniel received a letter bearing the tragic news of Edwin's death, foretold in advance through spiritual communion.

With the subsequent death of his mother, Daniel turned inward, morbidly preoccupied with death, religion, and ethereal resurrection. His aunt assumed the child's care and was a woman with strong religious convictions whose faith would soon be tested by a series of mysterious events. It all started one night when Daniel was settling in for sleep and was startled by three loud knocks. As might be imagined, Daniel searched his room for the cause, but finding none, he returned to bed. The series of knocks continued twice more before leaving the boy restless and struggling to fall asleep.

Daniel related the previous night's noise to his aunt, perhaps expecting a reassuring explanation, but the horrified woman ascribed the matter to deviltry and in an effort to drive the malevolent force from her house secured the services of three local preachers. A sort of crude exorcism followed their arrival, with pious supplications imploring the evil one to leave. Their prayers only seemed to incite the sounds, as the rappings continued unabated. Having failed in their mission, the bewildered preachers left Home and his aunt to cope as best as they could.

The uncowed spirit became a permanent resident of the house, with regular rappings reverberating from the walls and floors. Unleashed from the shackles of the afterlife, the restive spirit impishly moved furniture to and fro, further unnerving Home's aunt. And just like the Fox sisters, the spirit in Greeneville slowly rapped out messages as enraptured neighbors asked questions about their lost loved ones.

Home's aunt never reconciled the rappings with her religion, remaining steadfast in the belief that her nephew was satanically controlled. That combined with the steady stream of curiosity seekers forced the woman to abandon Home by ordering him to leave her house. Surely chagrined at the turn of events, Home complied and packed his meager personal possessions, launching a spiritual renaissance that dominated his remaining life.

Rufus Elmer described a typical Home séance that took place in Springfield, Massachusetts, in 1852. With the young spiritualist in charge, a group of six people sat at a table and "within a few moments the table seemed very uneasy, and to disregard the 'wholesome law' of gravitation, and seemed disposed to remain a portion of the time in midair." Home proved there were no gimmicks involved in the movement by placing a light under the table.[30]

Table moving was just the appetizer. The main entrée was served by Home communing with the spirits. With a glazed look, the spiritualist informed one of the female guests that her dead husband and daughter were both present and proved the claim with facts supposedly only known by the woman. Homes then directed his attention to Elmer's wife and described a vision of her deceased daughter as a beautiful angel.

Home was a traveler and his peregrinations took him across the northeastern United States, so that "in sickness or in health, by day or night, my privacy was intruded on by all comers, some from curiosity, and some from higher motives." At each stop along the way his audiences marveled at the table tippings and perceptive communiqués from the spirit world.[31]

Home rapidly achieved a cult status by eclipsing the Fox sisters and other spiritualists with his unequaled feats. His exploits baffled his detractors and amazed his admirers. By avoiding all remuneration Home added another element of credibility that further burnished his flourishing reputation.

Home's séances were beguiling, enigmatic exhibitions that rarely left attendees disappointed. "On one occasion ... the 'spirits' communicated through him the whereabouts of missing title deeds ... on another, they enabled him to prescribe successfully for an invalid ... and time after time they conveyed to those in the séance room messages of more or less vital import." The young, shy medium was tapping the spirit world to benefit humanity.[32]

Levitation was one of Home's more remarkable displays, first demonstrated in Connecticut in 1852. Imagine the surprise when "again and again he was taken from the floor, and the third time he was carried to the lofty ceiling." Persons present vouched for the airy display that added mountains of mystique to the man in what would become a trademark spectacle.

Successive séances took their toll on Home, who was always sickly and increasingly fatigued by his mental exertions. Instead of seeking solace from the spirit world, the young medium took more banal medical advice urging him to seek a better climate outside the United States. Home left for England in 1855, spreading Spiritualism's magic across the continent by entertaining nobility and converting stalwart skeptics.[33]

While most mediums eked out a meager existence, fame and fortune favored a few such as Daniel Dunglas Home, whose transatlantic trips created a financial windfall.[34] Almost immediately after disembarking the steamship in Liverpool, England, Home began making the rounds of the famous and fashionable elite of London. During his three-month whirlwind tour he met Mr. Rymer, who provided the financial means for Home to visit Paris. Two months later he traveled to Italy, conducting séances for inquisitive artists and aristocrats. Home briefly returned to America for the express purpose of bringing his young sister back to Paris.

The highlight of Home's return to Paris in 1857 was a lunch date with Emperor Napoleon III and the Empress Eugénie, and Maximilian II, King of Bavaria. As usual, Home amazed his distinguished audience as "invisible hands have touched the hair of his Majesty, knocked his knees and patted his hands; the furniture was removed to considerable distance."[35]

Home's demeanor cultivated the accommodating ambiance that mystified and mesmerized his audiences. A reporter gushed, "There is something in his look, in his presence, in the very atmosphere of his room, which imparts happiness and sunshine to those about him.... In an earlier and more superstitious period ... he would have passed for a being of divine origin."[36]

Home's persona was magnetic and attracted like-minded believers, among them the Rev. Jesse Babcock Ferguson, who spread the gospel of Spiritualism through Kentucky and Tennessee. In the years before he died Ferguson traveled to England with the Davenport brothers (described later), often receiving a cold reception but always warmed by his fervent faith, which never wavered.[37]

Ferguson was born January 19, 1819, in Philadelphia, Pennsylvania, but his family moved a few years later to Winchester, Virginia, a Southern sojourn that would forever mold his patriotic and political loyalties. As a teenager his singular interest in religious matters led to an invitation to teach school since his morals closely aligned with the rural community. His academic proclivities suffered a blow when the family's finances failed, forcing the young man to abandon any hopes of higher education. Disappointed but determined, Ferguson became an apprentice printer, which was a useful trade, but a succession of failed jobs led him briefly to accept a position as a book printer in Baltimore, Maryland. It was during this time that Ferguson had his first premonition of things to come.

While he was in Baltimore, Ferguson became seriously ill, the consequence of a painful and ulcerative bone disease affecting his leg. His grandfather had died of a similar affliction and that morbid outcome naturally depressed the fifteen-year-old boy. Ferguson left Baltimore behind and returned home full of dread and fearing death, but attending school and working kept the thoughts at bay.

Ferguson awakened one morning refreshed, with a strange peacefulness replacing the endless gloom. It was a welcome change that Ferguson celebrated by taking time off from school. His absence from school was noticed by a worried friend, the son of a local physician who visited the ailing boy, after which "Ferguson, directed as by an inaudible voice, asked his companion to inquire of his father what article ... would produce the same effect as a burn... and was then told in his sleep to ask for an antidote."

Ferguson's friend alternately applied caustic sulfuric acid to his diseased leg and when the pain became unbearable applied a soothing compound that reversed the burning. Three weeks later, by following the mysterious directions, Ferguson's leg had completely healed.

After his recovery Ferguson completed his education but his prospects for employment in Virginia were limited, so he set off for Ohio and Indiana. However, the westward trip was a disappointment. Ferguson returned to more comfortable turf in Kentucky and preached throughout the area for several years before accepting a prominent position at the Church of Christ in Nashville, Tennessee. For 11 years his sermons met a receptive audience, but his increasing infatuation with Spiritualism led to his dismissal in 1857.

In the years preceding his dismissal, Ferguson was actively engaged in attending séances accompanied by the typical table tippings, rappings, and mirthful musical instruments. His wife eventually developed psychic powers and supported her husband's spirit communications. Ferguson also forged an enduring relationship with H.B. Champion, a local Nashville spiritualist steadily gaining a reputation as a remarkable medium. Champion and Ferguson specialized in psychometry, which they advertised as a psychic ability that revealed a person's innermost character.

Ferguson also discovered and perfected his psychic healing, and he and his wife together would relieve a person's suffering. In one example, an esteemed member of his Nashville congregation severely injured his leg jumping from the third floor of a burning building. Eminent physicians predicted Mr. Freeman would be lame for life, which seemed entirely plausible given the severe nature of the injury.

The injured man's predicament weighed heavily on Ferguson's mind until his wife relieved the burden, and "I was overjoyed to hear Mrs. F, from deep entrancement say 'We can relieve Mr. Freeman, and he will walk again.'" With that insight, Ferguson and his wife hurried to Mr. Freeman's home, hoping he would permit their spirit inspired intervention. Freeman agreed and Mrs. Ferguson immediately set about entrancing her subject. After awakening from the mesmerized state Freeman literally jumped for joy.

With the war looming in 1860, many of the leading citizens in Tennessee turned to their learned pastor for inspiration. Ferguson obliged and delivered stirring oratories to politicians and soldiers, hoping for peace but resigned to fighting an unavoidable war. With the fall of Fort Donelson, Nashville became a threatened city beset by fear but calmed by Ferguson riding his horse through the streets and reassuring the alarmed residents. In the following days he encouraged embattled Confederate soldiers, and he narrowly escaped arrest by Union forces by fleeing to Canada.

Ferguson returned to America and made his way to Richmond, Virginia, in 1863. To those who would listen he railed against the war's cost in human suffering, and he considered slaves "the only innocent party in the terrible conflict in America." As a man of peace with Southern loyalties, he advocated for a two-nation solution that would preserve the Confederate states' autonomy. Ferguson died in 1870, having lived just long enough to realize the folly of that fantasy.

John Murray Spear combined the attributes of Ferguson and Home. He was a serious man steeped in religion who was compassionate, curious, and contemplative. He was born in Boston, Massachusetts, in 1804 and raised in the Universalist religion. In 1830 he became the pastor of a Universalist church and preached a gospel of equality that extended to slaves. His passionate support of abolition riled audiences and nearly cost his life in Portland, Maine.[38]

Spear confronted other controversies of the time, and by the mid-nineteenth century his name was synonymous with prison reform. He traveled throughout New England providing sustenance and support to prisoners and their families. From his meager earnings he bailed inmates from jail, lectured on crime and its causes, and nourished prisoners' souls with piety. His prison crusade soon gave way to a new infatuation. It was 1851 and spirit rapping signaled the emergence of American Spiritualism and with his Universalist theology and open mindedness the man seemed tailor made for conversion.

Spear's life changed forever on March 31, 1852, when an invisible force seized his hand and compelled the man to write a short missive signed by "Oliver." Spear seemed to take the automatic writing in stride because he apparently recognized the note's author as Oliver Dennet, the Portland, Maine, resident who had saved Spear's life during an antislavery sermon.[39]

Oliver's cryptic message instructed his host to travel to a nearby city on an errand of mercy and meet with David Vining, a man hobbled by severe leg pain. The two had not met before, but Spear's awkward explanation for his spirit-directed mission apparently convinced Vining of his honorable intentions. Spear took a seat next to Vining, and with Oliver in control he set about curing the man's suffering by first lightly touching his patient's ear and then unexpectedly grabbing the injured limb. As might be imagined, Vining jumped from his seat and screamed, but after regaining his composure Spear's patient was completely free of pain.

Spear continued making house calls throughout the region, relieving pain and suffering as directed by Oliver, but his psychic skills were evolving to include drawing and speaking. It was during a spirit drawing that John Murray, the founder of the Universalist theology in America, made contact with Spear. What followed was a series of transcribed meetings between the two, with Murray revealing insights from the spirit world. According to Murray, a person's death initiated a spiritual metamorphosis where echelons of redemption successively cleansed the spirit, after which even the vilest mortals entered a utopian afterlife.

Murray's predictions from beyond the grave described a world of peace and universal equality. His premonitions harmonized with Spear's antislavery stance and ominously forecast that "My poor brother ... toiling day after day with no earthly prospect before him; and another standing over him with the heavy lash ... cannot long continue."

Spear contributed to another phase of Spiritualism when his guides directed the construction of a perpetual motion machine, fueled by limitless spirit energy. With the aid of a female medium, the incongruous assemblage of metal was born in 1854, a feat even hailed by Andrew Jackson Davis. Spear moved his "New Motor" to Randolph, New York, a move designed to improve the machine's performance, but local neighbors were not impressed and promptly destroyed it.[40]

Even though the "New Motor" failed, it suggested that Spiritualism could potentially benefit America's booming industrialization, and perhaps even more importantly, it was another path to legitimacy.

Two

Science, Religion and Mysticism

America's industrial revolution inspired a creative genius that mechanized labor, improved communications, and built vast transportation networks. It ushered in a more scientific view of the world that competed with religion and mysticism as the dominant ideology. Spiritualism participated in the competition, using scientific methodology to explain its mysteries while at the same time carving out a distinct religious philosophy.

Robert Hare was a well-known scientist recognized for his contributions in chemistry, invention of powerful batteries, academic appointment as a professor of chemistry at the University of Pennsylvania, and member of prestigious groups such as the American Academy of Arts and Sciences.[1]

If any person on the surface seemed unlikely to embrace Spiritualism it was Robert Hare. Yet he did just that in 1853, in a quixotic quest that cost him scientific respect as he proudly announced, "I sincerely believe that I have communicated with the spirits of my parents, sister, brother, and dearest friends."[2]

Conviction did not come easily to the elderly scientist. He had an uphill struggle scaling years of skepticism, but he eventually conquered his doubts by employing the same scientific strategies successfully used before. Hare desperately wanted to believe that his long-departed loved ones could reach across time and metaphysical space, but he harbored a scientist's uncertainty and sought truth through trials.

Hare wanted to eliminate deceit and used his immense mechanical knowledge to construct a series of spiritoscopes specifically designed to defeat fraud. These were elaborate machines that seemingly made it impossible for a medium to control a spirit table's rappings. Hare described an early example as a table fitted with a large revolving disc with neatly printed letters of the alphabet. Cleverly connected pulleys and weights controlled a pointer that identified spirit selected letters on the disc, "so contrived that neither the medium seated at the table ... nor any other person so seated could, by tilting the table, bring any letter of the alphabet under the index [pointer] nor spell out any word requested." With this instrument and a series of successors, Hare enlisted the services of willing mediums in testing the veracity of spirit communications, and with each experiment Hare dispelled suspicions of deceit.

Hare's experiments added a touch of scientific validity to the claims of Spiritualism, but the faith still needed converts, and testimonials from celebrated individuals were especially welcomed. A particularly noteworthy person among this group was John Worth Edmonds, a New York State supreme court judge whose open and unabashed support surprised his colleagues.

John Worth Edmonds was born in Hudson, New York, in 1799, and after graduating from Union College he began his law practice in 1820. From 1831 to 1836 he was a familiar figure in New York State politics, followed by a return to his law practice. In 1845 he accepted an appointment as a circuit judge and then two years later joined the Supreme Court of New York, a position he forfeited in 1853 after publicly announcing his conversion to Spiritualism.[3]

Readers scanning the morning edition of the *New York Herald* on August 6, 1853, might have noticed a "Very Curious and Interesting Letter from Judge Edmonds." It was a public proclamation defending from innuendo and vilification his new-found faith in Spiritualism, with a jurist's sense of equity: "I am bound to acknowledge the right of others to question my faith, and my own obligation to defend it."

Edmonds's letter was written like a legal brief, with facts flowing from the author's research and assembled as a cogent argument. He began the narrative with his wife's death in 1851, a tumultuous period during which "I was at the time withdrawn from society; I was laboring under great depression of spirits. I was occupying all my leisure in reading on the subject of death, and man's existence afterward."

Edmonds's existential crisis deepened when his traditional religious beliefs could not bridge the bottomless emotional abyss created by his wife's death. Confused and desperately seeking spiritual reunion, the vulnerable man accepted a woman's invitation to attend a séance. The séance was a mind-altering experience that left Edmonds preoccupied with "what I witnessed, and I determined to investigate the matter and find out what it was."

Edmonds's pseudoscientific inquiry of spirit rappings, table tipping, and clairvoyance inextricably and point by point led to his unalterable belief in Spiritualism. It was a personal journey rewarded by a faith that "comforts the mourner and binds up the broken-hearted; that which smooths the passage to the grave and robs death of its terrors." The passionate jurist concluded his case by appealing to the public for a favorable verdict on Spiritualism—and on himself.

The response was rapid and ruthless, cloaked in ridicule, and obliquely questioned Edmonds's mental competence. Of particular concern was the judge's supposed reliance on Spiritualism for deciding complex legal issues, which undermined the Court's integrity. An even more damaging insinuation challenged Edmonds's mental stability, an inference based on his "study of the subject to find relief from profound grief at the loss of his wife.... What is more natural than that a mind so predisposed ... should seize upon these pretended revelations and be gradually drawn into a belief in their truth."[4]

Flummoxed reporters and readers grappled with the implications as the upstart new-age faith collected a consequential coup in Edmonds's conversion. More charitable critics couched their incredulity by emphasizing the judge's sincerity and sound mind before concluding he was a victim of a clever, artful pretense, perpetrated by psychic mediums whose masterful machinations eluded exposure. Other critics were less forgiving and firmly believed that the judge's endorsement would legitimize the illegitimate and claim even more victims as vulnerable citizens fell prey to the siren call of Spiritualism.[5]

Edmonds offered a rebuttal in the 1853 publication of *Spiritualism*, a book co-authored with physician George T. Dexter and embellished with a supportive supplement contributed by Nathaniel P. Tallmadge, the territorial governor of Wisconsin. Content came from twice-weekly séances attended by Edmonds, Dexter and his wife, spiritualist Owen G. Warren, and two unnamed mediums who received communications from the phantoms.[6]

Edmonds used the pages of his book to banish his foes and burnish his image. Curiously, he began his assault on traditional church attendance, extrapolating from census data and personal observations in concluding that most Americans, despite their pledges otherwise, were mostly irreligious. He bolstered that argument by declaring that the proliferation of splintered congregations and factional faiths was symptomatic of an unsettling degree of social drift and dissatisfaction.

In finding reality in Spiritualism, Edmonds abandoned the legal rigor that defined his professional career by accepting "evidence addressed to the mind only, and not to the senses." By rejecting physical evidence and substituting a metaphysical test, Edmonds probably sent shudders through conventional halls of justice.

Judge Edmonds was fully convinced that Spiritualism was real and he was eager to persuade others. Newspapers could broadcast his message, and so it was that an intrepid reporter from the *New York Herald* patiently awaited admittance to the judge's home on October 22, 1853.[7]

Edmonds greeted the keen eyed reporter in his library and immediately impressed the man with his calm, studious demeanor. During this initial encounter the reporter clinically analyzed his subject, noting "his forehead, though not exhibiting to the phrenologist the highest order of intellect ... is by no means an insignificant one.... The impression conveyed was that of acuteness, quickness of perception, and truthfulness."

A flood of emotions carried the reporter's imagination away as he soaked in the ambiance of the judge's library: "If half of what I heard and read of Judge Edmonds and the spirits were true, I was then upon holy ground.... I ought to have taken off my shoes." After recovering his poise, the reporter began interviewing the judge. It was a difficult three-hour meeting because Edmonds repeatedly bristled when the reporter raised the possibility of fraud, but he was far more peaceful when expounding at length, proclaiming Spiritualism a religion "calculated to reform the world."[8]

Edmonds's energetic evangelism spread the gospel of Spiritualism across the country. His proselytizing "lectures are well attended and a strong desire is evinced by the public to hear and investigate the doctrines," despite the nominal admission fee and the ridicule this generated.[9]

In between traveling and holding séances, Judge Edmonds was busy preparing a sequel to his first book, in collaboration as before with Dr. Dexter. Edmonds published the second volume of *Spiritualism* in 1855, and during the brief span separating the two books his daughter and a niece both became spiritual mediums. Edmonds's second volume was a book of revelations with the spirits providing dreamy visions in a way that "not only teaches us that we do indeed live after death, but it teaches us what that life is, affording us the inestimable advantage of knowing how to prepare for it."[10]

Life after death was a blissful garden of delights where "Everything was so full of joy and gladness ... birds, beasts, plants, man; all—all were full of it, overflowing with it ... [there were] innumerable spirits moving about ... some sitting beside a murmuring brook, some reclining on beds of flowers ... some sauntering around sparkling fountains ... no one alone. No sad recluse harbored there."

Edmonds's two books on Spiritualism sold well and suggested the presence of a receptive audience. At the same time, preachers of the prevailing faiths pushed back by mounting multipronged attacks that ranged from mildly ridiculing the beliefs as eccentric to more vigorously denouncing Spiritualism as a sacrilegious cult.

The Rev. William H. Ferris attacked Spiritualism in a series of articles appearing in the *Ladies' Repository*, a Methodist Episcopal publication marketed as a moral alternative to more materialistic magazines. Ferris recognized that the foe he faced was effectively tapping a trend by proving how "the belief of a future life sways the mind of man" while at the same time taking a swipe at Edmonds and others like him by questioning why these individuals were receiving "revelations from eternity more important than any prophet or apostle ever had."[11]

With every step Spiritualism seemingly made in credibility, it inevitably slipped back as public exposés slowed its advance. Janette Waldron was a case in point, a spiritualist speaker and medium whose second sight could not foresee her own future.[12]

Andrew Anguish posted a newspaper advertisement that offered a reward of $500 for information about his missing brother. A short time later, Anguish received a letter from Amos Flyn, who promised to share recently acquired information about his brother in exchange for $50. It seemed suspicious but Anguish accepted the proposal.

Immediately after mailing his response, Anguish rushed to the letter's destination in Utica, New York, and by sharing his suspicions with the postmaster and local police secured their assistance in setting a trap. Acting on the tip, the postmaster notified the police when a woman called for the letter, a timely intervention that led to the woman's arrest "for attempting to obtain money under false pretences." As it turned out, the woman arrested was Janette Waldron, a local spiritualist who sheepishly admitted sending the letter under the guise of Amos Flyn while under influence of bad spirits.

Critics of Spiritualism seized on a potent question when they wondered why the spirits did not extend their efforts to preventing the calamities of life such as "stopping a locomotive when it runs off the tracks—arresting children when about to fall into accident or mischief—restraining the hand of crime." Instead of such noble interventions, the spirits seemed content with parlor tricks like floating furniture, a barely uplifting spiritual experience.[13]

Despite the determined onslaught from naysayers, Spiritualism continued to attract interest in America as evidenced by the burgeoning number of mediums, and finding a spiritualist in 1858 was easily accomplished by scanning a newspaper's advertisements. Mediums marketed their various skills with small advertisements in the same columns typically shared with patent medicines, common merchandise, and more mundane business notices.

The list seemed endless, with Mr. A.B. Whiting, a trance medium, surely hoping that large audiences would attend one of his two lectures on

Spiritualism in Baltimore, Maryland, during which he promised a ghost writer would extemporaneously author a poem of an attendee's choice.[14]

Dr. William Pratt offered two lectures on Spiritualism in Baltimore, with the morning session dispensing with the evening's 10-cent admission.[15] Mr. Laning had a similar promotion in Baltimore on February 7, 1858, with two soothing lectures. His morning lecture offered an emotional argument contending that "Spiritualism [is] not opposed to Christianity or Bible Truth," followed by an evening discourse devoted to the scientific evidence underpinning the faith.[16]

Alonzo Newton was an editor of *The Spiritual Age*, which probably ensured an enthusiastic audience would attend his two lectures in Baltimore on November 14, 1858. *The Spiritual Age* was a weekly publication "devoted to rational Spiritualism and practical reform," with offices in Boston, New York City, and Chicago. Annual subscriptions cost $2 and informed readers about "the mysterious capabilities of departed human spirits" through supposedly scientific investigations.

The first edition of *The Spiritual Age* was dated January 2, 1858, following the merger of Newton's former publication the *New England Spiritualist* with Samuel B. Brittan's *Spiritual Age*. Articles on spiritual philosophy and the many manifestations of mediums graced the pages. A cautionary story titled "Vagabond Mediums" lamented the rise of roving spiritualists traveling through America's rural communities, trafficking in detestable deceit but easily distinguished from their honest counterparts through their "bluster, extravagant pretension, egotism, and big-eyed, open-mouthed credulity."[17]

A variety of advertisements supplemented the subscription cost of *The Spiritual Age* while providing readers with useful resources. For example, visitors to Saratoga Springs, New York, could consult I.G. Atwood, a magnetic and mental physician with spirit healing powers. A.C. Stiles, M.D., promised prospective patients in Bridgeport, Connecticut, an accurate diagnosis and cancer cure and reassured the risk-averse with a money-back guarantee.[18]

Spiritualists fielded an impressive array of enterprising businesses, but the Poughkeepsie Seer's mission was a single-minded focus devoted to building the philosophical foundation for Spiritualism. Andrew Jackson Davis, otherwise known as the Poughkeepsie Seer, was born in 1826 in the small village of Blooming Grove, New York. At the age of 13 his family moved north to Poughkeepsie, New York, and until 1843 nothing remarkable transpired.

The agent of change was animal magnetism, brought to the sleepy community by Mr. Grimes, a self-styled professor who enlightened and entertained the citizens with lectures and demonstrations. Davis was among the curious crowd, but Grimes's efforts to single out and mesmerize the teenage boy failed.

A local tailor by the name of William Levingston seemed an unlikely practitioner of the mysterious art, but after attending one of the itinerant entertainer's exhibitions he left the meeting with the express intention of duplicating the deed. His enthusiasm had barely cooled when young Andrew entered his store. Levingston seized the opportunity to practice animal magnetism and soon succeeded in magnetizing his subject. As proof, Davis read a book with his eyes bound, described distant, unvisited cities in detail, and performed other acts of amazing clairvoyance.

The newly branded Poughkeepsie Seer quickly grew tired of amusing the curiosity seekers and turned his clairvoyant proclivities to the practice of medicine. Over the next three years Davis ministered to a steady stream of the afflicted. His talents caught the attention of Dr. Lyon, who regularly magnetized Davis and then used the young clairvoyant to consult with medical authorities in the spirit world.

Ambitious spirits had bigger plans for Davis and during an enchanted state directed that William Fishbough, a casual acquaintance, help launch the next phase of his career as a traveling philosopher. Fishbough's job was laborious, requiring a written verbatim record of Davis's messages from the spiritual world. With a touch of humility and a ring of incredulity, Fishbough later wrote that "this appointment was entirely unsolicited (we will not say undesired) by ourself ... and so far from anticipating such an honor ... wrote Mr. Davis' first lecture at his dictation."

With Dr. Lyon as his magnetizer, Fishbough as his secretary, and three people proclaiming his prowess, Davis's little entourage launched the lectures. Aside from this small group the only others admitted were observers carefully selected and chosen to exclude those deemed to be unbelievers or troublemakers.

Davis's communion with the spirits was a tedious affair testing the patience of all in attendance. Lyon would induce the 20-year-old man's altered mental state with a few passes of his hands, followed by a series of dramatic contortions in Davis which signaled his connection with the spirits. Once in contact with the spirits, Davis "opens his mouth, uttering a few words at a time, which the clairvoyant requires to be repeated by Dr. Lyon, in order that he may know that he is understood. A pause then ensues, until what he has said has been written, when he again proceeds."[19]

With the passage of up to four hours and the transcription of three to 15 pages of carefully handwritten notes, the exhausted group would retire for the day. The process was repeated for 157 lectures over 423 days, with the last on January 25, 1847. At that point complete, Davis's lectures were bound together and published as the spiritual manifesto, *The Principles of Nature, Her Divine Revelations, and a Voice to Mankind*.

Adding apparent authenticity to the spiritual revelations was Fishbough's assertion that the Poughkeepsie Seer was an illiterate lad with a mere five months of education, with the implication being that such profound prose in *The Principles of Nature, Her Divine Revelations, and a Voice to Mankind* was beyond the cleverness of Davis. At the same time, Fishbough admitted some editorial license when transcribing the medium's message.

Fishbough and Lyon jointly published *The Principles of Nature, Her Divine Revelations, and a Voice to Mankind*, a ponderous tome consisting of three chapters that began by introducing Andrew Jackson Davis. As might be expected, the sympathetic story was carefully crafted to convince an incredulous reader. Fishbough positioned the Poughkeepsie Seer in this manner by declaring that "it is known to an absolute moral certainty to Mr. Davis's most intimate acquaintances, that he was, while in the normal state, totally uninformed on all the great leading subjects treated in this book, until he perused the manuscripts of his own lectures."

Established theologians schooled in the traditional tenets of the Old and New Testaments were variously appalled, dismissive, contemptuous, and perhaps even amused at sophistries such as "the doctrine of the trinity was thus derived from the early conception of three original beings that were supposed to have been engaged in creating the earth and man ... and as I clearly perceive the origin of the doctrine, I hesitate not to declare that it is strictly a mythos."

Readers making it through the second part of *The Principles of Nature, Her Divine Revelations, and a Voice to Mankind* found the third chapter devoted to "The Application; or a Voice to Mankind." With the spirit guides controlling his voice, Davis discussed the social and psychological state of humanity. According to Davis, humans are rather miserably grouped as "the poor, ignorant, enslaved, oppressed, and working classes ... the semi-wealthy, learned, enslavers, oppressors, and dictating classes ... and the rich, intelligent ... and idle classes." From their inner world the spirits lamented class inequity, profiteering, religious dogma, and despotism, offering in their place a plethora of liberal moral antidotes aimed at overcoming corrosive communal conditions.[20]

Perhaps the twists and turns, the convolutions and contortions, and the unmitigated hubris of Davis's magnum opus provided some readers the necessary aura of believability. As a prophet, Davis based his supposedly unassailable authority on his intimate connection with the all-knowing ghosts of the dearly departed. For believers in Spiritualism, that was enough.

Davis extended his literary efforts to the publication of the short-lived *Herald of Progress*, an eight-page weekly periodical positioned as "a Cosmopolitan Journal of Health, Progress, and Reform ... an airy platform from which the editor offered urbane commentaries on 'spiritual mysteries and things from the inner life.'"[21]

Readers intrigued by the subject could subscribe to the *Herald of Progress*, from roughly a year before the Civil War started, until the publication's demise in 1864. With a life span from 1860 to 1864, The *Herald of Progress* included the tumultuous period preceding the war, while the onset of full-scale hostilities offered Davis the opportunity to philosophically weigh in.[22]

The first editions of Davis's *Herald of Progress* debuted on February 4, 1860, and included a question-and-answer section. In a brief exchange, an unnamed speaking medium asked the editor "whether the number of mediums in the United States is as great this year as last." Davis's response provided his best estimate of Spiritualism's presence about one year before the shots fired at Ft. Sumter signaled the start of America's Civil War. Claiming a careful analysis before opining, Davis imagined two million converts to Spiritualism, ministered to by more than 38,000 psychic mediums.[23]

Dr. J.H. Rae, a self-styled electromagnetic physician and healing medium located in New York City, took advantage of the *Herald of Progress*'s advertising with a lengthy proclamation offering relief for prospective patients suffering from nervous headaches, joint pain, impotence, blindness, and pretty much every other ailment that plagued people. Rae accomplished his miracles by studying "the magnetism of the mind as well as that of the body ... and then I operate to remove both the voluntary and involuntary cause of disease, by Animal and Electro Magnetism."

J.B. Conklin was a well-known test medium from New York reveling in the accolades bestowed as early as 1854 in the pages of the *Spiritual Telegraph*. When news of mysterious manifestations leaked out of Athens County, Ohio, Conklin joined fellow psychic Stephen Dudley and two unnamed women for a journey westward. The investigators began their trip by train, leaving Buffalo, New York, and civilization behind as they made the trek through the wilderness. Their destination was roughly 80 miles southeast of Columbus, Ohio, the last portion of which the travelers traversed over rough, mountainous terrain in an uncomfortable stagecoach before finally arriving at the celebrated Koons's Spirit Room.[24]

Conklin and crew joined the festivities along with a much larger group of mostly local skeptics gathering for an evening's diversion. Jonathan Koons was the master of ceremonies and reserved special seats for the luminaries from New York, and after brief introductory comments a thunderous, room-shaking blow on a bass drum signaled the spirits arrival. As usual, the spirits were in a playful mood, singing, and playing a violin.

The group from New York wanted a private sitting free of the distracting naysayers, a request granted by Jonathan Koons and scheduled the next evening. At the appointed time the party of four took their seats along with Koons, his wife, and his son. As before, the spirits announced their arrival with a banging of the drum and then took up the violin and voice in an angelic choir. Following this melodious manifestation a spirit hand appeared and, seizing a pencil on the table, began furiously writing on a piece of paper, at the end of which the cold interloper shook hands with the visitors.

Stephen Dudley and his fellow passengers returned to New York and published the spirit hand's missive in *The Age of Progress*, a newspaper sympathetic to Spiritualism. It was a high-toned message recognizing humanity's endless anxiety and quest for life's meaning, revealed at last "to show the infidel and skeptic that there is a brighter state of existence beyond the shadow and valley of the grave."

Spirit rapping popularized by the Fox sisters spread to Ohio and infected Jonathan Koons as early as 1852, when the Athens County farmer began holding séances in that remote stretch of land. Groups of both profane and probing neighbors attended Koons's spirit rapping sessions, but tempers and tolerance sometimes took a toll. One late evening a fanatical few filled with alcohol and animosity set fire to Koons's barn, destroying his farm implements and a year's worth of crops.[25]

Koons professed his piety and purity in a letter published in the *Spiritual Telegraph*. With an air of indignation and exasperation, Koons exclaimed that skeptics examined every inch of his little spirit room and found little more than dust. Dark exhibitions and those performed during the light of day were the same, with neither producing any evidence of trickery. To his critics, Koons caustically concluded, "I cannot be responsible for their ignorance ... which, I fear, is too often willful."[26]

It was a perplexing personal period of introspection that led Koons to Spiritualism. In his younger days he rebelled against orthodox Christianity and in return was shunned and scorned, in a painful epoch that did little to mend the breach. Atheism was not the answer, and with his empty reservoir of faith the man turned to Spiritualism, hoping to fill that void.[27]

In the beginning he was a skeptic, determined to prove the practice a fraud, but in the end he failed. With resolute determination Koons trained his sights on a young female medium, and with her acquiescence they both attended a séance. To his wondering amazement a spirit rapped out the right answers to question after question. Returning home,

Koons discovered his own spiritual powers as a writing medium, and soon thereafter his entire family, consisting of nine children and his wife, were similarly affected.

Despite the setbacks, Koons and his family graduated from mundane spirit rapping and began their new calling with a novel gimmick. Claiming inspiration and direction from the spirit world, Koons built a spiritual machine, an impressive-looking mechanical conjuring contraption. Visitors could not avoid marveling at the large device: a wooden base two yards long and two and a half feet tall upon which an assortment of glass rods, metal drums, and copper wires gave the appearance of a galvanic battery. Koons claimed the spirits charged the device with electricity as a performance prerequisite. Once again the spirits joined America's march toward industrialization.[28]

Koons's spirit room was a rough-hewn structure set in the woods, roughly six feet from a larger dwelling where the family lived. The spirit room was a log building about 12 by 16 feet with a seven-foot ceiling. Furniture was spartan, with wood benches for spectators and chairs for the Koons family. After Jonathan closed the window shutters, the spiritual machine sent sparks flying as a prelude to the spirit's arrival.[29]

Clark Williams spent four days in late October 1854 at the Koons spirit room. With a party of 20 others, Clark noted the "retainer of electricity" prominently placed in the small room, and looking around spied Jonathan Koons and his 17-year-old psychic son. A long tin trumpet, a tambourine, drums, and violins scattered about the room set the stage for the spirit's antics. A loud, boisterous concert shook the little frame house, followed by a deafening silence, heralding the floating hand's entrance. Once again the disembodied limb took pencil to paper and scribed the wisdom of the ages.[30]

Clark fell ill the next day, threatening an early departure. His host suggested he postpone his decision and seek the counsel of Mr. King, Koons's most faithful phantom. At the next séance Mr. King spoke through the tin trumpet and diagnosed the ailing man's disturbance as dyspepsia and recommended a draught of pipsissewa tea, a soothing remedy that unsurprisingly quelled the man's queasiness.

In spite of the spirit hand's entreaties, not everyone attending a Koons séance left convinced. A withering letter written under the pseudonym "Common Sense" deconstructed the materializing events step by step. Common Sense took issue with the dark séance and the phosphorous-coated spirit hand, questioned when the lengthy letters were actually written, and dismissed the whole affair as the result of "a good psychologist [who] can make many persons believe the same thing at the same time, no matter how ridiculous."[31]

Incensed spiritualists probably fumed at Common Sense's criticism, but William W. Conkle burned with rage. He wrote a stinging rebuke attacking the author for hiding his name and then engaging in a guerrilla campaign lobbing libels at Spiritualism. Conkle aggressively assumed the moral summit and from that vantage point questioned "whether his own heart and acts are free from improper motives, ere he makes such sweeping charges against so large a class of persons."[32]

It all ended rather quietly. A short notice in the *Spiritual Telegraph*'s March 26, 1859, edition sadly informed readers that "Koons' trumpet medium has lost all his medium powers, and is no longer subject to spiritual influence."[33]

In the years immediately preceding the Civil War, Spiritualism was a familiar feature filling the pages of Northern newspapers. Stories oscillated around doubting dismissals, cautious conviction, and absolute acceptance, with many tilting toward some degree of belief.

Among those hedging their belief was a *New York Herald* reporter in 1858 summarizing the advent and advance of Spiritualism, in a personal narrative explaining an evolution from downright distrust to a discreet acknowledgment of its legitimate existence. The reporter began his journey of spiritual enlightenment with a farcical flair, "having a good time generally among the defunct who have consecrated their invisible existence to my amusement for an indefinite period."[34]

In tracing this history of Spiritualism, the reporter paid due homage to Andrew Jackson Davis before turning his acerbic sights to the proliferation of table tipping, rapping, writing, and healing mediums, with a frostiness that melted "when the medium is a young, beautiful, and interesting woman." Warming the reporter's heart were Cora Hatch, Emma Jay Bullene, Lottie Beebe, and "Miss Sprague, Miss Hardinge, Miss Hesier and others have spoken in our principal cities ... and the least that could be said of them is that they make out a plausible case for spiritualism."

With the potential for three million believers, the reporter scanned the environment seeking an explanation for Spiritualism's rapid rise before settling on its acceptance by such a wide swath of the upper class, the haute bourgeoisie populated by notable jurists, academics, scientists, and theologians. If any one group had an outsized influence, it was the class of ecclesiastics who tipped the tables on traditional religion with their embrace of Spiritualism. All in all, the reporter's personal pilgrimage concluded on a modest note that "whatever be its intrinsic merit as a philosophy, it is now a power in the land that is rapidly increasing."

Academics jousted with Spiritualism using science as their foil. The Rev. Asa Mahan, President of Cleveland University in Ohio, authored a magnum opus on "Modern Mysteries." His erudite examination of Spiritualism did little to settle any debate and in fact clouded the subject even further. Mahan conceded that some of the spiritualist's manifestations were genuine, but he adamantly rejected ghosts as the agency, leaving room for an alternative explanation.[35]

Mahan imagined the presence of an odylic force, an invisible power similar to a magnet's ability to attract and repulse, which was concentrated and transmitted through space by susceptible people. Instead of sprightly spirits, Mahan insisted that "the odylic force developed in the human system acts upon other objects ... without any physical touch, such as chairs, tables, and various articles of furniture." Mysterious rappings emanated from the same force bouncing off walls. Clairvoyance was nothing more than the odylic force of one person controlling the thoughts, behavior, and actions of another.

By accepting the manifestations of Spiritualism as genuine, Mahan added an academic's credibility to what many people considered fraudulent. His rejection of spirits did not offend established church doctrine, but it left the puzzle unsolved. Mahan fashioned his own secular, pseudo-scientific solution that in many respects was simply unbelievable.

A determined group of rogues, rowdies, and scoffers dogged spiritualists. In Portland, Maine, a local newspaper featured an advertisement promoting a lecture aptly titled "The Humbug of Spiritualism," in the course of which the self-appointed emissary of truth promised to let "the cat out of the bag." A packed audience eagerly awaited the presentation. They were motivated by the bargain ticket price of five cents and perhaps they simply sought the thrill of debunking Spiritualism. Shortly after taking the stage, the lecturer casually opened a large bag and almost immediately a large cat jumped out of the bag and scurried off stage. It probably stunned everyone, but after a moment's reflection the room erupted in laughter, sparing the entertainer what could have been a very rough rebuke.[36]

Some spiritualists retreated to the safety of higher ground by conceding deceit and admitted through their confession what many skeptics suspected. Dr. Randolph was a well-known fixture of the traveling seer circuit and cast aspersions "that spiritualism was one-third imposture, one-third insanity, and one-third diabolism." Perhaps his revelation was an attempt to prevent a spiritualist's descent to insanity, which Randolph considered the end result of a life devoted to Spiritualism.[37]

In another case, mischief makers upended a methodically planned exhibition and revealed through their feats the deeply guarded secrets of a spiritualist by exposing the trickery. George P. Payne was a theoretically trustworthy table-tipping telekinetic whose powers of persuasion converted scores of nonbelievers to Spiritualism. Unfortunately, he suffered an epic failure one night when confronted by Mr. Coles, who was a member of a renegade class, a psychic medium turned humbug buster.[38]

Payne glowed with an aura of adoration that was the result of a carefully crafted phony façade hiding a fatal flaw: a brash, in-your-face, challenging arrogance. Expecting to slay any naysayers, Payne traveled from his headquarters in Worcester, Massachusetts, to Geneva, New York, for the express purpose of convincing Cole of his table-tipping talent.

Cole enlisted the help of two other men and together they joined Payne at a séance. The group had barely assembled when Cole peremptorily demanded the table be repositioned, prompting Payne's refusal. Doubt and determination drove the inquisitive trio to carefully examine the floor, and through their careful inspection they exposed a small tear in the carpet under the table. With no escape, Payne capitulated and freely but glumly admitted that the table-tipping artifice was the result of a cleverly contrived stout wire rising invisibly from the carpet. Payne was bent but not broken, and in a shameless, face-saving pretension he insisted he "had resorted to deception in order to meet deception, and ultimately expose it."

While some fakers failed their inquisition, other psychics dodged detection. In the years leading up the Civil War, Cora Hatch continued her propitious promenade across America with her trips announced in advance to ensure a favorable reception by fawning reporters. Midway through 1857, an advertisement served notice that "Mrs. Cora Hatch, whose lectures have excited so great an interest in New York and Boston, is expected in Baltimore."[39]

Mr. A.S. Gibbs managed various aspects of Cora's cross-country performances, including helping or perhaps steering the audience's selection of the committee that would try to stump the young medium. On one occasion the committee asked Cora, "Is the law of God a unit; or is a violation of one command a breaking of the whole law?"[40]

Cora pondered the question as she gazed contentedly upward, a pious posture perfect for receiving the emanations from beyond. At last, she began a ponderous dissertation oscillating around a metaphysical notion that "Man had three natures": physical, intellectual, and religious, each with its own immutable laws. An enraptured audience listened thoughtfully and betrayed no doubts as the woman's musings meandered to and fro.

Cora avoided the withering criticism that other mediums sometimes suffered. A male medium reached to the heavens and flummoxed his audience with a supposedly divine demonstration of several foreign languages. The revelation of such knowledge from the spirit world led a reporter to wryly observe "that the medium ... becomes conscious of everything, except the fact that he is making a fool of himself."[41]

Conjuring spirits sometimes had sinister side effects. Psychic mediums mostly sidestepped these potholes, but some were tripped up giving cudgels to Spiritualism's opponents. Every now and then a spiritualist committed suicide, which was an unfortunate outcome that antagonists eulogized as the natural course of succumbing to sacrilege. Another moral bomb thrown at spiritualists was a proclivity toward infidelity, a self-inflicted perception promoted by a free-love faction. Critics also claimed Spiritualism fostered fraud and foul play. Taken together, a reporter facetiously opined, "if spiritualism were true, we should need to be very careful what sort of spirits, we put ourselves in connection with."[42]

By 1860 Spiritualism was still courting controversy and counting converts. Miss M. Johnson traveled from Boston to Brooklyn, perhaps hoping to find an elusive success, but her first spiritualist meeting in New York netted only three people. Three weeks later she tried again and this time she welcomed a larger crowd. As the audience waited and watched, Miss Johnson settled easily into a comfortable chair, closed her eyes, and was silent and seemingly somnolent for about 15 minutes. She then dramatically rose and with her eyes still closed began a one-hour lecture describing the beauty of heaven and the perils of hell and the pathways to each. The reporter attending the event was not impressed but sarcastically supposed enough dupes would keep her busy.[43]

Opposition to Spiritualism took many forms, with some convinced that its practice led to insanity. Cavorting with ghosts could only warp the mind, and publishing the occasional sensational story served that point. With the heading "another victim," readers might have noticed the sad story of Charles Higby, a retired postmaster of a small Pennsylvania community who succumbed to the seduction of Spiritualism. With nothing more than supposition, the short news story claimed that Higby "became crazy from the effects of spiritualism," an insinuation furthered by his subsequent death in an insane asylum.[44]

Impugning Spiritualism through innuendo was an indirect attack, but damning revelations by members of the cult were a direct hit. Among the subjects a newspaper advertised as "just published" in 1860 was a curious title "Confessions of a Medium."[45] Interested readers could find the anonymously written article in *The Atlantic Monthly*.[46]

On the surface, "Confessions of a Medium" suggested a scintillating exposé of Spiritualism, revealing the tricks from an insider's perspective. Readers expecting such were probably disappointed with the author, who narrated his personal evolution from a passionate partisan to a disillusioned disciple after his faith was damaged but not destroyed.

Despite the public's wavering waves of belief in Spiritualism, many entertainers of the faith rode the crest, thrilling audiences with their antics. In California, Professor J.H. Anderson and his two daughters Louisa and Flora joined together for a spellbinding night of magical manifestations with a spirit table taking center stage. Audience members asked questions and the professor's spirit table obligingly rapped responses. The self-styled "great wizard of the north" commanded a premium by charging $1.50 for orchestra seats and a lofty $5 for those seeking some anonymity in a private box.[47]

Two years later, in 1862, the originally anonymous publication revealed its author when Bayard Taylor added "Confessions of a Medium" as a chapter in a book otherwise best characterized as part diary and part American travelogue. Taylor's end-of-the-book addition of "Confessions of a Medium" seemed out of place, given the other mundane topics, but viewed from a broader context it simply described a different journey, in this case a metaphysical excursion.

Taylor was introspective and from his earliest years displayed a mix of sensitivity and sensibility that proved to be traits he recognized in his parents. It was an unequal mixture, with the former prevailing in his youth and contributing to a vivid imagination with pleasant dissociative daydreams offering a retreat from reality and particularly when suffering a Sunday sermon. During one abominably long sermon the young boy's daydreaming took a different turn as seemingly disembodied voices left an indelible impression: "If there is any happy delirium in the first stages of intoxication ... it must be a sensation very much like that which I felt."

Not surprisingly, his parents were alarmed by the young boy's behavior and sensing a connection between the sermons and the somnambulism spared Taylor subsequent sessions. As Taylor matured, the daydreaming receded but his philosophical proclivities intensified, an anxiety driven by thoughts of life's meaning and mortality but partially assuaged by animal magnetism.

Taylor's fundamental question, "Does the human soul continue to exist after death?," was not fully answered by animal magnetism, but another event unfolding at the time did. The sensational Rochester rappings captivated and calmed his tortured mind, and for further affirmation Taylor traveled to New York City to witness the marvelous manifestations of the Fox sisters. As they did with many visitors, the Fox sisters impressed Taylor as honest and forthright, encouraging the man to summon the spirits he sought. Conversations with his mother and several other dead family members diminished doubt and strengthened his resolve to dig deeper into Spiritualism.

Taylor began attending séances after meeting with the Fox sisters.

At his first circle he joined hands with "a girl of sixteen, Miss Abby Fetters, a pale, delicate creature, with blond hair and light-blue eyes." Shortly after that touching moment, the table began dancing about as Fetters and Taylor tenaciously held fast, finally releasing their grip and watching in wonder as the table settled silently to the floor.

Now convinced beyond all doubt, Taylor devoted every waking moment to studying Spiritualism and refining his newfound mediumship. Two factors propelled the man: the warm, almost erotic sensation attached to the somnambulistic mental state and a special pride in being selected as a channel for the spirit's return. Present at every séance was the charming Miss Fetters, whose spiritual evolution impressed Taylor, a growth that took a dark turn and snuffed out any budding romantic thoughts the young man may have entertained.

Taylor's circle expanded and contracted as members came and went over time, but a nucleus of believers constituted the core. A man named Stilton eventually joined the group and quickly established a dominant role aided by his appearance as "a stout, strongly built man, with coarse black hair, gray eyes, large animal mouth, square jaws, and short, thick neck." His presence stimulated the spirits and Miss Fetters.

Shortly after Stilton's arrival a change came over the social circle. Miss Fetters was far more animated and conjured crude ghosts more interested in liquid spirits, a request Stilton granted by ensuring the young girl always had a glass of whiskey nearby. Fetters's disgraceful descent shocked Taylor's moral sensibilities, an assessment sharpened by a growing familiarity between Stilton and the young girl.

Taylor watched helplessly as Stilton manipulated Fetters and his wife, a woman described in the most pitiful terms as loyal and endlessly abused. Claiming divine inspiration and instruction, Stilton promoted the adulterous affair, even as his weeping wife meekly protested. Taylor was disgusted and confused, recognizing the exploitation but unwilling to abandon his faith, an agonizing mental state that left the man on the brink of insanity. As he teetered on the edge, a young woman of traditional convictions rescued the man because "Agnes loved me, and in the deep, quiet bliss, which this knowledge gave I felt the promise of deliverance."[48]

For his part, Taylor realized that dark, evil forces lurked in the phantom world and could corrupt susceptible psychics. It was a cautious conclusion that left his belief in Spiritualism intact. Taylor's tale, like so many others, left Spiritualism tattered but not totally torn on the eve of America's Civil War.

Three

Spiritualism During the Civil War

Spiritualism's growth slowed during the early years of the Civil War as passions and patriotism replaced festering philosophical ponderings. The war riveted the nation's attention, diverting and draining doubts about the meaning of life and the hereafter with these heavy topics displaced by the rumbling realties of a coming conflict. A sense of invincibility among glory-hunting soldiers swelled regimental ranks and served as a psychic shield fending off the Fates. Chaos, carnage, and discontent battered that mental buffer exposing the naked reality of war, a revelation requiring a somber reassessment of aspirations.

Most soldiers stayed the course by placing their faith in military commanders, along with an untold number who relied on religion and turned to unit chaplains for comfort and compassion. Communications with far-away loved ones also softened the hard edges, but dependable mail service was not certain and sometimes callously subtracted its benefit. Less resilient soldiers succumbed to the tragedy of war, sometimes by drowning their doubts in alcohol or perhaps gambling that a disgraceful desertion was a better bet than a battlefield death.

An imponderable future shaped by war naturally included private thoughts of death. Breaching that boundary and freely discussing such anxiety could be condemned as cowardice, an unconscious social strategy that prevented a fear-laden contagion. Some soldiers surely settled on Spiritualism's soothing solution offering a life after death, and conniving mediums dutifully dispensed the balm.

With the dawn of a new decade and war on the distant horizon, the apostles of Spiritualism doggedly pursued their faith across the country. In 1861, just a few months before the Civil War began, a group of believers made an exodus to Hammonton, New Jersey, prompting a newspaper's derision: "about eleven hundred fools are already there or on their way thither, most of whom are spiritualists."¹ Hammonton attracted spiritualists as early as 1858, welcoming both local citizens and peripatetic preachers to regularly scheduled meetings.[2]

Just before war engulfed the country, J.B. Conklin enlightened and entertained audiences in Louisville, Kentucky, and Nashville, Tennessee.[3] In Iowa, Miss Laura E.A. DeForce invited the public to a series of lectures, including "Do we live as spirits after death of the body, and if so can spirits communicate with their friends on earth?"[4]

Bubbling passions predicting the coming conflict were on full display in Ann Arbor, Michigan, when a small group of abolitionists and spiritualists, both fervently antislavery, announced a conclave discussing the subject on January 26, 1861. Noted abolitionist Parker Pillsbury from Boston, Massachusetts, and Mrs. Jane Griffing were the keynote speakers. The meeting took place at a spiritualist church and attracted a sizeable crowd of partisans, some favoring abolition, and a larger, boisterous group determined to denounce Parker and Griffing's views. With emotions escalating, the "rowdies" took the upper hand, threatening the speakers and destroying the building.[5]

Newspapers still paired suicide and Spiritualism with not too subtle hints to avoid the practice or risk insanity. Suicide was bad enough, but casting traditional religion aside made for an even more ignominious death. In one of the innumerable short stories readers may have noticed was the death of Harvey McAlpin, an attorney in Port Huron, Michigan, succumbing to suicide after years of devotion to the faith.[6]

The moral crusade combatting Spiritualism catalogued conspicuous cases of fraud until the realities of the Civil War refocused the crusader's energies. It was hoped that such examples would warn wavering citizens considering the faith. In Pittsburg, Pennsylvania, Tennessee Clafin was a 12-year-old girl locally known as a "wonderful child" for her supposed sixth sense. By word of mouth, visitors from the surrounding area learned of Tennessee's miraculous healing powers and, forsaking traditional doctors, put their faith in a young girl.[7]

A school teacher who perhaps should have known better consulted Tennessee for a chronic, painful eye disorder, After eight weeks of treatment that included mesmerism and spirit medicines the teacher was $11 poorer and still suffering. Another victim was a music teacher seeking relief from bronchitis who, despite paying $5 and receiving similar treatments, fared no better. An unfortunate side effect of the treatment left the music teacher "crazy at times, and [she] didn't know what she was doing."

Tennessee's father was the ringleader of the little clan and exploited his daughter and gullible neighbors in a get-rich-quick scheme. Dozens a day showed up seeking consolation but leaving disillusioned, distraught, and drained of their meager money. Uncouth manners, brash boasting, and disenchanted patrons eventually led to the Clafin family's arrest.

America's collision of wills turned lethal when Confederate forces took aim at Ft. Sumter, South Carolina, on April 12, 1861, and explosively transformed a war waged with words into more deadly deterrence. The dramatic escalation left little room for neutrality, finally forcing most to cast their fate with like-minded Southern or Northern sympathizers. Spiritualists opposed slavery and philosophically aligned their movement with the Northern states. At the same time, their reinterpretation of established religious views conflicted even more with the traditional teachings in the Southern states.

Madame Lucy A. Cooke, a clairvoyant physician in Vermont, professed her pride by hoisting a 12- by 18-foot flag, a patriotic display of "the workmanship of her own hands, and wholly at her own expense, and [she] was *wide awake* all the while."[8]

Spiritualists thoughtfully struggled with war and debated pacifism versus participation. Before the war between the states, Andrew Jackson Davis, the doctrine's dean, addressed war in classical terms, considering the cost of conflict to be the price for the evolution of humanity's freedom.[9]

With the Civil War now a reality, Davis reconsidered the role of spiritualists in the army in his characteristic, convoluted manner, distilling the debate as a moral crusade pitting liberty against slavery. After elevating individual freedom from tyranny to the loftiest pinnacle, Davis concluded that "resistance should be moral and spiritual, but sometimes the *physical* is most effective, and for this reason it is sometimes the best prevention of formidable evils to mankind."[10]

Davis's spiritually informed opinion did not quell dissent. In a letter to Davis published in the *Herald of Progress*, Milo Townsend respectfully disagreed with the editor, offering instead an apocalyptic assessment of the Civil War. Drawing on his faith in Spiritualism, Townsend's soul searching probably resonated with other spiritualists with pacifist proclivities, as he argued that violence only begets more violence, trapping the protagonists in a vicious spiral. Townsend believed war was both retribution and salvation, much like the biblical account of Noah's Ark and the great flood.[11]

Palpable, partisan bitterness split families previously separated only by geography. A Southern woman wrote a passionate defense to a relative's denunciation of secession by accusing Northerners of flagrant aggression and anti-Christian sacrilege. "In the South we have no conscience higher than the Bible ..., we do not worship... spiritualism, abolitionism, and all the other isms in the North which poison the springs of domestic and public virtue ... while your churches are filled with sewing machines to manufacture clothing for the minions of a tyrant who would enslave us, ours still contain the affairs of our God."[12]

A Southern newspaper's editorial struck a similar defiant note portending a lengthy conflict. "As enemies, we fear them not.... We have no need of them, or of anything they have ... their hollow philosophy, their sanguinary religion, their Spiritualism, Mormonism, Free Love or Abolitionism."[13]

Standing alongside the serious social discourse were seers peering into the future, hoping to find fame and fortune. In Indianapolis, Indiana, a well-placed, unnamed citizen confidently broadcast a message from his spiritualist brother. In what was surely one of the worst predictions, perhaps transmitted by mischievous spirits, the brother relayed that the bloody conflict was forever over if no battle occurred on June 22, 1861, in Virginia between the opposing forces. The reporter's tongue-in-cheek commentary concluded: "As we have no intelligence of any battle on the 22d ... we are a little curious to know how the difficulty is to be settled. Will our friend enlighten us?"[14]

Faithful followers turned the pages of spiritualist newspapers and were reassured by the litany of telling testimonials. Mainstream periodicals spanned the spectrum, with some ridiculing Spiritualism while others vacillated between what seemed to be a community-minded effort warning readers of the perils and a more banal circulation building sensationalism. Whatever their motive, the print media brought attention to the obscure belief and through the process magnified Spiritualism by adding elements of visibility and credibility.

Eyewitness accounts of mysterious manifestations, both pro and con, rippled through various periodicals, leaving voracious readers whipsawed. Anonymous or pseudonymous reports cast doubt on their authenticity but probably reinforced a reader's inclinations nonetheless. "Enquirer" authored a letter to the editor of a Wisconsin newspaper describing a meeting with a medium in Chicago, Illinois. It was clear from the outset that the author was a skeptic, and accompanied by two friends, he set about proving his point.[15]

Miss Hoyt greeted the trio, and after forming the circle she asked each participant to write the names of those in the spirit world they would like to contact. "Enquirer" listed Yankee Doodle, an implausible choice but one that Miss Hoyt had no trouble summoning. With the channel to the spirit world opened by Miss Hoyt, Yankee Doodle identified the skeptic as a soldier and looking into the man's future saw his safe passage through many bloody battles.

It was a cleverly constructed ruse. "Enquirer" had assumed the role of a soldier and attended the séance in a uniform, completing a devious trap that felled Miss Hoyt. Sensing a setup, Miss Hoyt and her spirits clammed up, but the skeptic left the séance convinced that his $1 admission was money well spent.

Incredulity met inconsistency through advertising. Buried in the back of many newspapers were advertisements hawking all types of psychic services, and even while page one might lambaste or lampoon Spiritualism, phantom profits were real and tangible. As a consequence, periodicals of every stripe welcomed the adverts of people like Madame Victorine Hollard, a clairvoyant and magnetic doctor whose attractive promise of curing the incurable was a deceptive draw. During Hollard's cooing clairvoyant canard she asked "no questions, nor does she require invalids to explain symptoms, telling their cause and location with so much satisfaction as to merit and receive the confidence of all who have consulted her."[16]

Even the mighty *New York Herald* sold psychics some space in a section for astrologers. Mrs. Alexis offered her services as a test medium and second-sighted specialist for medical and business matters. Madame Milton was a sympathetic seer, commiserating with those duped by misleading mediums and promising to restore their faith. Her expertise extended well beyond curing the typical medical maladies with a special gift as "the only lady who can restore drunken or unfaithful husbands." Unfortunately, Madame Byron, "the greatest wonder in the world," claimed the same.[17]

Sometimes the spirits were dead wrong. Two men from Vermont left their wives behind and journeyed west to California and during their several-year sojourn never sent a letter home. Their wives solved the silence by contacting a spiritualist, who provided intricate details about the duo's deaths. How long they waited was not mentioned but the women remarried, with the reporter quipping, "There was a funny time when the long absent husbands returned."[18]

As might be imagined, soldiers were reluctant to openly embrace Spiritualism, making estimates of its prevalence in the ranks impossible. That is not to say that the practice was unknown, as suggested by anecdotal reports that surfaced throughout the Civil War era. An early example just a few months after the war began came from Camp Dennison, a Union Army recruitment and training site located near Cincinnati, Ohio.[19]

Idle soldiers at Camp Dennison turned their pent-up energies toward perpetrating pranks, and a sutler received their special attention. To his later regret, the merchant had confessed his belief in spirit rappings and other marvelous manifestations, admissions that mischievous military members instantly seized upon.

The quartermaster's office was the stage, and soldiers designed the scene to spook the stalwart. After drilling holes through the roof in a contrivance inspired by puppet plays of the day, the soldiers fastened nearly invisible strings to clothes, cups, and other lightweight objects and watched in delight as the articles danced about the room, stringing the sutler along.

As the sutler was the camp's expert on immaterial matters the soldiers urged him to summon the spirits. Unbeknown to the sutler, "the 'spirit' on this occasion had a piece of iron under the leg of his pantaloons which was dropped and raised by a string extending to his pocket." The sutler took the bait and asked if any spirits were present, and immediately received three affirmative raps in reply. Having established a connection, the sutler asked a series of questions that culminated in responses identifying the spirit as one of his departed relatives who had returned to accuse the man of unnamed crimes. Now totally unnerved by the invisible accuser, the sutler confessed his wayward drift from religion and subsequent preoccupation with liquid spirits. Over the coming days his tormentors continued the pranks, but finally gave it up as the sutler succumbed to Spiritualism and they feared for his sanity.

A tempest in a teapot threatened to spill over when a small contingent of controversial chaplains brought forth angry calls to reduce the pay of all military ministers in an effort aimed at eliminating any salary-serving incentive.[20] In reality, some considered the hue and cry a sinister ploy that disguised a desire to eliminate religion in the ranks, an avowedly anti-Christian stance that motivated one soldier to complain, "Why not go on a little further, and, considering that there are many unbelievers in the army, suggesting appointment of a spiritualist."

Like a messianic Johnny Appleseed, James Martin Peebles traveled the country spreading the fruit of Spiritualism. Peebles spent a year in California logging countless miles crisscrossing that state's byways, captivated by the climate and scenery. But Peebles was first and foremost a missionary, bringing the Spiritualists' gospel to cities large and small and providing financial backing to fledgling like-minded communities. Tragedy interrupted his evangelism when a devastating flood at his Michigan home led to the death of a child, and the subsequent loneliness of his wife forced the man's return. Both parents still had bitter memories of three other dead children that prompted a pious wish from Peebles: "I shall see them stand on the shining strand, their white arms oe'r the tide, waiting to twine their hands in mine, when I reach the farther side."[21]

Peebles's humble, heart-tugging homily cinched a sense of sincerity, projecting veneration and indirectly supporting Spiritualism. It was a far cry from the self-aggrandizing hucksters who filled metropolitan meeting rooms, mixing revelry and reverence for a fee. Such contradictions bedeviled Spiritualism, but true believers simply sifted supposed grains of truth from the chaff.

Cora Hatch spent the early war years dazzling audiences with lectures and holding interactive sessions with the spirits, taking trap-filled questions and providing ethereal answers. In a typical New York City venue she welcomed visitors to a morning question-and-answer session but reserved the evening for a more refined lecture on the "Age of the World."[22]

A few months later the 22-year-old woman was in Cleveland, Ohio, and earning gushing praise from a reporter: "In listening to this remarkable lady one cannot but be convinced of an attendant power altogether above her own." Cora impressed audiences with her serene demeanor and well-known lack of higher education, a credibility contributing combination. She also challenged all onlookers and engaged her critics with irrefutable repartee guided by assistance from beyond.[23]

Chicago citizens in 1862 played host to Mrs. Anderson, a healing medium and clairvoyant who counseled female clients for 50 cents and men for $1.[24] Mr. and Mrs. T.S. Price performed clairvoyant examinations at their hydro-electric clinic in nearby Rock Island, Illinois.[25] Miss Nettie Colburn was a trance medium who lectured on Spiritualism in Baltimore, Maryland, toward the end of 1862, charging a nominal 5 cents for women and twice that for men.[26] At nearly the same time in Cleveland, Ohio, Dr. L.K. Coonley was another trance medium who held a series of lectures on Spiritualism.[27]

In the early years of the Civil War Dr. O. Phelps Brown advertised mail-order medical mentalism, presumably for the feeble homebound or reluctant traveler. In a novel twist, Brown provided a free "prescription," the makings of which were furnished by a young clairvoyant girl. With the medical treasure map in hand, the buyer found the prescribed common ingredients at any drugstore. Brown's clairvoyant concoction cured consumption, dyspepsia, and fits. Gratified customers could purchase the doctor's book describing other herbal preparations.[28]

Hobbling Spiritualism's every step were warning signs urging caution. After seven years of cavorting with ghosts, the Rev. O.D. Miller of Nashua, New Hampshire, resolutely renounced Spiritualism, claiming unspecified personal harm from its practice.[29]

Jacob Brown denounced a phony pair of psychic physicians by declaring his dissatisfaction in a notice to the public. The object of his ire was an advertisement promoting "Dr. S.W. Howard and Lady, Clairvoyant and Cancer Physicians." Brown consulted the male member of the group in Greenfield, Indiana, on his wife's behalf and, whether through confusion or connivance, believed the doctor was "Dr. E. Howard & Son, of Indianapolis, the celebrated Cancer Doctor." His wife's condition worsened under the pair's care, provoking Brown's condemnation and warning to the community.[30]

Biographer George C. Bartlett reverently remembered Charles H. Foster, otherwise known as The Salem Seer, for his novel performances beginning around 1861. Foster traveled to every large city in America and then circled the globe, demonstrating pellet reading and skin writing, his two trademark tricks which fascinated his séance spectators.[31]

Pellet reading was spiritual mentalism with a twist. Foster would invite his guests to write questions or more commonly the names of dead people on scraps of paper, which were then "crushed into the shape of bullets, then placed in tin-foil, and rolled and re-rolled" into a shape variously described as pellets or bird shot, after which he dramatically revealed the contents by consulting with the spirits.

Foster truly made his mark as a medium when answers to séance attendees' questions were mysteriously scrawled on his forearm or the back of his hand as eerie red welts that raised devotion and doubts. For some the angry red lettering was reminiscent of the Devil's Mark, an unfortunate association that bedeviled the man from Salem, Massachusetts.[32]

In other localities Foster's performances left skeptics agnostic and not quite ready to accept Spiritualism as fact but trending in that direction. A brief visit to Springfield, Illinois, in 1861 created such an impression when amazed visitors saw the names of long-dead loved ones mysteriously appear as red welts on his hand. The exhibition was done with a scrutinizing public in attendance under the bright glare of lights, seemingly preventing any duplicity. A reporter admitted that while "not yet a believer in spiritualism ... [I] recommend the curious or those earnestly seeking to elucidate these mysteries, call on Mr. Foster."[33]

A crushing review came from a performance in England, originally written in London's *Saturday Review* and subsequently adopted as a piece in the *Brooklyn Daily Eagle* in 1862. The reporter attended a Foster séance along with eight other distinguished men and left the circle sarcastically concluding the man was certainly no imposter since nothing occurred. During the two-hour debacle the medium was discombobulated and disturbed the reporter with endless inaccuracies. "The pellets inscribed with the names of departed friends were manipulated, and about one in twenty times they came right." Even when Foster revealed "John" crudely drawn on his arm, the suspicious story writer concluded it was a hoax, drawn at an earlier moment by the performer.[34]

When not casting aspersions, Spiritualism's skeptics resorted to scare tactics. The wife of George Ford from Glastonbury, Connecticut, was offered as a cautionary tale for readers of northeastern newspapers. Ford's wife was deeply distressed by the deaths of her two children, a tragedy that the soothing scriptures of Spiritualism could not soften. As in a whirlpool, she was mercilessly dragged down as her mind descended into a frenzied swirl. Heeding the husband's plea for help, her parents, both ardent followers of the upstart faith, rushed to their daughter's aid. Over the next four days the entire family teetered on the edge of insanity, alarming neighbors with their rampages, with furniture thrown about and ear-piercing screams shattering the area's tranquility. Neighbors rescued George but probably believed the others could not be saved from their abyss, an accurate assumption, with the remaining trio transferred to a nearby insane asylum.[35,36]

When it came to reading newspaper accounts of Spiritualism during the Civil War, separating supposed facts from fiction and the critical from the complementary was a tough task. Writers were often anonymous, and stories meant to sway public opinion lacked authenticating details. In some cases a reporter's comments clearly revealed their disdain, disbelief, or devoutness. But whatever their stance, a seemingly insatiable public was regularly treated to tales of the supernatural.

A Michigan newspaper matter-of-factly reported that a famous local spiritualist was recruiting like-minded soldiers to fill the ranks of a new regiment. Whether true or not, the story might have shaped a patriotic feeling that some spiritualists could march to a different drummer, a welcome rap knocking the faith's critics.[37]

By late 1862 a slow trickle of articles, sometimes amusing or supportive but mostly snide snippets, connected Spiritualism with the war effort. Even in the few periodicals devoted to Spiritualism a curious lack of interest in the war was evident, suggesting perhaps a belief that the conflict would end quickly or an unwillingness to openly commit the faith politically. The *Herald of Progress* hinted at this political vacillation since "the upper world does not neglect the soldiers of either army."[38]

Occasionally a spiritualist would make a newsworthy contribution to the Union war effort. At an ebullient war meeting in Brooklyn, local politicians and other luminaries rallied a large crowd unified in their support of the war. Joseph Hoxie was among the speakers who roundly denounced the traitorous Confederacy, earning whoops and hollers from the rowdy crowd. Hoxie concluded his passionate crowd-stirring rhetoric with help from the spirit world, relying on the credibility of a psychic's communication with former President Andrew Jackson, who thundered from beyond that "Abraham Lincoln was the choice of the people, and if they loved the country and its institutions they must support him."[39]

Spiritualism's adversaries occasionally used the faith like a sword smiting their foe, sometimes slashing, sometimes scratching, but always with an aim to maim an enemy. Truth also suffered from the attacks, making verification of an incident nearly impossible.

Readers of the *London Herald* received a particularly jaundiced view of the developing American conflict from the newspaper's New York City correspondent in 1862, with a caustic commentary chastising the Union Army's early reversals. According to the reporter, President Lincoln's inability to quickly vanquish the Southern rebellion bred Northern anxiety and undermined Northern confidence in the military, with Major General George B. McClellan receiving the lion's share of scorn. The *London Herald*'s man in America retained a reservoir of goodwill for President Lincoln but wondered how "he can stand such nonsense as to put up with a General-in-Chief who is guided by spiritual mediums.... General McClellan married Miss Marcy. Her uncle, Dr. Marcy, is the chief of spiritualists in this city. I believe she is a medium.... McClellan depended upon these mediums."[40]

Another dubious declaration targeted Confederate Brigadier General Gabriel J. Rains, a soldier and inventor credited with the skillful development and deployment of landmines, which was a tactic used at the battle of Yorktown in 1862 and was severely criticized by McClellan.[41]

Joining the attack were Northern newspapers. In one example the *New York Times* skewered Rains by poking holes in the Confederate general with a supposedly substantiated smear. The reporter claimed that a captured Confederate soldier named Grover made a sworn statement that "the construction and planting of these torpedoes has been the special work of Brig.-Gen. Rains, who goes among the Rebel soldiers by the soubriquet of 'Sister RAINS,' on account of his devotion to Free Love and Spiritualism."[42] Another Northern newspaper joined the chorus of criticism and, citing similar insinuations, concluded that Rains was "just the sort of man to undertake such a work."[43]

A cryptic story in the *Herald of Progress* was short on details but left the impression that psychic phenomena could not be suppressed. An unnamed aide-de-camp "involuntarily uttered a 'sentiment,'" a premonition that led to his prompt arrest. The arresting officer was probably influenced by a similar event a day earlier, when an apparition supposedly appeared in the camp and unnerved soldiers.[44]

Perhaps not surprisingly, a dry academic lecture debunking Spiritualism drew little attention, especially when competing with an evening's rival offer of entertaining marvels. Professor Grimes chose a New York courthouse as his venue to attack the faith as a fraud but most seats remained empty, a sad scene for a reporter in attendance who complemented the professor's vast knowledge but admitted, "He has not succeeded in converting any one from that ridiculous faith."[45]

Ridiculing Spiritualism took many forms, but foisting a festive fraud was an amusing sport that pranksters enjoyed. A mischievous man bet his boardinghouse landlord that he could ring a dozen bells without touching them, relying on his recently developed psychic powers. Seeing a chance to make a quick $20 the landlord agreed, fully expecting to win the wager. Much to his chagrin he lost as the jovial jester swiveled in his chair, opened a closet door, and turned the gas off to the upper rooms. In mere minutes residents sounded their displeasure at being plunged into darkness, urgently ringing room bells in the landlord's office. After a moment's reflection the bamboozled landlord admitted defeat and paid the trickster's bet.[46]

Southern newspapers such as the Richmond, Virginia, *Daily Dispatch* considered Spiritualism a by-product of the irreverent liberality of Northern communities, insisting, "Spiritualism has enlisted most of its multitudinous disciples from men who could not credit the Bible."[47]

An occupation newspaper published in Beaufort, South Carolina, brought news from a Northern perspective to the Deep South state. In one edition the newspaper lampooned Spiritualism with an amusing anecdote. According to the story, a true believer recalled a memorable séance at which his long-deceased wife made an appearance and fondly hugged and kissed him. A skeptic hearing the story challenged the man, questioning the reality of such an amorous spirit. The believer reflected a moment and then sheepishly revised his story, admitting that his wife's "spirit took possession of the body of a female medium, and through her embraced and kissed me."[48]

Despite the back-and-forth publicity, Spiritualism's adherents steadily plowed ahead, breaking new ground in the fertile northeastern fields while steadily expanding westward. Mrs. Nellie L. Wiltsie brought the word to Springfield, Illinois, lecturing while in a trance at the courthouse on Spiritualism.[49]

Kentucky jerks seized scores of citizens in rural hamlets, first afflicting a preacher, wrenching and writhing at the pulpit and then rushing like a madman into the nearby woods. Like a wildfire, jerking spread and "people were often seized at hotels ... ladies would at the breakfast table suddenly be compelled to throw aloft their coffee.... The long plaits of hair then worn down the ladies' backs would crack like whips." While some attributed the widespread phenomena to deviltry, others ascribed the jerks to malicious or mischievous spirits.[50]

Warren Chase visited Bloomington, Illinois, in early December 1863 and despite the frigid weather attracted large audiences with eloquent essays on the war and Spiritualism. Chase chastised the religious orthodoxy, earning high praise and converts, many of whom were apparently well-placed local citizens.[51]

While Chase was mesmerizing audiences, William T. Church from nearby Springfield offered séances, a sort of back-to-back course in Spiritualism. Church was no ordinary medium simply channeling messages from beyond. His particular expertise was the physical materialization of spirits and not just their voices.

William F. Jamieson visited Grand Rapids, Michigan, in the latter weeks of July 1863, devoting his energies over the next three months to setting up a choir. Shortly after arriving, the fledging group settled on a novel and, for the time, scandalous scheme to promote Spiritualism. At irregular intervals the female spiritualists held dance parties and invited the local men to the well-attended soirees. Jamieson objected at first, but his moral reluctance soon yielded to the "flitting fairy forms, 'entangling,' alliances with crinoline … their faces every line of which betokend the utmost sincerity, and felt reassured." If nothing else, Jamieson was pragmatic, and the dance parties filled the group's coffers with money and brought the men, mostly nonbelievers, into close contact with female spiritualists.[52]

California in 1863 was a prosperous region flush with mineral and agricultural wealth. According to Andrew Hartman, Spiritualism was represented in the larger cities, but the rural highlands were more likely infatuated with vices such as gambling and not ethereal spirits. Even so, "many of the miners have rappings and table-tippings in their cabins, in the dark ravine."[53]

Nevada City, California, located northeast of Sacramento, boasted nearly two dozen converts, including several ministering mediums and a small meeting room. Hartman's wife was a healing medium who tended mostly to women. Hartman was a medium, too, and claimed the role as a clairvoyant physician, pioneering Spiritualism in a hostile environment. His motivation for advancing the faith developed after his son died in a mining accident.

The social maelstrom enveloping America in 1863 forced commentaries from the few periodicals devoted to spreading Spiritualism. War was anathema to many spiritualists because "human beings, who openly speak of superior intelligence … are not less ready than born barbarians in resort to bloody warfare to settle their differences and ventilate their passions."[54]

By 1863 the tide of the Civil War was turning against the Confederacy, but the *Banner of Light*, a newspaper dedicated to spiritualist-minded readers, saw a silver lining in the death and destruction cutting such a wide swath across the country. While saddened by the loss of men from both sides, the newspaper editorialized that the men's valor would not be in vain as their spiritual immortality and wisdom would guide the path of America's future.[55]

Momentous battles in 1863, including the carnage at Gettysburg, tilted the tables toward a Union victory, or so the *Banner of Light* prematurely concluded. With the demise of slavery in sight, ending "the barbarous practice of selling men for a lifetime for no crime," the newspaper turned its attention to another cause: the emancipation of women, which the *Banner* earnestly hoped would be accomplished without bloodshed.[56]

Cora Hatch weighed in on the war with a lecture at the Lyceum Society of Spiritualists in Boston on May 17, 1863. Bowing to what seemed inevitable, the entranced woman claimed that war and peace were both inseparable and indispensable ingredients of human societies. War was like a violent thunderstorm wreaking havoc through pent-up passions, but once the skies cleared all was fresh and pure and peace reigned. Hatch sentimentally sermonized that war's ultimate sacrifices, such as a mother's son marching off to an uncertain fate, her husband's long absences fighting in distant places, or a father mourning a lost son, all kindled feelings that eventually led to peace.[57]

A week after the battlefields lay quiet in Gettysburg, Cora Hatch gave another lecture focusing on "the national struggle." In tracing the conflict's root cause, Hatch cited three factors: intemperance, gambling, and political corruption. By blaming intemperance she was indicting a different type of spirit, one that befuddled minds and promoted reckless actions. Gambling was a game, one that imprudently and disproportionately weighed risks, making it more likely that men wagered in war. Political corruption came in many forms but in each example sullied governments and soured citizens, with slavery receiving special condemnation from the spirit world.[58]

Laura Cappy addressed the Lyceum Society of Spiritualists in Boston on November 8, 1863, with prophecies that would follow the war's end, some good, others not so. Like Hatch, Cappy pointed to the end of slavery as the greatest good coming from the conflict, but she saw storm clouds gathering on America's horizon with "the return of the soldiers—who, in camps and battlefields, have laid aside ... respect for just laws and the proper preservation of the people's peace." It was a sweeping condemnation of the soldiers, but an even more cynical conclusion followed.[59]

Cappy confidently predicted that the war would expand the influence of Spiritualism. With an oblique swipe at traditional religions, Cappy wondered what solace they offered for a grieving person's battlefield loss. Capitalizing on that supposed breach, she rhetorically pondered, "Who will reveal to us the continued existence of our dead? And here Spiritualism comes with its mighty consolations."

As spiritualists gained a semblance of respectability, a clamor arose to include their faith among the ranks of military chaplains. Even as military ministers were under attack elsewhere with calls for their elimination, spiritualists saw another pathway to legitimacy. It was a reach too far for one ardent believer, who realistically settled instead for a plea that spiritualist newspapers such as the *Banner of Light* be freely and widely disseminated among the troops.[60]

Spiritualists were savvy enough to understand that the spirits could benefit from political influence. A lack of representation in Washington, D.C., prompted Alfred Horton to issue an open appeal for mediums and sympathetic speakers to visit the city in 1863. A small cadre of advocates carried the torch, of whom two illuminated the War Department with their messages, but Horton hoped the true luminaries such as the Davenport brothers would make a visit.[61]

Uriah Clark figured the faith was moving mainstream in 1863 and offered the masses his *Plain Guide to Spiritualism*. As with most books of this ilk, he leaned on the credence of ancient mysteries and biblical miracles to span the gulf of most people's disbelief by building a bridge between the past and the present. Clark's literary truss work explained Spiritualism as a revival and not a revolution, softening objections through moral equivalencies. A typical example began with the reimagined Rochester rappings. "From that humble home in Hydesville, as humble as Nazareth, the tidings spread with a joy and wonder akin to the angel tidings over Bethlehem; and the mediums were as credible as were Mary Magdalene and the other Mary who first heralded the news of a risen Christ."[62]

Clark addressed the skeptics head on, aiming to overcome doubts and suspicion with testimonials from everyday people and those in positions of esteem. At the same time, he acknowledged the head winds Spiritualism faced with strong gusts of disbelief.

Infesting the ranks of spiritualists were fraudulent practitioners who used the faith to advance various nefarious interests, ranging from the pecuniary to the salacious. Clark proposed a litmus test to distinguish the prevaricating purveyors from the pious providers, principally premised on a strict adherence to Spiritualism's core belief in extraterrestrial communications, egalitarianism, and a fervent desire to reshape America by abandoning what they believed were orthodox practices corrupting society.

Among the corrupting social influences that animated Clark and like-minded spiritualists were their views on marriage. Spiritualists enshrined individual liberties, which led to their adamant disavowal of slavery. In a similar fashion, they argued for equality in marriage: an unpopular stance attacking the husband's paternalism. While maintaining a steadfast faith in the sanctity of marriage, spiritualists were not opposed to its dissolution if irreconcilable differences stood in the way. Loosening the bonds that held women in marriage fostered claims that spiritualists were ardent advocates of divorce, a claim Clark protested. Clark also tried to distance Spiritualism from the free love advocates.

Clark adopted a reverent tone before discussing the known spectrum of mediums' manifestations, admitting the futility and folly of a mere mortal divining the endless ways the spirits could communicate. Humbled by the task, he nonetheless plunged forward and identified dozens of psychic proclivities, including mediums who rapped, wrote, saw spirits, healed diseases, and predicted the future.

Spiritualism earned the undying ire of Christians alarmed by the rise of the heretical faith. A Vermont newspaper could not fathom how the gullible multitudes so easily accepted rappings and table tippings and similar manifestations as evidence of spirits. As proof of guile, the newspaper offered "the trick of one Mr. Fay, who in a room made intensely dark by the exclusion of every possibility of light, ties himself, or, as he says, is tied by 'spirits,' with his hands apparently securely fastened behind him." While Fay was seemingly immobilized, the audience was treated to ringing bells and strumming musical instruments.[63]

The Vermont newspaper suspected a hoax, a claim given weight by the medium's refusal to have his hands held by a spectator or to perform the feat under the glare of bright lights. Cinching their case was another performer who not only replicated the trick in daylight but quickly unraveled tightly fastened ropes through a series of contortions and freed his hands to perform those mysterious manifestations.

Spiritualists roundly rebuked accusations correlating their faith with insanity and insisted that any religious fervor could unsettle a person's mind. Dr. Andrew McFarland, Superintendent of the Illinois State Hospital for the Insane, disagreed and insisted that the hospital's crowded condition was not due to the Civil War, because "the war excitement has been healthful upon the public mind; hence its great contrast with those gales of popular delusion, such as Spiritualism, etc., which has wrought such ruin."[64]

In 1864 a large Spiritual convention and grand exhibitions dominated the headlines, offering distractions for some people from a lingering war and a bitter election that kept President Lincoln in office. At the same time, even the reduced newspaper coverage kept Spiritualism from fading from the public's mind.

The *New York Herald*'s attention descended on the Eddy family, a new sensation hailing from rural Vermont and bringing to the big city performances so perplexing that "there may be some occult influence at work in the human constitution about which we know nothing." The publicity implicitly inflated the spiritualists' stock by urging a serious investigation of the occult sciences, an inquiry the newspapers insisted was best conducted by scientist-philosophers and theologians.[65]

Among the big acts, few could rival the Davenport brothers, and their success continued through the war years. Like many others, they arose from the Rochester rappings heard around the world and by 1855 were full-fledged mediums. Ira Davenport was born in 1839 and William in 1841, and both grew up in Buffalo, New York. Their paranormal experiences began with the dining-room table tipping to and fro, followed by the ubiquitous floating violin, which was quickly surpassed by the two boys floating to the ceiling. Curious neighbors soon learned about the Davenport brothers and overwhelmed the family house, but their enterprising father procured a larger room to accommodate the overflowing crowds.[66]

The Davenport brothers supposedly channeled the spirit of Johnny King, the nom de plume of Henry Morgan, better known as a fearsome privateer and later Governor of Jamaica, who for unknown reasons preferred to be an incognito ghost. Morgan seemed a perfect choice for the adventurous, imaginative young boys.

With their father as escort and impresario, the boys took their show on the road, traveling to New York City, but all along the way suspicions of duplicity were a constant companion. After uneven performances, the family returned to Buffalo with a determination to hone its exhibitions and dispel all doubts of trickery. It was during this period of refinement that the Davenport brothers previewed their spiritual escape acts, one of their signature performances aided by the omnipresent fun-loving Johnny King.

The Davenport brothers' innovation was a spirit cabinet, a piece of furniture large enough for the two brothers to sit opposite each other on specially designed chairs with holes strategically placed for purposes of fastening the ropes that bound them tight. Alert observers also noticed various musical instruments on the floor. An audience member closed the cabinet doors and the stage manager extinguished the house lights, after which the stringed instruments came to life and filled the theater with their discordant notes. When the cabinet doors were flung open the Davenport brothers were still tied tight.

People flocked to the Davenport shows from Ohio to Maine, and the brothers received a similar reception when they traveled to Europe. Many were awestruck, shaking their heads in bewilderment, but suspicions of

The Davenport brothers' séance cabinet (Henry Ridgely Evans, *The Spirit World Unmasked: Illustrated Investigations Into the Phenomena of Spiritualism and Theosophy*, Laird & Lee, 1897).

imposture shadowed the shows. Some venues were openly hostile, resenting the irreverence and likening the brothers' presence to that if carnival barkers and similar shady characters. Local authorities arrested Ira Davenport in Sturgis, Michigan, in 1864 following his steadfast refusal to purchase an exhibitor's license. A magistrate hearing the case set his bail at $200, and after a moment's freedom the police again arrested Ira for the same offense.[67]

The Davenport brothers accepted challenges from skeptical audience members whose sole intent was exposing what they considered to be a fraud or clever trick. Skeptics endlessly tried immobilizing the brothers' movements using stout ropes and intricate knots threaded in every imaginable way. In most cases the ligatures only succeeded in burnishing the Davenports' mystique.

Occasionally a performance was foiled. In Kenosha, Wisconsin, the Davenport brothers accepted an invitation from a scalawag to join them in their spirit cabinet. Unknown to the brothers, the interloper had smudged his hair with oil and lampblack. All three were then plunged into darkness as the cabinet doors closed, with the visitor between the bound brothers. Shortly after the doors closed a spirit hand rested lightly on the man's head, and upon inquiry he learned it was his long dead mother. When the cabinet doors were opened the Davenport brothers were still tied up "but the hand of one of them was thoroughly besmeared with the sable compound, showing that whatever spiritual agency might be connected therewith the Davenport boys had a hand in it."[68]

America's capitol hosted the Davenport brothers in February 1864 at Willard's Hall, with politicians and judges among the many buying a ticket to watch the performance. Taking center stage was the spirit cabinet and, as was their custom, the brothers invited a spectator to strap them to their chairs. A local judge and another man accepted the invitation, and for 15 minutes both did their best to bind the brothers. The doors were closed and with the passage of mere seconds were thrown open, revealing the brothers unshackled. In another scene, the same men again tied the brothers' hands, arms, and feet and placed several musical instruments on the cabinet's floor. Again the doors were closed and the audience listened as popular tunes filled the theater. As expected, when the men opened the doors ropes still fastened the brothers firmly to their seats.[69]

A reporter attending the show at Willard's Hall glanced about the packed room and noted several members of Congress. Before the festivities began a short speech introduced the night's topic, after which "the mediums [who] are two very modest young gentlemen, and appear upon the stage without the usual swagger of too many of our public exhibitors."[70]

Baltimore received the Davenport brothers in March 1864 following their successful engagement in Washington, D.C. Fifty cents admitted the curious to an evening's exhibition at the Maryland Institute to witness the "Greatest Phenomenon of the Nineteenth Century."[71] Instead of Spiritualism, it was "sleight and delusion" that would confound theatergoers.[72] The brothers "challenge the scrutiny of experts of every degree" and extended their stay for another week to meet the demand.[73]

The brothers' journey to New York City and subsequent tableau excited the nation. Local newspapers covered their exhibitions in dramatic detail, often sandwiched between war news on the front page. It was an odd juxtaposition, but it guaranteed a prominence rivaling the reader's attention for news of the war. For the war-weary it was a distraction from the dreary drama unfolding on the battlefields.

The Cooper Institute hosted a mixture of believers, skeptics, and rowdies for the Davenports' debut performance. Ardent spiritualists angrily confronted cynics and scoffers and the heated exchanges disrupted the performance multiple times. Mr. Lacy, the Davenport's stage manager, eventually quelled the arguments and began selecting the committee that would inspect the cabinet and secure the mediums.

Selecting the committee was another boisterous undertaking, made even worse when the Davenport's manager refused an army officer's participation. After the brouhaha simmered down, Gordon Conklin, an elderly well-known spiritualist, offered his service and after some opposing banter gingerly came forward. E.P. Bradbury, a local businessman, also met the crowd's approval and joined Conklin on the stage. Conklin painstakingly examined every nook and cranny, even peering underneath the cabinet and after exhausting the audience's patience he finally pronounced it free of trickery.

The Davenport brothers now made their appearance and the two committee members spent the next thirty minutes roping them to their chairs, while a restive audience alternated between jeers and cheers. At long last both men finished their task and closed the cabinet's doors, the house lights dimmed and grew dark, and a spirit trumpet mysteriously issued forth from the cabinet's front facing small window. Conklin's inquisitive nature got the better of him as he leaned forward to inspect the trumpet and in return received a loud thump on his head, to the utter amusement of the audience.

The night's entertainment now began in earnest. From the cabinet a tambourine jangled and a violin strummed a merry tune. A hand thrust through the cabinet's window rang a bell and flung it across the stage. From inside the cabinet a raucous din arose, as if some spirit was violently protesting its confinement; at the peak of this, the cabinet's doors sprang open, revealing the two brothers calmly and securely restrained.

Again the doors were closed and a few minutes later the brothers emerged with the ropes lying on the cabinet's floor, but an even more amazing feat followed. The brothers reentered the cabinet and a few minutes later when the doors were opened they were tied tight, provoking gasps from the audience. Soon a chant arose from the audience insisting that Conklin join the brothers in the cabinet. Yielding to the popular pressure Conklin took a seat in the cabinet with a hand on each brother's shoulder, the doors were closed, and a musical ensemble ensued. A visibly shaken Conklin emerged from the cabinet, insisting that neither brother, still firmly bound, moved a muscle even as his head was cracked with a violin by playful spirits.

The final spectacle was a mind boggler as the Davenport brothers entered the cabinet: the theater's lights darkened and an eerie ghostly white hand emerged from the door's small aperture "like the arm of a corpse through a new made grave amid gleams of moonlight. Back and forth moves the arm as it rings a bell with each passage, while inside the cabinet the musical instruments take up a violent concert. Mr. Lacy unceremoniously opened the doors and the guitar, violin and tambourine came flying out as if animated by an unseen force; revealing at the same time the composed, bound figures of the Davenport Brothers."[74]

The *New York Herald* took the Davenport brothers' presence as an opportunity to muse philosophically about the state of affairs in nineteenth-century America, or at least in their myopic view from a big city. Seeing a revolution in progress and with the Civil War heralding tectonic technological and social shifts led the newspaper to fold the Davenport brothers into that assessment. With an odd twist, the newspaper discounted Spiritualism and conjectured instead "that the power to produce such manifestations has been bestowed upon them; and it is perhaps the same occult power, differently developed, as that shows in the telegraph and the steam engine.... It is evident that we are upon the threshold of a new era of human development."[75]

Newspapers across the country trumpeted the Davenport brothers' spirited shows. Readers in Chicago, Illinois, learned about the exhibitions at the Cooper Institute and speculated that electricity played a part in the manifestations. In an effort to insulate the Davenport brothers from criticism when they opened in Chicago, Mr. Lacy placed glass tumblers under the brothers' chairs. In a replay of prior exhibitions the committee chosen from the audience bound the boys, locked the cabinet, and the music from several instruments filled the hall. When the doors were opened the brothers were still tied.[76]

For the night's grand finale, Mr. Lacy placed flour in the hands of the bound brothers, closed the doors, and the typical musical ensemble ensued, the spirit hand protruded from the door's small opening, and the spirit trumpet was thrown out. Lacy opened the doors and there stood the brothers, unbound with flour in hand and not a speck seen elsewhere. It was a magnificent closing act.

A newspaper published in Atlanta, Georgia, wryly remarked that "They are having an excitement in New York which even dims the interest taken in Grant. It appears to be a sort of spiritual demonstration which is peculiarly attractive to the Yankee nation." After presenting a detailed account of a night's show the newspaper struck a more sympathetic note, deciding that the show was worth the admission price, evidenced no deceit, and was simply inexplicable.[77]

Out west in Kansas also, readers learned about the manifestations enthralling New Yorkers. After extensively quoting a New York City newspaper's account of the Davenport brothers, the Kansas paper announced that "modern Babylon is all agog with a new excitement."[78]

As a hurricane spawns tornadoes, the Davenport brothers' whirlwind tours gave rise to look-alikes. These acts copied the core elements of the brothers' performances, such as the spirit cabinet and the escapes, while adding dramatic fringes that set their shows apart. As a whole, their impact was less consequential, but the lure of fame and fortune was sufficient motivation for many.

Without a blush the St. George sisters took direct aim at the Davenport brothers, hoping to blow them away with an uplifting, copycatting performance. They debuted in Washington, D.C., on July 4, 1864, at Canterbury Hall with a bold advertisement hyping "the most startling phenomenon the world ever witnessed."[79]

Although the Davenport brothers ambiguously attributed their magical acts to Spiritualism, they never fully attributed the manifestations to spirits. Emilie and Kate St. George nonetheless made that connection and sensationally advertised their ability to outperform the same Davenport demonstrations without the spirits' aid. The sisters insisted that the Davenport brothers' spirit cabinet was a fraud and they would convince a skeptical audience with their own cabinet, from which Emilie and Kate would reveal spirit hands, bell ringing, and airborne musical instruments, and escape more quickly from shackles than their male counterparts.[80]

The St. George sisters claimed great success, supposedly impressing capacity crowds in New York City, Philadelphia, and Boston that, according to their newspaper advertisements, even exceeded those drawn by the Davenport brothers.[81] It was an audacious boast since the St. George sisters seemed to fizzle out after several well-received performances in Washington, D.C., during the hot month of July 1864.[82]

Another troupe copying the Davenports' show was the Thorpe brothers. While the St. George sisters seemingly eschewed Spiritualism, the Thorpes did not. At Hope Chapel in New York City the Thorpe brothers demonstrated their spiritual manifestations before a small but curious group of onlookers in 1864. It was a performance with all the hallmarks of a Davenport act, complete with spirit cabinet, but instead of ropes the brothers' hands were pinioned in wooden stocks. Spectators considered the act marvelous and were certain the Thorpe brothers would meet similar enthusiasm when they started touring the country.[83]

A few months after their Hope Chapel show, the Thorpe brothers entertained the patrons at Niblo's Saloon in New York City. Both brothers were mediums and held private séances, honing skills that were now on public display for only 50 cents a seat. While the brothers were seated opposite each other in the cabinet, a committee selected from the audience clamped the stocks over their forearms, bound their feet with ropes, and for an added measure placed a mug of beer in each one's outstretched hand. Shortly after closing the cabinet, a banging drum, ringing bell, and musical hand organ announced the spirit's arrival. As always, when a committee member opened the cabinet doors the Thorpe brothers were bound as before with nary a drop of beer on the floor.

The Thorpe brothers teased the public with provocative advertisements asking prospective attendees, "Would you draw the curtain of another existence and view the apparition of your spirit friends? Go and see the Thorpe Brothers."[84] According to the newspaper advertisement, true believers would confirm their faith and skeptics would leave bewildered.

Two reporters attending "an evening with the spirits" prefaced their lengthy commentary by proclaiming the death of Spiritualism, rejoicing that the great moral corrupter undermining traditional religion was now as faint as the ghosts those spiritualists conjured. It was a premature conclusion, but the reporters buttressed their argument by dismissing bogus spiritual manifestations and ascribing those wondrous marvels to human magnetism or electricity, an explanation that sidestepped Spiritualism's beliefs and instead offered a pseudoscientific sophism.

William Fitzgibbons shrewdly invited both reporters to his Brooklyn residence "to witness some of the peculiar and highly interesting phenomena in Human Magnetism and Human Electricity."[85] Joining the reporters were 18 other individuals, roughly half of them women, and all among the higher social class. The private show was a prelude to public exhibitions and was cleverly designed to drum up business.

The event took place in Fitzgibbon's rather Spartan home with a cabinet dominating the exhibition room and leaving just enough room for chairs. It was a typical but less elaborate cabinet with benches for seating and shelves for the usual musical instruments. Fitzgibbon invited the guests to examine the cabinet, and once everyone was satisfied the night's entertainment began.

Fitzgibbon magisterially introduced to the guests the Eddy family, an appearance the reporters glibly described as two brothers and one sister, all "homely, awkward, and badly dressed." All three exuded no excitement; devoid of patter and with a matter-of-fact, almost bored approach they took their seats in the cabinet and the selected committee members bound them securely.

The Eddy family followed the Davenports' script through four routines, with the only variance occurring when the young girl fainted while bound in the cabinet, requiring her revival before the performance continued. Following the cabinet performance was a dark séance attended by a small group that included a reporter. Mrs. Ferris, "a more intelligent and attractive medium," officiated and insisted that everyone firmly hold hands around the small table and await the spirit's arrival. The most dramatic moment occurred when the young Eddy girl floated slowly upward, with a soft thud suggesting contact with the ceiling.

Overall it was a rather routine performance, mystifying and amusing the reporters, who attributed the manifestations to unseen magnetic or electrical influences harnessed by the Eddy family. Having dutifully and in their opinion objectively reported the night's events, the reporters awaited the public's response to the Eddy family.

As predicted, the Eddy family moved out of Fitzgibbon's house and began its public expositions at Hope Chapel, a fashionable location on Broadway in New York City. Audiences were enthusiastic and the crowds overwhelmed Hope Chapel's limited seating capacity, leading to a change of venue to the larger Cooper Institute.[86]

Critics raved and the Eddy family soared in popularity. The *New York Herald* gushed that the performers were "the ablest troupe of media since the days of the Foxes," as they baffled spellbound audiences with inexplicable and awe-inspiring feats. Without a rational explanation, the newspaper speculated that "Eddyism" was certainly an unknown and possibly occult force that animated the performances.[87]

The Eddy family, the Davenport brothers, and similar shows constituted the thespian side of Spiritualism. They played to packed theaters in large cities in Union states. Southern states rebelled and mostly kept the spiritualists at bay, firmly believing that they undermined traditional Christian values. This was yet another schism between the two warring sides.

Eddy brothers' séance, William E. Robinson (*Spirit Slate Writing and Kindred Phenomena,* Munn & Company, New York City, 1898).

Four

Doctrine, Dilemmas and Doubts

The summer of 1864 brought no relief from the fiery passions embroiling America, but the leading spiritualists of the nation decided that it was time for a grand convention: a conclave of believers designed to showcase their strength in numbers and marshal their forces for maximum social impact. Spiritualist chose Chicago, Illinois, for the opening session of the National Convention of American Spiritualists at Bryan Hall on August 9, 1864. It was a gathering that included representatives from the northeastern states, along with Tennessee, Kentucky, Missouri, California, Ohio, Michigan, Illinois, and Indiana.[1]

A temporary chairman gaveled the morning convention's start, and for the next 12 hours the work of the day proceeded, dominated by disputes and airy efforts aimed at appeasement. The first order of business proposed by the acting chairman was the establishment of various groups, with the organizing committee provoking the most concern as its mission dictated the structure, goals, and objectives of the movement.

Harnessing the interests of spiritualists was a daunting task, and the room soon succumbed into chaos after the organizing committee left the great hall to begin its deliberations. Speaker after speaker expressed their concern that individualism and their unique creative energies were at risk. Dr. Parker personified this view, claiming that "he had no care that anybody should labor with him or for him ... he had carried the sledge-hammer of truth on his shoulder for fourteen years, striking at error wherever he could find it."

James Peebles argued for harmony and suggested a progressive spiritual creed that would unite humanity since "we are one great family, having one father, being all brothers." According to Peebles, the discord on display weakened that resolve and discouraged the collective effort required by spiritualists to reshape American society.

Four—Doctrine, Dilemmas and Doubts

When the Committee on Permanent Organization returned to the hall, Stephen Jones of Illinois became the newly elected president and addressed the gathering with soothing words, proclaiming that their united presence and participation would signal a historic shift in American Spiritualism. Jones was an obvious choice for the position, given his central role supporting a staunch spiritualist group in St. Charles, Illinois, which became an established institution when his son-in-law Colonel John Bundy joined the effort.[2]

The conference ended the first day on an upbeat note as a succession of speakers urged the faithful to spread Spiritualism by emphasizing a sort of virtual hand holding harmony and promoting the lifelong pursuit of a person's spiritual prowess.

The second day of the spiritual convention counted an even larger audience, in spite of the admission fee charged to help defray the meeting's costs. A reporter in attendance glibly remarked that the absence of apparitions "was because they had not the wherewithal to pay the admission fee." Sarcasm aside, the reporter set about describing the second day of the grand convention as appeals for harmony alternating with dissent.[3]

Disagreements spilled through the second day, with themes of subordination to a centralized spiritualist authority fracturing the group's harmony. Dissidents formed their own competing committees, championing their individual positions, and in the end they won the approval of the larger body, sidestepping another contentious controversy.

The remainder of the second day was devoted to lectures such as George Linn's expostulation for a universal freedom, a component of which was "free love ... which he believed ... would cause no man to love his wife the less." Lizzie Doten philosophized about freedom with her allegiance squarely aimed at a heavenly banner that transcended the battle flags of the two warring parties in America.

After an afternoon break the lectures continued into the early evening hours, with two speakers starkly describing the consequences of challenging orthodox religion. Elizabeth Packard was first and she related a harrowing tale of abuse. Elizabeth's husband was the Rev. Theophilus Packard, the Old School Presbyterian Church's preacher when they lived together in Manteno, Illinois. Over the course of a 21-year marriage they had six children and by her reckoning it was a happy marriage.[4]

Elizabeth's life took a dramatic turn for the worse with an innocent request from Deacon Abijah Dole that she take over an insipid, lifeless bible class. She successfully animated the subject and brought new pupils to the classroom by encouraging debate and openly questioning supposedly settled spiritual matters. Her husband and a newly appointed deacon recoiled and sternly admonished her for blasphemy. Elizabeth did not see the darkening clouds, and while trying to reconcile her position with her husband she was quietly labeled mentally ill.

Illinois state law in 1860 permitted insane asylum admissions based on a husband's uncontested testimony, and so it was that Elizabeth Packard became a resident of the Jacksonville Illinois Insane Asylum from June 18, 1860, to June 18, 1863. According to Elizabeth, Theophilus justified the action because "I must protect the cause of Christ!"

Elizabeth's travails did not end with her asylum discharge. Months afterward, Theophilus locked her up in their house, and only by surreptitiously delivering a letter to a friend did she gain her release. A legal battle followed, with her husband once again contesting her sanity. In a remarkable turn of events, Andrew McFarland, the asylum superintendent during her previous stay, testified that he discharged Elizabeth from the asylum knowing she was still insane. In spite of what seemed an uphill struggle, Elizabeth prevailed when a jury deliberated for seven minutes and set the woman free.

Packard's story surely resonated among spiritualists accustomed to the slings and arrows launched by religious stalwarts defending their beliefs and authority. Spiritualist T.B. Eddy suffered a similar fate in a Chicago insanity trial where "they called in all the priests of the city, to see what constituted insanity, and notwithstanding all their quibbles and dogmas, they were considered perfectly sane, while he who simply believed in plain immortality, was considered ... to be out of his mind."[5]

The convention's third day was entirely set aside for the war.[6] As a group, spiritualists opposed slavery, considering the practice an abomination that fundamentally struck at one of their core beliefs, that of human equality. While united in supporting slavery's abolition, they disagreed over the means to achieve it. A vocal, mostly pacifist, minority fiercely put forward an antiwar argument, prompting another spiritualist to ask whether their principled position involved "kissing the rebels into submission."

President Lincoln was on the minds of many, with most members supportive of his policies. The pacifists did not approve of the war effort and openly acknowledged their dissatisfaction. For the most part, when speakers lauded the President the packed room erupted in praise as the majority loudly expressed their support.

Colonel Dorus M. Fox strode to the stage and revealed that his infatuation with universal freedom was his principle motivation in fighting the Rebel cause over a three-year span but that "he was now severely wounded, or he would be there now; his two sons had fallen in that cause." Unsurprisingly, Fox admitted that in 1860 he did not vote for Abraham Lincoln but opted instead for Stephen A. Douglas, but now, war weary

Four—Doctrine, Dilemmas and Doubts

and surely agonizing over his sons' deaths, he urged the convention goers to fully support the current administration.

On the fourth day the speakers rehashed similar themes, with some continuing to protest a national organization while others took up the controversial subject of free love. Dr. Abel Underhill favored free love, and after mesmerizing many women "believed thousands of women had fallen in love with him." At the same time, the egalitarian man insisted that his marriage did not prevent his wife from seeking happiness elsewhere.[7]

Spirits seemed to shun the convention, with political and philosophical matters taking center stage. Occasionally a medium channeled the thoughts from the spirit world that along with many mortals expressed dissatisfaction with the convention's 10-minute time limit on all speakers. Interestingly, the trance talks swayed few people.

A case illustrating the convention's irreverence took place on Saturday, August 13, 1864, the fifth day of the spiritualists' meeting, when Mr. Pinkham, a representative from California with "remarkable physiognomy and hair of Absolomic extensiveness," peremptorily captured the stage before being ruled out of order by the attentive chairman. As he was leaving, Pinkham began jerking and shaking, with his agitation indicating possession by a restive spirit. In this case the spirit chose script as the means of commination, and Pinkham dutifully transcribed the message from beyond, after which he asked for and received permission to convey the missive to the crowd.[8]

Pinkham timorously delivered the phantom's preamble: "We have noticed the angry discussions of this Convention, and have determined that they are useless, for we have taken charge of the matter ourselves and will read what is intended to settle it." The spirits came down firmly on the side of an even larger convention of spiritualists to be held on Washington's Birthday in 1865 in New York City, during which time a new Bible would be revealed, inaugurating the onset of Spiritualism's social dominance.

Pinkham's presentation elicited jeers, not cheers. Perhaps it was his physical appearance or the drama preceding his presentation, but in any event the phantoms' proposals triggered ridicule and rebuke from a largely unsympathetic audience of spiritualists.

The *Chicago Tribune*'s reporter faithfully and matter-of-factly described the spiritual convention's week-long meeting, waiting until the last day to supplant facts with opinion. Delegates held their last get-together at Chicago's Metropolitan Hall, and as on the previous days it was soon mired in controversy and conflict. In the end the delegates did not agree on establishing a central organization, resolving instead that "attempts to control the opinions or the practice of any man or woman, by an authority or power outside of his or her own soul, is guilty of a flagrant wrong."[9]

Another resolution the delegates approved was Lizzie Doten's patriotic appeal supporting the Union war effort. Doten was a favored speaker at the convention, and in recognition of that status she brought the meeting to a close by reciting a poem supposedly channeled from the famous poet Robert Burns. The day following the convention's conclusion, Colonel Benjamin J. Sweet, in command of the Confederate prisoners-of-war at Camp Douglas, saluted Lizzie Doten's patriotism with a serenade performed by the 5th Regimental Band.

After a week chock-full of spirited meetings, the reporter found little evidence of progress since the main object of the convention was the creation of a unified central command, abandoned because "not one of all that motley throng but thinks him or herself the one commissioned by the spirits to turn the world (or tables) upside down." In his final assessment, the reporter dismissed the conventioneers as a ludicrous lot with "few grains of reason and common sense."[10]

Despite the dissension and derision, Spiritualism thrived in the arid environment, nourished by an evangelical zeal that sprouted mentors, missionaries, and mediums across the country. Thomas Gales Forster lectured on Spiritualism in 1864 and offered two free lectures on the subject at Saratoga Hall in Baltimore, Maryland.[11]

Forster was born in Charleston, South Carolina, on May 14, 1816, and was reared in the Unitarian faith by his father. He spread the gospel of Spiritualism through a series of roving lectures published for posterity by his wife after his death. A fundamental tenet of his faith centered on the notion that the soul was eternal and the physical body merely a transient chalice that death liberated for ascension to higher planes of spiritual existence.[12]

Forster argued that the main appeal of Spiritualism was its philosophy of death. At a time when death permeated America, it surely resonated in a country saturated with sorrow. In explaining what came after death, Forster first took aim at the nihilism of nonbelievers, a group that dismissed any religion, favoring atheism or agnosticism, both of which relegated a person's fate to an eternal nonexistence.

Followers of traditional faiths fared little better, with many religions consigning their followers to eternal damnation. As one of Spiritualism's sirens, Forster seductively steered society toward a belief where "natural death ... is to the Spiritualist the grand step of life ... through which man is to attain to the highest possibilities of his nature."

Baltimore's Saratoga Hall was a favorite haunt for Spiritualists. Samuel H. Paist, a test medium, took up residence there and met with daily visitors for 50 cents each.[13] Paist was another prophet of death claiming communication with Dr. Horace Abraham Ackley. Ackley's spirit took the time to reassure the medium that "death is not so bad a thing after all." In fact, it sounded joyful, with Ackley's spirit emerging from his mortal remains, airily rising to the world beyond, greeted by angelic hosts, and then escorted to an ethereal paradise.[14]

Mrs. Augusta A. Currier was another spiritualist speaker at Saratoga Hall in 1864, offering two lectures: one devoted to "Observations on Spiritualism" and the other "the Childhood's Days of Science," both without charge.[15] Currier was a multitalented test medium, clairvoyant, and lecturer who combined the words from beyond with loud spirit raps. Adding to her spells was "a pleasing external appearance, and naturally graceful bearing."[16]

Washington, D.C., hosted spiritualists at Smeed's Hall, with Mrs. L. Smith and Mrs. E. Wren beckoning all interested individuals for an afternoon discourse on April 17, 1864.[17] Smith also lectured at Temperance Hall, speaking "under the divine influence of Jesus Christ, about Secession, its heavenly results, the good times coming."[18]

The Rev. John Pierpont dabbled with Spiritualism late in life following a tumultuous adulthood as he careened from educator, to lawyer, and to merchant before finally settling on preaching the gospel in Boston, Massachusetts. Pierpont's clerical career ended in controversy, and with six decades of life leaning heavily on him he turned his attention to animal magnetism, hoping to heal suffering with a pass of his hand.[19]

Tragedy turned Pierpont toward Spiritualism. A string of family deaths that included his wife left the man grieving, but his greatest concern was his impressionable young granddaughter. In an effort to relieve her trauma, Pierpont mesmerized the girl and succeeded in reducing her anxiety, but not without a mysterious side effect developing. It soon became increasingly obvious to Pierpont that a spirit controlled his mesmerized granddaughter. From this time forward, Pierpont increasingly immersed himself in Spiritualism and as an itinerant lecturer sought to educate the public.

The Reverend Pierpont enthusiastically made a case for Spiritualism at Smeed's Hall on the last day of January 1864. Pierpont took his audience on a sentimental journey recollecting personal manifestations, presenting them as factual proofs of Spiritualism. In one example, his granddaughter channeled the spirit of the Unitarian minister William Ellery Channing, who urged the Reverend Pierpont to "impress on the congregation the great truths of spiritualism!"

Pierpont initially demurred but Channing's spirit insisted, and through the young girl he wrote a majestic sermon. After memorizing the words, Pierpont repeated the spirit-summoned sermon in a pious prayer at the same Boston church where a mortal Channing previously preached, after which Pierpont "noticed at the time that the congregation settled down in a silence almost appalling." It was an act of courage and conviction from a man converted to Spiritualism.[20]

Ridicule was a favored tool to undermine Spiritualism, and amusing stories, whether real or fanciful, often did just that. In one embarrassing anecdote, a somber séance connected with the spirit world and a woman asked the invisible agents how many children she had. After a moment's pause, four distinct raps filled the room, evidently providing the correct answer. Her husband joined the circle a bit later and for whatever reason asked the same question. This time the spirit rapped twice. There were nervous glances around the table, but no one dared question the spirits or the married couple.[21]

Out West in San Francisco, California, an interesting juxtaposition of lectures straddled a weekend at Platt's New Music Hall. Henry Gibbons was a California physician, and his lecture on Spiritualism and insanity was preceded a day earlier by the psychic medium Emma Hardinge Britten. The back-to-back discussions offered a sort of point-and-counterpoint debate amiably separated by one day, perhaps in an effort to avoid any unpleasant confrontations.[22]

As for many erudite individuals of the time, Spiritualism attracted Gibbons's interest, but his analytic and scientific turn of mind could never accept its claims. His interest in the subject and first experience with mesmerism came about when the traveling team of Robert H. Collyer and "Frederick" stirred his imagination as a young boy. From the outset, Gibbons was suspicious and determined to trap the mesmerist. Collyer's clairvoyance seemed contrived and limited to identifying common concealed objects among the patrons.[23]

In an effort to foil the performer, Gibbons distributed a variety of uncommon objects such as a razor strap and brush among obliging audience members and then invited Collyer and Frederick's clairvoyance to identify the hidden items. It was a spectacular failure, with both blindsided by Gibbons's trick. In later years Gibbons honed his skill as a fraud buster, eventually earning a reputation that led many mediums to bar his participation as a committee member vouching for the veracity of an exhibition.

Gibbons marveled at spiritualists' gullibility and their delusional conviction, arguing that such certitude unsettled unbalanced minds and precipitated insanity. While not condemning all believers to that fate, Gibbons remarked, "I will not say that all such would find in the belief and the pursuits of Spiritism a cause sufficient to lead their minds out of the domain of right reason; but I will venture the statement that no other one cause is capable of doing so much mischief in that direction."

On the other hand, Emma Floyd Hardinge Britten was a devout

Four—Doctrine, Dilemmas and Doubts 73

spiritualist and her lectures fostered the faith. She was born in London, England, in 1823, and during her younger adult life she took a fancy to performing on stage and through those efforts achieved sufficient acclaim to win a role on Broadway in New York City. Emma was 34 years old when she left England with her mother on the mail ship *Pacific* for Broadway's theater district. Once she had arrived in America, Emma's fascination with Spiritualism steadily evolved and her powers as a trance medium and eloquent speaker shaped her future career.[24]

Emma described a lonely childhood, with her fondest memories arising from a vivid imagination when confined to a sickbed. Tragedy struck when the 11-year-old girl's father suddenly died, a crisis that left her "longing to join my father.... I resolved to follow him, and thus I stood one dark night by the river's bank, and was only saved ... by the sound of my dead father's voice bidding me return to school, and leading me back, as I distinctly felt, by the hand."[25]

Emma's suicidal ideation gave way to somnambulism soon after she arrived in Paris to further her musical education. Night after night, loud screams and aimless sleep walking took a toll on Emma, as she eventually lost her golden voice to chronic irritation. All was not lost, as she quickly shifted to playing the piano and through that conversion developed her clairvoyance, mystifying audience members by playing their unspoken selections. Shortly thereafter, Emma began attending séances on a regular basis.

Her arrival in New York was turbulent and beset by homesickness, even with her mother present. Conflicts with the stage manager spiraled out of control, leaving her with a binding contract but no work. Emma was unhappy and bored but determined

Emma Hardinge Britten (*Nineteenth Century Miracles, or, Spirits and Their Work in Every Country of the Earth: A Complete Historical Compendium of the Great Movement Known as "Modern Spiritualism,"* **William Britten, Lovell & Co., New York, 1884**).

not to buckle, a mental state relieved by a married couple's animated discussion of Spiritualism at the home where she boarded. After some hesitation, Emma started attending séances in New York City with Ada Foye, a rapping medium who introduced Emma to many long-lost family members.

Many séances later, Emma became an accomplished medium: "I could give tests of spirit identity by personations, impressions, writing, and automatic movements of my fingers over the alphabet." But her greatest skill, aside from her passionate elocution of Spiritualism, was a clairvoyance that even detectives valued in solving crimes.

Along the way, she collected accolades from admirers and countless criticisms. A visit to Cleveland in 1864 was much the same, but a local reporter roundly ripped the spiritualist. After sarcastically referring to Emma Hardinge as "the great High Priestess of spiritualism," the reporter begrudgingly acknowledged her oratorical eloquence and her large spellbound audiences. Even so, the reporter caustically commented that "in personal appearance Miss Hardinge is a non-attractive, elderly maiden."[26]

Emma rose to the top ranks of influential American Spiritualists, hobnobbing with the Fox sisters, Conklin, Edmonds, and others, a public prominence achieved through riveting lectures unapologetically promoting Spiritualism. Her travels across the country included an extended sojourn in Nevada and California.

She was a staunch advocate of the Union cause, which in one instance paid a handsome dividend after she donated a large sum of money to a Soldiers' Refreshment Room in Philadelphia, Pennsylvania. As the casualties of the war mounted, local officials converted the refreshment room into a hospital and Emma's charity was warmly appreciated by the soldiers. She had no idea that her compassion would rebound.

Emma was lecturing in Virginia City, Nevada, in 1864 when she accepted an invitation to do the same in a more remote town. Friends in Virginia City counseled otherwise, citing the arduous journey and ubiquitous outlaws that roamed the area, but Emma dismissed their concerns. It was a rough three-day ride, bumping along in a stagecoach, that nearly ended in disaster. A few miles from her destination a small band of outlaws surrounded the stage coach and after ordering the driver to halt began systematically threatening Emma and the other passengers. As the outlaws rummaged through the passengers' baggage they found Emma's name neatly lettered on a package. With a gasp one of the outlaws exclaimed, "God Bless you Emma Hardinge, you have helped to save my life, and my poor brother's—since dead."

The grateful outlaw painfully recalled a grievous wound suffered during a battle near Philadelphia. Along with others, he was carried in a cart to Philadelphia and forced to spend the night outside. Later that night a group of nurses relieved their pitiful plight by transporting the blood-soaked soldiers to Emma's refurbished Soldiers' Refreshment Room, now outfitted as a hospital. Following his reminiscence, the outlaw handed Emma a hastily scrawled note guaranteeing her future safe passage.

Emma left Nevada in 1864 and during an extended stay in California spent her final months campaigning for Lincoln's reelection. Her unequivocal support of Lincoln combined with her grand eloquence as a speaker guaranteed large audiences, a politically diverse group surely united in their favorable impression of Emma's patriotism. After Lincoln's reelection Emma left California and resumed stumping for Spiritualism in the Northeast.

Every now and then an enigmatic story surfaced, obliquely reinforcing a belief in ghosts. A Vermont newspaper was one of many reporting these curiosities. In its version an unnamed person reputedly held in high esteem by the local community approached the newspaper with a fantastic revelation. From sound sleep one night, the elderly man awakened with a start, a sudden jolt "as if he had been shot through the head." A moment later a vision of his son, an officer on a distant battlefield, appeared and silently seemed to convey the morbid news of his death. Three weeks later the father learned of his son's death from a bullet wound to the head, on a date that exactly coincided with the father's macabre nighttime experience.[27]

Every ardent spiritualist spawned a seemingly equal number of fraudulent performers and those determined to expose them. Professor Sands razed the faith in Ohio in 1864 with feats of magic that simulated spirit manifestations and in the process earned a newspaper's high praise for his work that should "serve as a warning to all to beware of tricksters and sharpers."[28]

Charles Reed was another roving phantom plyer earning a reputation and little else. Reed's psychic specialty was ringing bells, and his spirits apparently preferred clanging to rapping. At a performance in Cleveland, Ohio, in 1864, cantankerous spirits confounded his show. Try as he might the bells would not ring, and a frustrated and embarrassed Reed left the stage, ostensibly seeking a better connection with the spirits. A restless audience waited and waited, and then a few of the more energetic began searching for the performer. Reed was eventually found apparently under the influence of liquid spirits.[29]

It was a bad night for Reed. His ruse unraveled when a young boy commissioned by the medium to ring a bell at a nearby fire station at a precise time suspected the man was planning a robbery and was using the ploy to distract local authorities. At the agreed-upon time a large audience eagerly awaited the spiritual bell ringing but nothing happened. Reed was furious and, racing from the stage, accosted his young accomplice, who had the foresight to have a fire engineer on standby.

The gig was up and Reed knew it. "As soon as he was caught ... he commenced staggering violently, talked incoherently, and assured the officers that he was 'very tight,' or else he would not have hired the boy to ring the bell." A judge rewarded his act with a $5 fine, a debt paid by the moneyless medium with jail time.[30]

Henry Melville Fay was a traveling test medium and with his psychic wife Anna toured the country; they were always looking over their shoulders for the Rev. Abraham Smith Dobbs, the pair's inveterate bête noire. Dobbs dogged Fay in the early 1860s in the oil-rich Titusville, Pennsylvania, region, denouncing the medium and effectively driving him out of the area.[31]

After leaving Pennsylvania behind, the Fay troupe went west and started performing in Ohio. Toward the end of July 1864 they opened in Cleveland before a boisterous crowd. As protégés of the Davenport brothers, the Fays' act presented a similar show, with Melville entertaining the crowd with a coffin-like cabinet from which he variously emerged, tied or untied, and the usual mysterious bells, drums, and spirit hands exciting the audience.

Fay concluded a performance prematurely rejoicing the night's success, when his arch advocate arose from the audience and challenged the medium. Dobbs turned to the audience and begged the assemblage to join him the following night at Brainard's Hall for an exposition debunking Fay. As might be imagined, the audience greeted the interloper with a mix of derision and disbelief, but Dobbs's dedication conveyed a sense of honesty and dispelled those initial doubts.

Dobbs was a Methodist minister, and when he strode onto the stage around eight o'clock the next night he opened the event with a short homily denouncing the use of magic tricks to foster faith in religion. A committee comprised of two men then carefully inspected Dobbs's spirit cabinet and after pronouncing it free of gimmicks bound the minister securely inside. As usual, bells, drums, and spirit hands mysteriously made their appearance, and when the committee members opened the cabinet's doors a demure Dobbs was still fastened tight.

Dobbs was a nimble man, flexible and flamboyant, and used both characteristics to upend the Fays. In full view of the audience, the committee men once more tied him to a chair and within seconds the ropes lay on the floor. A reporter in attendance cheered that "it was a most searching,

Four—Doctrine, Dilemmas and Doubts

thorough and successful exposition of one of the vilest, boldest swindles and humbugs ever practiced."

Robert Heller was among an emerging group of entertainers deftly duplicating spiritual manifestations but never ascribing the marvels to ethereal agents. From his Salle Diabolique on Broadway in New York City, the performer promised "to besiege the Spiritualists in their own citadel and with their own weapons."[32]

Heller was born in London and from his youth trained as a musician, but his life changed forever after witnessing the magic of Jean-Eugène Robert-Houdin. Houdin's protégé perfected his skills in England before coming to America in 1852. Heller's debut in New York City was a financial failure and the disappointed showman retreated to Washington, D.C., where he traded the stage for a decidedly more banal living as a piano teacher. Heller married one his students, a woman from a well-to-do family, and with her support he abandoned music for magic.[33]

Magic proved more rewarding the second time around. On the stage at his Salle Diabolique, Heller's revival entertained the audience with masterful piano concertos, humor, feats of legerdemain, and his amazing mentalism, "seemingly supernatural marvels surpassing all spiritual manifestations."[34]

Heller's second sight act was the show stopper. It was performed with Haidee Heller, billed as the magician's sister, which was possibly a fictitious relationship allowing both to disguise and to assuage the sensitivities of the Victorian audiences of the nineteenth century.[35]

Second sight was variously described as mind reading or clairvoyance. When performing the act, Robert Heller would obtain some item from the audience and Haidee, who was unable to see the item, would invariably describe it in minute detail to the utter amazement of all present. The magician did not credit spiritual influences for the second sight, joking that "some learned folks say that my second-sight experiment is accomplished by ventriloquism, some magnetism, some spiritism. But they are all wrong, it is simply Hellerism."[36]

Hellerism was not some occult practice but according to Robert was "a system: an understanding between two people whose minds are in active sympathy … by the exercise of peculiar faculties of the brain." Heller would never reveal the method behind Hellerism, although Harry Hermon, his longtime assistant, did so after the entertainer's death. According to Hermon, Robert and Haidee communicated through elaborate verbal codes that provided clues to an item's description.[37]

As America entered the last year of war in 1865, Spiritualism seemed to flounder much like the South's rebellion. Trials and tribulations dominated the newspaper headlines even as Spiritualism's stalwart champions stubbornly soldiered on. All the notables like the Fox sisters, the Davenport brothers, Cora Hatch, Andrew Jackson Davis, and Judge Edmonds continued their crusades.

Spiritualists in Maryland proudly banded together, forming The First Spiritualist Congregation in Baltimore, a religious union holding regular meetings at Saratoga Hall.[38] From Bloomington, Illinois, the spiritualist and clairvoyant Dr. Smith offered the services of a machine designed by the spirits for the express purpose of producing an image of a person's future spouse, a revelation for the nominal sum of 50 cents and one stamp.[39]

The Thorpe brothers held cabinet séances in New York City and private séances offering spirit-guided healing for those with chronic medical problems.[40] Smith and Nixon's Hall in Chicago hosted E.H. Eddy for an evening's entertainment during which the performer promised "a view into the mysteries of the cabinet spirituelle, together with an explanation of the mode of producing these 'phenomena' which have astonished the world."[41]

Much of the national interest in 1865 was focused not on the mystical manifestations of the performers and mediums but instead on their misdeeds and miscalculations. Headlining this narrative was the trial of Charles J. Colchester, a famous medium with a reputation "only second to the famous Hume in notoriety as a spiritualist." Colchester ran afoul of the Internal Revenue Service in New York, with the agency claiming that he was "practicing jugglery without a license."[42]

Colchester refused to purchase a license labeling his practice as jugglery, countering with an offer to pay any stipulated fee that excluded the connotation of fraud, a negotiated position that the New York Collector of Revenue promptly refused, setting the stage for Colchester's arrest. As a spiritualist, Colchester insisted that his practice was genuine, an intractable dispute between the parties that propelled the matter to the United States District Court in Buffalo, New York, for resolution.

Newspapers of the day relished the fight and recast the dispute as a contest determining the legitimacy of Spiritualism. A Brooklyn newspaper sarcastically claimed, "It is high time that some official action was taken, as for years communication has been kept up between the spirits and their friends in the flesh without the use of postage stamps."[43]

The events leading to Colchester's arrest began on May 23, 1865, when the New York tax collector unceremoniously approached the medium during a private séance. After filling out the jugglery license the collector handed the form to Colchester, who indignantly protested the insinuation by countering that "I would like to take out a license as a spiritual medium—not as a mountebank." If Colchester expected a favorable reply he

Four—Doctrine, Dilemmas and Doubts 79

was sorely disappointed, and expressed his frustration by angrily ripping the license to shreds.

Colchester's arrest was a serious challenge for spiritualists. As the combatants squared off in the Buffalo courtroom, Colchester's defense team consisting of George B. Hibbard and Josiah Cook sparred with prosecutors William Dart and Charles H. Tappin. As it turned out, Cook pled illness, leaving Hibbard as the main attorney defending Colchester.

The trial began on August 19, 1865, in a courtroom packed with spectators. Colchester pled not guilty to the charge of practicing jugglery without a license, after which the proposed list of witnesses was presented by the respective attorneys, although in a portent of the outcome none of an extensive list of defense witnesses was present. After the customary wrangling, the attorneys finally agreed on the jury, signaling the start of the trial. Mr. Hibbard challenged the constitutionality of the law under which his client was charged, but an unimpressed judge dismissed the argument.[44]

District Attorney Dart put the case in perspective, alleging that the defendant simply violated a duly constituted law requiring the purchase of a license to practice jugglery. Dart believed the case an incontrovertible matter, openly wondering what defense Colchester could mount. Speaking to the jury and a courtroom packed with journalists, the prosecutor mused, "While I concede the inestimable value of the press, I cannot forbear the remark that it has been made the instrument of magnifying this case into undue proportions, and to cause the public to believe that it is a contest between the United States and a large body of citizens calling themselves spiritualists, and an endeavor, on the part of the former, to crush out a religious sect and to expose its heresies if it has any, and that the result of this trial will establish the fact whether Spiritualism is true or false. Nothing can be further from the truth."

James Rogers was the prosecution's first witness: a close associate and Colchester confidante whose testimony betrayed his former friend. Rogers testified that Colchester simulated spirit rappings with his foot and in an unguarded moment the medium actually admitted the humbuggery. It was an ominous start but just the beginning of Dart's prosecution.[45]

William McCarthy and George Thrall, both residents of Rochester, New York, testified next. Both lived in Rochester, New York, and had visited Colchester's place of business. Their experiences were similar: McCarthy and Thrall each wrote a series of questions on small pieces of paper, rolled them into small bullets, and placed them on a table near the medium. Colchester asked both men to write the name of a deceased person on another piece of paper and after receiving the information he dramatically threw it out a nearby window. A few moments later Colchester supposedly made contact with the spirits named by McCarthy and Thrall and through their inspiration began answering the questions posed by the two men. Both men were suspicious and suspected fraud but were unable to prove it.[46]

John H. Anderson was the prosecution's most profound witness, based on Colchester's proposal to make the man a partner in his performances. During the negotiations Colchester revealed some tricks of the trade, even going so far as teaching Anderson the finer points of clairvoyance. Despite Colchester's pressure and promise of rich rewards, Anderson dismissed the offer as a humbug.

District Attorney Dart's case concluded in the afternoon, paving the way for Colchester's defense. It began with Colchester's lead counsel George B. Hibbard attacking the jugglery law, insisting that his client did not conduct public performances as the law stipulated, opting instead for private séances. In dismissing Hibbard's argument the presiding judge referenced Colchester's public posters and fees for service.

Hibbard secured an interesting group of witnesses for his client's defense, including Judge J.C. Chumesew, Lewis Burtis, Lester Day, and two newspaper editors, William Ferrin and Thomas Kean. Each in turn recounted their meetings with Colchester and collectively testified that they detected no evidence of sleight of hand. Frank Kahn was a magician and a clever choice as a defense witness. He was familiar with some of Colchester's routines, but Kahn frankly admitted that he did not "know how the answers to questions in envelopes was made; thought the answering ... was supernatural."

A reporter attending the trial predicted the defendant's exoneration in a verdict that would leave Colchester's reputation untarnished. The jury had a different opinion, and on the morning of August 23, 1865, found Colchester guilty. Hibbard immediately protested the verdict and implored the court to revisit the constitutionality of the revenue law and the impingement of his client's religious beliefs, a request the court granted by permitting the attorney a few days to prepare a more formal appeal.[47]

Colchester's trial had predicable results, with ardent advocates of Spiritualism decrying the verdict as a witch hunt and partisans in the other corner rejoicing at the result.[48] Spiritualism's opponents expansively declared, "The jury decide[d] that spiritualism is jugglery; that raps and table-tippings ... floating guitars and all the other phenomena produced by the so-called mediums are ... merely the result of slight-of-hand." After indicting all spiritualists as Colchester co-conspirators, the newspaper derisively concluded that the verdict would not dissuade the deluded practitioners.[49]

Ridicule was a favored technique to demean Spiritualism, and Colchester's verdict was tailor made for mocking the movement. "It was expected by many that the defendant would fly thro' the keyhole of the courtroom when he heard the decision; but he didn't. The spirits evidently deserted him."[50]

If the spirits abandoned Colchester, they were joined by some prominent spiritualists who rushed for the exits following his conviction. Judge Edmonds was among those drawing a bright line between Colchester and the efforts of many to impugn Spiritualism based on the trial's outcome. He began his dispute by excoriating the illiberal newspaper reporters attacks: "I care precious little about the efforts at making me ridiculous; or about your penny-a-liner correspondents ... but when, through me, you and others attack what I regard as a grand principle ... I cannot, as a matter of principle, permit my silence to give ... sanction to the attacks."[51]

Part of Edmonds's pique stemmed from a widely reported and erroneous account of his participation as a member of Colchester's defense team. The judge freely admitted that Colchester requested his legal counsel but Edmonds refused: a repudiation based on Edmonds's disdain for Colchester's money grubbing, which smacked of business building manufactured manifestations. Colchester's conviction validated his assessment.

After discarding Colchester, Edmonds turned to the crop of critics who used the trial's outcome to broadly indict Spiritualism. In colorful terms the judge took issue with the ignorance of Spiritualism of the "flippant writers," misconstruing the faith as nothing more than physical manifestations, which glossed over its religious roots grounded in a spiritual belief of life after death. Contact between mortals and spirits was the fundamental tenet of the faith, and Edmonds educated the cynics by noting that the thousands, maybe millions, of believers who received messages from the those in the spirit world provided shared experiences simply too large to ignore.

Colchester's woes did not end with the trial's verdict. Hibbard's appeal was also dismissed, with the court finding that the revenue law was constitutional and not a religious tax. The court further reasoned that "if the defendant and these spirit mediums are not imposters ... the most obvious and direct mode of proving the defense set up was to put these so-called mediums upon the stand ... under oath ... that they do receive communications, from some spiritual ... source." The court relied on sworn testimony as a barometer of truth, and the fact that no spiritual medium testified was a glaring and suspicious omission.[52]

By and large the press coverage of the trial was negative, and the venerable *New York Times* joined the parade by castigating Colchester and the profit-focused phantom profession. Before warning readers about the perils of Spiritualism, the newspaper gave ground, heading off any criticism from grieving family members by insisting that the newspaper had no intention "to abridge by a single iota, the consolation which some profess to derive from frequent and tender communion with the spirits of the beloved and (perhaps recently) lost." With that concession, the editorial proceeded to lambaste the faith and strongly urged its readers to avoid the fakery and fraud.[53]

Charles Colchester was seemingly unfazed by the negative publicity and continued holding séances. Some simply dismissed the trial and considered the man a martyr crucified by legions of nonbelievers. What Colchester could not deny was the $40 fine and $473 in court costs.[54]

Religious conversions were influential fodder that Spiritualism's advocates and opponents lobbed with glee. A celebrity's about-face was particularly poignant, such as when Edward Askew Sothern turned the table on Spiritualism. Sothern was a popular stage actor earning praise for performances such as "Our American Cousin" in 1858 and "David Garrick" in 1864.[55]

Edward Sothern (*Frank Leslie's Illustrated News*, August 31, 1861).

Sothern flirted with Spiritualism, but the fascination faded. He was singularly irked by a piece in the *Spiritual Magazine* that coined the term "Miracle Circle," a reference to the actor's mysticism on display at regular séances attended by a clique of famous actors. It was factually inaccurate, as the peeved performer painfully pointed out, noting that the séance was not composed of actors but of curious, learned men and that his contributions were scientific and not spiritual.[56]

Sothern admitted a two-year relationship with

Spiritualism during which time he attended nearly weekly séances. As time went on, the actor lost faith in the spirits but not in the manifestations, boasting that his prowess duplicating any medium's magic exceeded all of his contemporaries such as the Davenport brothers. Sothern made it clear that prestidigitation and not phantoms explained his performances, but he did not reveal his secrets. In a further poke at spiritualists, Sothern reminded readers that his performances were always free and followed by a nice supper. Casting aside any further civility, Sothern considered Spiritualism "a chronicle of imbecility, cowardly terror of the supernatural, willful self-delusion, irreligion, and ... fraud."[57]

John McQueen traveled across Michigan and over the course of four years thrilled and amazed audiences with his psychic powers. It was the usual stuff, bell ringing, table tippings, and rappings, but his fame came to a screeching halt in early February 1865 when an alert audience uncovered deception during a performance in Kalamazoo.[58]

McQueen took the fall landing on his feet, and with a charlatan's mental agility took off in the opposite direction. The turncoat now admitted the fraud: a revelation apparently requiring the man's pious restitution in the form of a tell-all exposé, for a small fee of course. A waggish reporter drolly noted that "skeptics and believers in McQueen's spiritualism can be convinced in the light; that he has heretofore humbugged them in the dark."[59]

Another unmasking that threw doubt on Spiritualism involved a self-promoted Professor Cadwell. The man packed Brooklyn's Harmony Hall in the company of two attractive features: the young spiritual medium Laura V. Ellis, and a $500 reward to any patron proving dishonesty. It was a cabinet séance with the typical spirit shenanigans, but the real fireworks exploded at the conclusion of the young girl's performance.[60]

Albert Dean was a precocious 12-year-old boy from Great Barrington, Massachusetts, who confidently accepted Cadwell's $500 challenge. To the amazement of the audience the young boy recreated every aspect of Ellis's routine and by many measures exceeded her performance. If Dean expected the reward he was sorely disappointed. Cadwell hemmed and hawed but would not forfeit the money, even as a restive audience clearly supported Dean. Police prevented the disgruntled customers from destroying the Ellis séance cabinet.

Cadwell and Ellis made a hasty retreat after both were thoroughly disgraced for their cheating and welching. It was a sad outcome for Dean, but sympathetic citizens rallied to the poor boy's cause and booked Harmony Hall for an evening devoted to debunking Spiritualism by the very boy who defeated Cadwell, and as a final tribute the boy received the night's receipts.

Upending spiritualists was a cat-and-mouse game and spared no one. The Davenport brothers took their show to England and beyond, perhaps in an effort to avoid the sport. If the brothers expected a more sympathetic or gullible group, they seriously misjudged mischief makers who lived on the other side of the ocean.[61]

Something was in the air when the Davenport brothers appeared before an unruly, packed-to-the-gills audience at St. George's Hall in Liverpool, England, in mid February 1865. The pair's stage manager Dr. Ferguson anticipated a rough night, and standing before the crowd he laid out the ground rules. Ferguson expected those attending to be civil and avoid unseemly public reproaches cast against the performers, and while inviting a committee to examine the séance cabinet he reserved the right to expel those judged unfair. As a final warning, Ferguson demanded that anyone unable to comply should promptly leave the theater and their money would be refunded.

Ferguson asked for a committee, and two men, "Mssrs. Hulley and Cummins," both conveniently seated in the front row, immediately accepted the invitation. The stage manager recognized the men as virulent antagonists and refused their offer, which proved to be just the spark needed to set the audience aflame. A cacophony of indignation rattled the walls as the entire audience almost in unison loudly protested Ferguson's decision. As the stage manager tried in vain to calm the spiraling escalation, Hulley and Cummins ignored the hubbub and took a seat in the Davenports' spirit cabinet and began a minute inspection.

Ferguson had lost control of the crowd, and only the appearance of the Davenport brothers momentarily quelled the riot. The brief pause provided the stage manager the opportunity to further explain his concerns about Hulley in particular, accusing the man of blatant brutality if allowed to bind the entertainer's hands and feet to the spirit cabinet. Acquiescing at last, Ferguson permitted Hulley to tie up Ira Davenport.

After firmly binding Ira in the spirit cabinet, Hulley triumphantly turned to the crowd, followed almost immediately by the performer standing unbound but bleeding from a hand wound. For a moment the stunned crowd absorbed the scene, which seemingly confirmed Ferguson's sadistic accusation targeting Hulley. Ira silently added to the condemnation by angrily walking off stage.

Cummins was unfazed by the drama and, addressing an audience already primed to distrust the Davenport brothers, claimed the wound came about when Ira begged his stage manager to cut one unyielding knot. The house erupted and, like a dam holding back a swelling torrent, burst open, with indignant spectators streaming on stage and smashing the spirit cabinet to smithereens.

Four—Doctrine, Dilemmas and Doubts

A reporter in attendance excused the violence by arguing that "the proceedings, though turbulent, were exceedingly good humored," a comedy brought to halt when dozens of police brought the festivities to an end. The good-natured crowd sought in vain to find the Davenport brothers after their hasty retreat, perhaps hoping to tar and feather the performers for more fun.

The Davenport brothers eventually recovered, and in September 1865 they made their debut in Paris. Despite a steep 25-cent ticket, the theater was filled to the brim. Nothing happened for a considerable time, which set the audience on edge, but finally a festively plumed emcee broke the boredom and began a sonorous monologue denying spiritual influence for the forthcoming manifestations while exhorting the audience to be respectful.[62]

As usual, a committee composed of two men inspected the Davenports' spirit cabinet and after satisfying their doubts tied the brothers securely, the theater lights were extinguished, and musical instruments sallied forth. After the venue was relit, the brothers stood unbound, but one of the committee men cried foul and insisted that the ropes lying on the floor were not the originals. The audience members screamed, rattling the rafters with their disgust.

Unperturbed by the criticism, the brothers proceeded with their act and entered the spirit cabinet unbound. Again the lights were dimmed for a moment, and when the lights were relit the brothers faced the crowd bound to their cabinet's seat. This might have ended on a triumphant note except for an eagle-eyed spectator who rushed on stage, "put his hand on the bench round which the cords are wound, touches a spring, the bench bends in the middle, and the cords fall at the feet of the captives."

It was a humiliating disclosure and the audience erupted. The enraged mob dashed toward the stage but was stopped by the French Gendarmerie, who finally restored order after promising a full refund. During the melée the Davenport brothers performed their best escape by hurriedly disappearing from the theater.

Southern newspapers loved lampooning Yankee interest in Spiritualism. From Virginia, the *Richmond Daily Dispatch* ridiculed an 1865 performance in Boston but spared the performers any additional ignominy through anonymity. According to the story, "a shrewd person present, in order to satisfy himself as to the corporeality of a 'spiritual hand' which was shown from an aperture in a 'cabinet' used, supplied himself with a syringe filled with ink, and, watching for a favorable opportunity, squirted the dark fluid over the digits and wrist of the phantom member." With the lights restored the bound woman's hands were closely inspected and faint traces of black ink exposed the fraud. Members of a rightly insulted crowd voiced their disapproval by publicly denouncing the medium and her cabinet, but they abstained from any physical violence.[63]

Phineas T. Barnum, the great entrepreneurial showman whose name became inextricably linked to hoaxes, was in fact interested in debunking deceit, and it was just a matter of time before he turned his sleuthing eye to Spiritualism. Before casting his gaze on the seers of the afterlife, the famous impresario wrote a series of short stories in *The New York Mercury*, a widely read paper of the era. Barnum toppled quack doctors, patent medicines, and get-rich-quick schemes, along with other connivers and charlatans that eventually included psychic mediums. It was a popular series, and *The New York Mercury* urged readers to purchase back copies to complete any missing revelations about the "ancient and modern humbugs of the world."[64]

Barnum's American Museum, located in lower Manhattan, was a repository for repulsive, curious, eclectic, scientific, and educational exhibits. Wax figures vied for attention alongside a working iron foundry, steam engines, dramatic theatrical plays, glass blowers, and the signature oddities such as the living skeleton, the Circassian girl, and the eight foot boy. In the midst of this tableau Dr. F.W. Van Vleck held practical demonstrations revealing the tricks of the trade used by spiritualists.[65]

Phineas T. Barnum (*Frank Leslie's Illustrated News*, July 23, 1864).

Four—Doctrine, Dilemmas and Doubts

Barnum obliged a public captivated by all types of imposture with the publication of *The Humbugs of the World*, a revised compilation of the articles previously printed in *The New York Mercury*. For his temerity exposing the goings-on of supposed spiritual manifestations, the author suffered more than verbal slings and arrows, with threats of libel cast his way. Barnum countered by offering $500 to any medium who could deceive him, with the only stipulation being that the showman would select the location and setting, depriving the spiritualist of the controlled environment required to foist their fraud. Apparently the money went unclaimed.[66]

Nine chapters in *The Humbugs of the World* dissected and destroyed Spiritualism with explicit details describing the frauds. In one example, Barnum explained how a medium produced blood red writing on an arm, which always amazed the credulous. "Try the experiment yourself, reader. Hold out your left arm; clench the fist so as to harden the muscle a little, and write your name on the skin with a blunt pencil or any similar point ... pressing firmly.... Rub the place briskly ... this brings out the letters quickly."

In some cases the manifestations claimed by spiritualists strained common sense and bordered on the delusional. Armed with ridicule and humor, Barnum attacked a pair of mediums claiming a bizarre immaculate conception. In the late 1850s as the industrial age steamed forward, machines were still wondrous, mysterious marvels, attributes that clever mediums exploited.

In 1854 in High Rock, Massachusetts, a group of spiritualists was busily occupied in building a spirit machine. According to Barnum's account, the Reverend Spear, one of the principals building the contraption, received a spiritual sign that a famous female medium should visit the site. Spear transmitted the message to the unnamed woman, who agreed to make the journey despite being supposedly pregnant.

When she arrived, the pregnant female medium doubled over in agony, portending an imminent delivery but not of the human sort. The medium's labors instead gave birth to the inanimate spirit machine. Like any devoted mother, the medium nurtured the machine for a few weeks before it sadly succumbed.

For Barnum it was an incredulous but true story ripe for ripping. With a ribald touch the showman wondered, "Who was the Daddy? For if things like this are going to happen, the ladies will be afraid to sleep alone in the house if so much as a sewing-machine or apple-corer be about."

In some cases humbug turned to crime and exposed a medium's darker side. It was a warning sign that skeptics used to urge caution when approaching spiritualists. Mr. Hopkins of Little Hocking, Ohio, missed the message and fell victim to a pair of artful mediums from New Jersey. With his visions of wealth replacing common sense, the gullible man's inklings of belief in Spiritualism crystallized into certainty when the psychics promised to reveal a treasure trove hidden in his house.[67]

The first communion with the spirits was disappointing, as the spirits refused to reveal the treasure until Hopkins placed $3500 in a trunk. After complying with the spirits' demand, Hopkins prudently locked the trunk and pocketed the key. The spirits had further directed that the man wait five days before opening the box and reviewing the treasure map. In the ensuing interval the mediums disappeared, a fleet feat that left Hopkins bewildered at their sudden departure. At the end of the fifth day Hopkins opened the trunk expecting the spirits' gift but was mortified to discover only scraps of paper and pieces of tin. As the reporter telling the tale marveled, "Such is the power of these spiritualists to transform gold into tin, and greenbacks into old newspapers."

Even more disturbing was Sarah Leonard's sordid story, a woman otherwise known as Sarah Haviland who would stand accused of killing three of her children. Haviland hailed from Ypsilanti, Michigan, but fled that city, escaping what she considered an abusive husband, after conferring with the spirits. With little more than her ardent faith in Spiritualism and her five children, the woman began a new life in Battle Creek, Michigan.[68]

A local citizen discovered the bodies of three young children on December 16, 1865, in a shack on the edge of town, and on closer inspection recalled seeing them playfully cavorting about a few days earlier. Their deaths raised immediate suspicions of foul play and a coroner's inquest confirmed it.[69]

Shortly after arriving in Battle Creek, Sarah Haviland had met Daniel J. Baker, a healing medium who performed miraculous cures. Baker moved in with Haviland, a scandalous affair by itself, and soon thereafter Lizzie Merritt, a 23-year-old spiritualist, joined the growing congregation. Hattie Hannis was a 17-year-old girl who completed the core group that held séances every Sunday and Wednesday. Baker seemed particularly interested in promoting Hattie's spiritual growth, a cozy relationship that invited innuendo that "she being naturally quick-witted, we are assured she did 'develop' with exceeding rapidity, though not in the direction of work."

The spirits recognized the cramped living conditions and wisely suggested they move to a vacant lot on the edge of town. Baker borrowed the money from the hapless Lizzie and in doing so confiscated the young woman's entire fortune to procure the land and build a rough-hewn two-room shanty for five children, Sarah, Lizzie, Hattie, and two men, which included Baker and Lizzie's brother.

Four—Doctrine, Dilemmas and Doubts

Baker eventually settled on the notion of touring the countryside with Sarah lecturing on Spiritualism and Hattie adding the mystical component. As he thought through the logistics of the plan, Baker was stymied by the three children who were too young to travel or be left alone. Just in the nick of time, the spirits predicted the children's deaths and Baker disingenuously spread the spirits' word about town, perhaps in an effort to cover the coming crimes but his repeated pronouncements only caused suspicion. In the days before their deaths the three children pitifully suffered vomiting, severe stomach pains, burning throat, and unsatiated thirst. During a séance an Indian spirit foretold their imminent deaths.

A coroner's inquest convened shortly after the local citizen discovered the dead children. Three doctors examined the bodies and sent specimens to Ann Arbor, Michigan, for chemical analysis. A week later the inquest reconvened and heard conflicting testimony, but the officials expected the autopsy results to clarify the confusion, a fact already known by all the suspects.

Toward the end of the day's inquest on December 23, 1865, Sarah approached the sheriff to make a determined request to testify. On the witness stand, Sarah confessed that she came to Battle Creek to escape an abusive, alcoholic husband but was destitute upon arrival. Baker was her salvation, and when the other female boarders came the work was shared among them, which improved their collective lots in life. Still, all was not well when Sarah saw disturbing developments in her young children that suggested that her husband's bad influence was sprouting in them.

It was at this point that Sarah concluded, "It was better to send them to the Spirit world while they were innocent.... I have no one to blame but myself.... I feel that what I have done is to be settled between me and my God and the Spirit World.... Monday morning, a week ago, I came up town to get some sulphur and cream of tartar and arsenic, and mixed it together in molasses." Sarah's memory now grew foggy as she tried to recollect how many poisonous portions her children swallowed, but pretending a mother's tenderness she testified that "I took care of my children and watched over them until the last breath."

A jury convicted Sarah Haviland for murder and punished her with a life sentence at Michigan's first state prison in Jackson.[70] Not surprisingly, spiritualists resented the implication that their religion contributed to the crime, by questioning whether "devotees of a common faith are responsible collectively for the isolated act of a single member?"[71]

The less consequential but still sensationalized legal cases of Luther C. Tibbets were yet another opportunity to indirectly impugn Spiritualism. Tibbets was an irascible businessman with a penchant for violence that usually played out in a never-ending torrent of civil lawsuits aimed at what the man considered conniving conspirators intent on destroying him.[72]

Tibbets had a feisty relationship with members of the New York Corn Exchange, a long-standing simmering dispute that led to his banishment from the building. What provoked the members was his erratic behavior in attacking banks and brokers who spurned his business interests. This all came to a head when a righteously indignant Tibbets stormed the Corn Exchange and, brandishing pocket knives, battled police who were called to remove the impetuous interloper. From his jail cell Tibbets furiously launched a salvo of lawsuits.[73]

The objects of Tibbets's ire, the defendants in his many lawsuits, portrayed the man as insane and his court room antics and admissions helped make that case. Most imprudently, Tibbett preceded pro se and in so doing relegated his lawyer to spectator status as he sparred with the judge and rather ineptly examined witnesses.

It was Tibbets's avowed belief in Spiritualism that probably did the most damage to his cases, a revelation that the man tried to hide but the presiding judge refused to dodge. Tibbets was unable to escape the legal pincers and finally launched into a religious monologue long on Christianity but short on Spiritualism, which ended with the judge's rebuke. A brief interrogatory conducted by the opposing lawyer asked Tibbets, "Do you receive communications from the dead?" After first refusing to answer the question, Tibbets reluctantly relented by demurely declaring, "I believe in receiving communications just as Judge Edmonds, Andrew Jackson Davis and others do; the spirits are with us all the time."

Tibbets's bluster was simply not enough, as demonstrated by the judge's prompt dismissal of the frivolous lawsuit. In addition to Tibbets being pilloried in the press for his meritless lawsuits and spirit counselors, the judge ordered him to award $100 to the defendants to defray their legal costs.[74]

With the fading of the South's fortunes in 1865, bitterness born from privation crept into everyday life. In the soon-to-collapse Confederate capital in Richmond, Virginia, the local newspaper angrily bemoaned a starving city and soldiers weakened by want, a desperate situation that patriots in the countryside could not alleviate. Riding into this dire scene were General Philip Sheridan and his Union troops, who lobbed dispiriting propaganda with devastating effect.[75]

The *Richmond Dispatch* took aim at the North's blasphemous flirtation with Spiritualism. With derision the newspaper reported that "A party of Yankee spiritualists, under the direction of that famous wizard, Sheridan ... in the course of their travels, exhibited a series of wonders never surpassed in the days of witchcraft. They made a few raps with their electrical knuckles at the farm-houses they visited ... and potatoes, bags of meal, barrels of flour, and endless hams of bacon, came to the light of day.... Sheridan boasts, in his account of these miraculous transactions that he caused provisions enough to appear in this way to 'feed Lee's army for the three months.' It is ridiculous to suppose that these provisions existed before his arrival, and had been ingeniously concealed from public observation."

As the Civil War came to end in 1865, the steady drumbeat of negative news about Spiritualism also seemed to herald its demise, which turned out to be a conclusion upended when the death of Abraham Lincoln reinvigorated the human hope of reuniting with lost loved ones.

Five

Assassination, Resurrection and Exploitation

America's Civil War ended at a courthouse in Appomattox, Virginia, when General Robert E. Lee surrendered to General Ulysses S. Grant on April 9, 1865, in an almost amicable conclusion to a bitter conflict. The two generals' gentility was a first step toward repairing a social rupture that would take decades to heal.[1]

Demobilization of the two armies did not end the suffering, with an almost endless stream of wounded soldiers returning home, as a tragic and persistent reminder of the war's cost. Even this mixed blessing was denied the families and loved ones of those who would never find their way home, casualties of a conflict where many men died an anonymous death. Not knowing a soldier's fate was doubly difficult, particularly as time went by and extinguished the last flickers of hope.

Whatever satisfaction the successful Northern states could muster came to a dramatic stop on April 14, 1865, when John Wilkes Booth assassinated President Abraham Lincoln only about one week after Lee and Grant made peace their priority.[2] It was yet another dark cloud threatening more storms for a nation weathering the winds of war. In the Northern states, the assassination whipped and frayed emotions as mourners sought refuge from the tempest in churches of all denominations.[3]

Spiritualists joined the cortege, lamenting the "terrible national calamity."[4] The assassination was a sickening action that spiritualists morally tied to the war as the "last blind and brutal act of the Slaveholder's Rebellion."[5]

Among spiritualists, Lincoln's death resurrected rumors of séances at the White House. Those rumors began shortly after his inauguration in March 1861, like the snide commentary surfacing in a northern newspaper in 1862. A short paragraph related the gist of a lecture by Artemus Ward delivered in Detroit, Michigan, in late December 1862 that touched on the subject of Spiritualism. Ward mentioned that during a séance held at the White House a member of the circle inquired whether the spirit of Andrew Jackson could join their group, a request denied because "the spirit of Jackson had not been within a hundred miles of Washington for a good many years."[6]

Discerning readers decoded the composition, because Artemus Ward was a popular showman of the era known for his biting wit. He was born in Waterford, Maine, and christened Charles Farrar Brown. His last name

John Wilkes Booth (*Frank Leslie's Illustrated News*, April 29, 1865).

later changed to Browne and then with stage fame was dropped entirely in favor of the pseudonym Artemus Ward. Ward's early life progressed from printer to reporter, during which time he perfected his trademark down-home humor capturing country colloquialisms full of waggish wisdom.

As in his comic lecture in Detroit, Ward ridiculed Spiritualism from the stage and through satiric texts. In a short story aptly titled "Among the Spirits," he turned his droll repartee on Spiritualism in describing a séance: "The cumpany then drew round the table and the Sircle kommenst to go it. Thay axed me if thare was an body in the Sperret land which I wood like to convarse with.... I then called fur my farther. 'Ain't you proud of your orfurn boy?' 'Scacely.' 'Why not, my parient?' Becawz you hav gone to writin for the noospapers, my son. Bimeby you'll lose all your character for trooth and verrasserty."[7]

Lincoln reveled in Ward's writings, finding the man's humor a welcome distraction from his obligations as President. At the same time, Ward furthered suspicions and innuendo, even if comic in nature, that Lincoln's White House regularly hosted denizens from the spirit world.[8]

Despite the White House's denouncement, some in the foreign press used the President's predicament to undermine his administration.[9] There was a mean-spirited story that appeared in the *London Dispatch* in 1863 reporting the cavorting of supposed manifestations under the mediumship of Miss Sibylla Pythonissa Dodge, a scarcely disguised reference to the ancient Greek soothsayers inhabiting the Oracle at Delphi.[10]

Apparently taken as real by the English newspaper, the reported séance included the President, Dodge, Judge Edmonds, an unnamed British reporter, and Lincoln's Secretary of War Edwin Stanton. It was an absurd account that rational minds seemingly would have rejected, but the story unfolded with an undeserved seriousness.

Shortly after the circle was formed, a series of rappings heralded the arrival of a spirit who immediately made it known that an accordion was in order, and after receiving the instrument the spirit played "Yankee Doodle." After this rousing rendition, a spirit claiming to be George Washington rapped his entrance, but Judge Edmonds cried foul, claiming it was a mischievous ghost impersonating America's first president. After this, a series of famous guests from the world beyond came forth, with some offering Lincoln military advice while others drawled in a backwoods fashion similar to that of Artemus Ward, the well-known entertainer favored by the President. According to the reporter in attendance, the whole affair came to a close "and the company went to liquor up."

American newspapers could not resist the trend and occasionally mimicked their foreign counterparts, ridiculing supposed Spiritualism at the White House. Adding legitimacy to the lunacy were nuggets of truth that conferred credibility to the fallacy. Such was the case with a fantasied séance under the tutelage of Robert Dale Owen, apparently assembled for the express purpose of divining the victor of the presidential election of 1864.[11]

Scaling a mountain of mockery, the *New York Herald* wondered "why should our Court circle at Washington hesitate to avail itself of this new science.... Mr. Robert Dale Owen ... is a recognized light of spiritualism, his services in that capacity are in great demand in and around the White House." And so it was, according to the satire, that Owen presided at a séance with Lincoln and members of his inner circle by hoping to peer into the future and see who would win the coming presidential election. With an oracle's wisdom, Owen predicted that the conjured spirit would send a vision of the next president, which came to pass as a vague, indiscernible specter floated about the room, defying definition and leaving the circle's members in the dark.

Owen was a controversial character championing disparate social causes during a full life filled with politics, philosophy, and fanaticism. He was born in Scotland in 1801 and immigrated to America in 1823. He and his father invested in the utopian settlement established at New Harmony, Indiana, but that socialist community ultimately failed. Undeterred by its dissolution, Owen pursued his liberal beliefs as an elected member of the Indiana legislature and later in the U.S. Congress. He was an avowed abolitionist, fervent spiritualist, and founding member of the Smithsonian Institution.[12]

On one occasion Owen presented a detailed discussion on an esoteric, spiritual topic to a skeptical and bored President, who quipped at its conclusion that "for those who like that sort of thing, I should think it is just about the sort of thing they would like."[13]

Owen's egalitarian mind embraced Spiritualism, as evidenced by his publication of *Footfalls on the Boundary of Another World* in 1860 and *The Debatable Land Between this World and the Next* in 1871.[14,15]

Following the daily news of the war in 1863, the *New York Herald* moved onto lighter subjects, and the supposed séances at the White House were fair game. After raising the topic and revealing the content of conversations with famous spirit notables like Benjamin Franklin and Napoleon, the reporter blithely predicted that the "spiritual séance at the White House will attract even more general attention to the new system of religious philosophy," an admission that seemed to exonerate the rumor-mongering role of the press.[16]

Political opponents of the President used the rumors to undermine and belittle his administration. During the tumultuous period in 1863, Lincoln's Emancipation Proclamation added to the country's divisiveness since it was hailed as an act of courage in Northern states but derided in the South.

Reports soon surfaced linking the President's supposed fascination with Spiritualism and the Emancipation Proclamation. Without a blush and with the faintest evidence, the story making the rounds suggested that Robert Owen and a group of like-minded spiritualists contacted the long-dead wise ones, who urged the publication of the Emancipation Proclamation, a spiritual recommendation that an obliging President readily accepted.[17]

According to the widely circulated story, Owen's influence was part of a disturbing trend that elevated other known or suspected spiritualists such as Judge Edmonds, Horace Greeley, and Thaddeus Stevens to prominent positions in Lincoln's inner circle, prompting a warning that "we have an Administration controlled by Spiritualism." An unnamed New York spiritualist with regular visits to the White House made the accusation even graver, but the President's humor and skepticism helped dent the distress.

A funny farce, or from another viewpoint a biting bit of banter, filled in the blanks missing from the innuendo swirling around the White House séances. In a fanciful fiction, an anonymous participant opened the curtains cloaking the darkness hiding the mysterious manifestations of a spiritual circle at the White House. Herr Shockall and Madame Vonauvem presided as the psychics, with members of Lincoln's cabinet and various guests rounding out the circle with thirteen other attendees.[18]

Herr Shockall carefully set the scene, placing musical instruments on smaller tables arrayed around a large table in the middle of the room. Each person took a seat at the large table and touched their neighbor's hand while awaiting the spirits' arrival. The table started shaking and rotating with a violent force that threw everyone to the ground and then rose to the ceilings. It continued its flight to the heavens, leaving a holey White House roof behind.

As might be imagined, Lincoln was furious but Herr Shockall urged patience and, walking around the room, struck each musical instrument in an act that animated the spirits, playfully plying the Southern song "Dixie." Slowly but surely the long-lost table descended from on high, sealing the rent roof as it assumed its former position.

It was now time to get serious and seek advice from the spirit world. Prior President Andrew Jackson stopped by and implored his successor to keep General Joseph Hooker in charge of the Army of the Potomac, which seemed a curious request following Hooker's disastrous defeat in 1863 at the Battle of Chancellorsville.

Setting aside his suspicion, Lincoln wondered if a spirit would reveal the Confederate troop strength in Virginia. Much to his surprise, a Rebel casualty of the war came forth and declared "that the full strength of Lee's army at Chancellorsville has been correctly set forth in the NEW YORK HERALD." The stunning and irritating admission was more than the President and his cabinet could take, prompting their collective condemnation of Herr Shockall and his spirit entourage as frauds.

Parody was popular, and supposed Spiritualism at the White House served to simultaneously amuse readers and indirectly impugn President Lincoln. Toward the end of April 1863 a farcical séance story appeared in the *Boston Gazette* and was soon seeing print in other newspapers such as the *Cleveland Leader* in Ohio.[19]

Charles E. Shockle and a friend of the medium who reported the night's event hosted the spiritual circle at the White House, which in-

Five—Assassination, Resurrection and Exploitation 97

cluded President Lincoln, his wife, Secretary of War Edwin Stanton, Secretary of the Navy Gideon Welles, and two other unnamed guests. After the usual rappings and table tippings, the subject of the war took center stage. It was fortunate that Welles was in attendance when the President turned his attention to the fully enchanted medium and requested that "the spirits would tell us how to catch the Alabama."

Lincoln had good reason to inquire about the CSS *Alabama*. The Confederate warship was the scourge of the seas, scuttling Union trade and treasure and defying efforts to destroy her. Even more galling was the ship's English heritage, which seemed to reflect a blatant attempt by the Old World power to once again meddle in American politics.[20]

The spirits granted Lincoln's wish to peer into the future and see the fate of the CSS *Alabama*. As the séance room ominously darkened, a mirror mounted on the wall started glowing softly and the image of the enemy's ship came sharply into focus. The ship was moored near an English fort and seemed totally devoid of life, which prompted the President to muse, "So England is to seize the Alabama finally?" No definitive answer ever followed, and with the hour growing late Mrs. Lincoln suggested that the weary medium and his spirits depart.[21]

Thoughts of President Lincoln seeking a second term rattled his opponents, and the *Hillsdale Democrat*, a newspaper published in a small Michigan town, huffed and puffed that "it has been intimated that Mr. Lincoln has had some spiritual communications purporting that he should continue in power another term—that is, he is to reign, not serve the people ... so say the spirits, who have been consulted on this momentous subject." The city's competing newspaper, *The Standard*, bashed the "Copperhead" paper's hysterical hyperbole, openly mocking its gullibility in so readily and seriously accepting Lincoln's supposed spirit cabinet.[22]

Spiritualists by and large supported Lincoln's reelection, but a virulent dispute cleaved the group at the 1864 National Spiritual Convention in Chicago. A resolution proposed by a majority endorsed the President and assured him that "every magnanimous" spirit would do the same. For a minority the endorsement was sacrilegious and tarnished the sanctity of a religion that frowned on worldly pursuits at the expense of piety. The sanctimonious sect seceded and vowed to hold another convention attended solely by spiritualists untainted by political aspirations, a position leaving a reporter quipping that "even the spirits are going back on the President."[23]

Spiritualists and skeptics struggled with Lincoln's death with at least one question in common: how could the psychic prognosticators not foresee and prevent the tragedy? For nonbelievers it was yet another vindication of their disbelief, but for spiritualists the answer required a response consistent with their faith. Ever-faithful and supportive spiritualists turned to the various sympathetic periodicals such as the *Banner of Light* for solace.

The *Banner of Light* held regular séances and, with the authority granted to the spirits, routinely tackled and reported the responses to weighty issues. Lincoln's assassination was an obvious opportunity to assemble a circle and seek succor through informed spirits who could clarify the meaning behind his death.

It took just about three months after Lincoln's death for mediums to start questioning the spirits and openly wondering how a man they believed was guided and guarded by altruistic apparitions could come to such an untimely end. Any answer had to resonate with their beliefs.

In a typical response, the spirits reminded their mortal brethren that "you are in the habit of clinging to form ... and so you cling to these bodies, and when they fall off and leave the spirit free, you mourn ... when you change worlds, or are called upon to part with your physical bodies ... by the Infinite Power." To the spiritualist, death was not a mystery but a gateway to the Elysium Fields, offering transcendence to beauty and bliss.[24]

The soothing sophistry still did not fully satisfy the nagging question of why the spirits did not warn the faithful about Lincoln's death. After all, second sight was an essential focus of many séances. Preserving the phantom's omnipotence required the agile answer "that though they knew of this cloud that was to overshadow your nation, they were not permitted to prophecy of its coming." The "Infinite Power" issued the injunction without further explanation.

Even more comforting was a spirit's pronouncement that Lincoln would continue to exert a positive influence on American life from the afterworld. In fact, his death was actually reframed as a benefit to humanity, "an absolute blessing to himself and to the nation."

Of course, nothing was more uplifting than connecting with the spirit of Lincoln, and such communications became rather common among the postwar mystics. One of the first such contacts, strange as it may seem, took place not in America but in Bordeaux, France, as reported by J.M. Sterling, who apparently witnessed the resurrection.[25] French medium M. Rul contacted Lincoln's spirit on the third day of May in 1865 and quickly sought an opinion on America's fate following the war. Perched afar, Lincoln's spirit struck an optimistic note, forecasting peace and prosperity while thanking God for the wisdom and resolve he needed in preserving the Union. Following this heartfelt homily, the medium asked Lincoln's spirit to weigh in on the emancipation of the slaves.

With his characteristic sagacity the late President predicted that "it will require some years ere this sin can be entirely extirpated," a sorry state of affairs prolonged by the aggrieved slaveholders' losses.

Perhaps even more remarkable than a visitation by Lincoln was a connection with John Wilkes Booth. Miss Lizzie Doten was a famous medium renowned for reciting verses from dead poets, as in suitably macabre visits from Edgar Allan Poe. During one particular lecture during which Doten relayed a poem ostensibly from Poe, the audience alternately laughed and applauded the medium's aplomb, with one witty character proclaiming the performance rivaled those given by the Shakespearean actor Edwin Booth, who was a brother of the infamous assassin.[26]

Like most spiritualists, Doten admired Lincoln's stance espousing human rights, particularly his antislavery position. Shortly after Lincoln's death, an enchanted Doten mesmerized an overflow audience at Boston's Lyceum Hall with a passionate speech honoring the departed man. At the conclusion of her main points and while still under influence of the spirits, the medium narrated a poem titled "Sic Semper Tyrannis." The Latin phrase "thus always to tyrants" was the parting politics of John Wilkes Booth as he made his escape. Doten's poem turned the phrase against the perpetrator: "To the true loyal blood in the National Heart; and the future shall prove, when the conflict is done, that the hearts of the people are beating as one."[27]

On a Sunday evening, June 18, 1865, an entranced Doten once again packed Boston's Lyceum Hall with revelations on "the relative power of Abraham Lincoln and J. Wilkes Booth in spirit-life." It seemed that the ethereal transformation did little to dull Lincoln's luster, but Booth's transition shed some shame and led Doten's spirit guide to speak sympathetically of the assassin as he wandered around in the afterworld.[28]

Spiritualists had to reconcile their fundamental pacifism with the assassin's capture and killing, prompting a soul-searching quest to morally justify his death. Turning to the spirit world, the *Banner of Light*'s regular séance helped extricate stuck believers by condoning his death. A sagacious spirit acknowledged that mortal laws were imperfect in an imperfect world but in a hopeful tone predicted that "the time will soon come when you will cease to throw stones at those who sin among you."[29]

Booth made his debut from the spirit world toward the end of August 1865 through the mediumship of Lizzie Doten. A phantom poet, purportedly Booth, possessed Doten and voiced an ode about the man he'd murdered. It was an uplifting epic that stood in stark contrast to Booth's foul deed and once again presented an incongruity that obliging spirits resolved. According to the spirits, Booth's death liberated his soul from the mortal manacles of malignance and revealed the glory of God. As a consequence of the assassin's heavenly ascent, "John Wilkes Booth is in harmony with Abraham Lincoln, for he knows him to be his friend."

Attempts to reach Booth's spirit were not uniformly successful, but persistence sometimes captured a roving relative. Junius Brutus Booth, the father of the assassin, joined a *Banner of Light* séance and apologized for his son's intransigence by explaining that the spirit world's peace and quiet was an invigorating antidote to the venom of mortal life. With that in mind, the elder Booth's visit was an attempt to assuage curiosity. His son no longer harbored any animosity toward Lincoln but at the same time he would not renounce his Southern sympathies, which seemed like an implicit and troublesome lack of remorse.[30]

One of Spiritualism's most indomitable disciples added to the Lincoln lore from the spirit world. Judge John W. Edmonds received information from his brother Frank, who had died in 1862 after 57 years of mortal life. As often happened after a loved one died, Edmonds had premonitions of his brother's presence, and through the urging mediumship of Mrs. Tower he made contact. Frank began the conversation with the usual rappings but soon took control of Tower's writing hand, which offered a far more efficient method for the gabby ghost.[31]

Frank Edmonds reassured his brother that all was well. In fact, he had never been happier after reuniting with his mother, his father, and John's wife. It was an idyllic picture of death that Frank painted, with gorgeous artwork, blissful music, sweet, scented air, and complete contentment that led the spirit to exclaim that "I was overcome with joy, and wanted all my friends to die instantly, that they might realize what I was enjoying."

From his heavenly post Frank languidly witnessed the comings and goings of the prominent and not-so-prominent spirits, which were faithful mirrors that reflected their social positions from mortal life. It seemed that even the infamous mingled with their more respectable counterparts, upending any notion of segregation that more traditional religious views adopted, with Hell punishing ardent sinners and Heaven reserved for the virtuous. And so it was that Frank described the first meeting between the spirits of President Lincoln and John Wilkes Booth.

According to the spirit of Frank Edmonds, President Lincoln entered the spirit world dazed and confused. His sudden death left no time to process his pending fate. It was a temporary state, as Lincoln slowly recognized friends and associates whose death preceded his, while at the same time a warm feeling of peaceful belonging swept over him. Lincoln resolutely accepted his death, but a nagging worry about his country blunted the bliss. However, his faith in Andrew Johnson, his political successor, eventually quelled the concern.

Lincoln was happy. Adjusting to death was made easier by his reception, which included glad tidings from soldiers who died defending the Union and "many a slave emancipated through his instrumentality." All this stood in stark contrast to Booth's welcome.

Booth knew he was dying, which made his transition to the spirit world less traumatic. Through an unknown agency, Lincoln's spirit was made aware of Booth's imminent death and hastened to the assassin's side, resulting in an awkward meeting where "the first living thing that Booth encountered in the spirit-world was Lincoln; and he met him with a bold and defiant air, as if glorying in the act he had performed, and ready to fight in defense of it." As might be imagined, Lincoln's spirit, with true Christian benevolence, turned the other cheek and met Booth's demeanor with kindness and gentility.

Booth's punishment was isolation. He had no friends and sympathizers in the spirit world and was overcome with despair, vainly wishing for complete obliteration. Compounding his agony was Lincoln's magnetic persona, which relentlessly drew the assassin toward his victim. It was an attraction that forced Booth to confront the goodness of the man he executed and accept a bleak future without hope of absolution.

A reporter hiding under the name "Insider" could not resist the temptation to lampoon the resurrection of Booth and from the pages of the *Brooklyn Daily Eagle* did just that. Feigning psychic powers, Insider gratuitously admitted faking spirit messages while quipping "that some mediums could not evoke raps but could evoke tips."[32]

Careening further into his parody, Insider boasted of his attendance at a séance populated by high-toned believers during which he mischievously called forth a variety of well-known ghosts before invoking Booth's spirit. The assassin's appearance spooked the group of believers, who fled the sitting en masse, but their curiosity brought them back. Pretty much in line with other conjurings of Booth, Insider's version revealed a repentant man still tortured by his foul deed but hoping that purification in the spirit world might pacify his soul. Chuckling inwardly, Insider cast Booth as a spiritualist commanding "every one to embrace it, as well as the wickedness of those who rejected it."

The best answers as to why the spirits did not warn Lincoln of the assassination and whether he was a spiritualist purportedly came from the former President. A séance attended by Lincoln's spirit answered both questions toward the end of February 1867. It was a carefully crafted response reported by the *Banner of Light* that nimbly straddled the controversies surrounding the questions.[33]

In an attempt to resolve the first question Lincoln disclosed that his son Willie, speaking from beyond the grave, had warned his father of the dangers posed by his enemies and supposed friends. Many months before the assassination, Willie urged his father to take appropriate precautions such as sleeping under the watchful eye of trusted guards. To a certain extent Lincoln apparently followed that advice, but as the time of the mortal event approached Willie pleaded with his father to avoid public appearances, a request Lincoln could not honor, given his pledge to faithfully fulfill his presidential duties. Even though Willie assured his father that he would be the first to welcome him to the blissful spirit world, he understood his father's dedication.

Perhaps even more important to Spiritualism was whether the nascent movement could include President Lincoln among their group. At the séance Lincoln adamantly denied being a spiritualist while alive but had adopted an agnostic approach. His skepticism did not prevent a curious inquiry into the subject, and the various mediums and séances held at the White House were simply investigations that ultimately did not convince the man's mortal self. Lincoln acknowledged that such activities mistakenly contributed to the public's perception that he was a spiritualist.

Lincoln's spirit tacitly admitted an inner conflict, as the mortal man studied Spiritualism in a vain effort to prove the reality of the beautiful belief. While Lincoln was on the stump for his second term, a man supposedly asked Lincoln whether he was a spiritualist and received in return an avowed denial with a curious footnote that "when I get beyond the vale, I can answer your question, perhaps to the contrary."

The nudge that finally convinced Lincoln was his arrival in the spirit world. At the séance the President resolutely admitted his faith in Spiritualism, as evidenced by his presence at the séance. The admission added credence to the beliefs of Spiritualism's faithful followers, while at the same time blunting criticism from opponents by acknowledging Lincoln's mortal skepticism, which gave way in the afterlife to an unassailable and certainly unprovable conversion.

Resurrecting Willie was a cynical undertaking that exploited the boy's death and a mother's grieving in a shallow and callow effort to legitimize Spiritualism's core belief. Willie died on February 20, 1862, and naturally left the Lincolns sad and somewhat immobilized. According to one report, the President's moroseness contributed to a deepening isolation as the grieving father came to grips with the loss, a behavior most prominent every Thursday, which marked the weekly anniversary of his son's death.[34]

Mrs. Lincoln suffered her own private grief but intervened in her husband's decline by inviting the visiting Rev. Francis Vinton from New York's Trinity Church to meet with the President. Vinton agreed to the arrangement and used the meeting as an opportunity to both gently chide and console the President. The Reverend reminded the

President that his grieving, while natural, was interfering with his duties as commander-in-chief of a country in dire straits, but it was his comments on Willie that conquered the man's grief. Vinton relied on biblical scriptures to reassure Lincoln that Willie was "alive in Paradise" and through a miniature homily lifted the mental fog that had dulled the President's emotions.

Interest in Lincoln's spirit was widespread, as evidenced by enterprising mediums reaching out to the late President. A child medium excited citizens in Huston Township in central Pennsylvania in late August 1867 with spirit-inspired rappings. The orphaned girl lived with a respected family, which added credibility to the young psychic's manifestations.[35]

Every evening for a week the young girl entered a trance state, with rappings slowly filling the house in volume and intensity. Curious neighbors took the opportunity to pose various questions through the medium, including a question that dwelled on Lincoln. Apparently the answers satisfied visitors, who came expecting fraud but left convinced of the girl's mystical prowess. It was an evanescent connection to the spirit world that lasted less than a month.

Supposed contacts with Lincoln made entertaining reading, and newspapers fanned the phenomena far and wide. Obliging mediums who never knew the President in life somehow became trusted confidants in death. Mrs. Daniels, "the great Boston medium," was of that ilk and supposedly brought her show to President Johnson's White House. Although the report was short on specifics, readers were left to infer that Daniels would contact Lincoln, who in turn would offer Johnson sage advice.[36]

Details of Daniels's alleged 1868 White House encounter came from scattered reports in newspapers as far away as Atlanta, Georgia. In the version that originally appeared in the *Baltimore Gazette*, Colonel Thomas Florence, the editor of the *Constitutional Union*, paved the way for the medium to meet President Johnson. In what might be construed as a tongue-in-cheek accounting of the event, Lincoln's spirit laughed and cryptically commented, "let him laugh who wins." No one could decipher the meaning, but Lincoln promised to return another day and through Mrs. Daniels to hold a more meaningful conversation.[37]

Whether fact or fantasy, the Daniels story traveled around the country. In commenting on the visit, the *New York Herald* bemoaned the trend of respectable men "consulting spirits," while at the same time suggesting that President Johnson's dabbling in Spiritualism was not an isolated event.[38]

Former Confederate state newspapers joined the chorus, probably delighting their audience by impugning Johnson through his supposed interest in Lincoln's spirit. Sharp-eyed readers of Virginia's *Richmond*

Dispatch might have chortled at reports of Lincoln reappearing at the White House and laughing, leaving his chuckling to their imaginative interpretation.[39] The same story showed up in *The Daily News*, a Charleston, South Carolina, newspaper.[40]

Cynicism's ascendancy seemed to have no constraints confining it, so Willie returned through the beguiling mediumship of the *Banner of Light*, offering soothing words for Mrs. Lincoln. What prevented her husband from delivering the message is unknown, but conjecture would suggest that Willie still held the foremost tender spot in his mother's heart.[41]

Setting speculation aside, the *Banner of Light* reported that Willie carried a message from his father to his mother affirming that "she may rest assured if it is best for her wishes to be fully carried out in that which seems to trouble her so much, they will be." From afar, Willie assured his mother that her husband was constantly monitoring her well-being, hovering invisibly about her, providing comfort and safety, and looking forward to the day when they would all be reunited in spiritual bliss.

Booth continued his redemption tour aided by agreeable mediums attending an 1870 Brooklyn spiritualist meeting. A large crowd gathered with Mary J. Wilcoxson headlining an event attended by a respectable, curious group, and even the faith's believers lacked "the long hair … cadaverous countenances … [and] extravagant deportment," as witnessed by the reporter's roving eye.[42]

Following Wilcoxson's late-afternoon spiritual sermon, an attendee made a motion of invitation to form a circle. Ultimately, two men and four women joined hands while a larger group outside the circle observed the séance. The female medium turned her attention to the women first and, taking their inquiries about lost love ones, received reassurances from the spirit world that all were happy in their afterlife.

A more probing question came from one of the politically motivated men, wondering whether John Wilkes Booth felt any remorse for the President's assassination. After a pause, perhaps reflecting Booth's contemplation, his psychic mouthpiece conceded that "he has become reconciled to Abraham Lincoln. They walk out daily. He says the assassination was based upon an unfortunate misunderstanding. He has now gone through two states of progression. He is entering on a third."

Another controversy was Mary Surratt's complicity in Lincoln's death. The same man wondered whether she was guilty, a question that caused the medium's hand to violently shake as if adding a dramatic exclamation point to the spirit's answer declaring that "she was wholly innocent."

Following her husband's death, stories began circulating about Mrs. Lincoln's interest in Spiritualism. One of the more sensational supposedly took place in 1869, when Mrs. Lincoln traveled to Boston to meet William

Five—Assassination, Resurrection and Exploitation   105

Spiritual photography (*Harper's Weekly*, May 8, 1869).

Mumler in his studio. Mumler achieved almost instant fame by claiming the ability to photograph spirits. Photography was in its infancy and still a mysterious marvel that captured images for posterity at a time when paintings were a memorial luxury unavailable to most people. Instead of his guests leaving a séance with mere memories, Mumler offered them a tangible, treasure, token from the spirit. It was among the meanest deceptions that exploited the yearnings of the living by reaping phantom profits.[43]

Mrs. Lincoln met with Mumler enshrouded in secrecy, no doubt hoping to avoid the probing press in her emotional quest. She was not successful in that venture, but during this visit to Mumler's studio she left with a picture of Captain Todd, a Confederate soldier assumed by all to have died. The picture's value precipitously fell when the subject was later found alive.

William Mumler was the impresario of the first spirit photography emporium, and in his personal memoirs he dwelled at length on a supposed visit by Mrs. Lincoln. His recollection of the encounter was published in 1875 in the third installment in a series of six that were mostly testimonials designed to "prove that these forms are actual likenesses of those who have passed to spirit-life."[44]

According to Mumler's recollection, a heavily veiled woman entered his studio and while awaiting the proprietor casually questioned a man on the verge of leaving after sitting for a photo. The woman seemed reassured by the conversation, and when Mumler asked her if she desired a spirit photograph she quickly agreed.

Mumler needed the woman to remove her dark veil, which totally obscured her features, an arrangement that his visitor would only grant in the moments before the photographer snapped her image. After Mumler captured her picture on the photographic glass the woman identified herself as Mrs. Lindall, a name the photographer neatly printed on the envelope with the negative inside. Mumler advised his mysterious customer to return in a few days, during which time he would develop and print the photograph.

Mumler's studio was a one-stop supernatural shop, with the man selling spirit photographs and his charming wife a medium. When the inscrutable woman returned, Mumler was out of town, leaving his wife in charge, and at the behest of the customer she retrieved the previously taken spirit photograph.

Immediately after fetching the photograph and handing it to the mysterious customer Mrs. Mumler fell into a trance and, speaking in a boyish falsetto, asked Mrs. Lindall if she recognized the photograph's phantom. Overcome by the photograph and the disembodied voice, Mrs. Lindall

Five—Assassination, Resurrection and Exploitation 107

timorously ventured, "I do recognize it; but who is now speaking?" The spirit replied, "Thaddeus." It was more than the poor woman could bear, hearing from her dead son supposedly returning from the spirit world.

A long, emotional conversation followed with her son as it became clear that Mrs. Lindall was actually the heavily disguised wife of President Lincoln. Mrs. Lincoln left Mumler's Boston abode with a warm glow and a spirit photograph showing her husband "standing behind her, with his hands resting on her shoulders, and looking down, with a pleasant smile."

A gossipy insert in a Vermont newspaper from 1872 spread the word that Mrs. Lincoln had visited a medium in Moravia, New York, and through that agency had seen her husband, and while a motherly hug might have been more satisfying, she settled for shaking hands with Tad.[45]

Like today's paparazzi, reporters kept an eagle eye out for any sightings of the former President's wife, and when discovering her they dutifully dished out the details. Mrs. Lincoln attempted to avoid the scrutiny by adopting disguises, by hiding her visage behind dark veils, and by furtively traveling under a nom de plume.

In another report, Mrs. Lincoln supposedly journeyed to Boston during the winter of 1872 for the express purpose of meeting with a well-known local spiritualist. Between visits she stayed at the Parks House using the name Mrs. Linder in an effort aimed at anonymity, but it failed when a fellow lodger recognized the famous woman. Although the next step was not specifically described, the lodger probably conveyed his suspicions to a reporter, who in turn dug a bit deeper and discovered the reason for Mrs. Lincoln's stealth. According to the published story, Mrs. Lincoln attended a series of séances, during which her husband consoled the grieving woman.[46]

President Lincoln's spirit seemed to favor the *Banner of Light*'s public séances as a means to reconnect with those he left behind. On the seventh anniversary of his assassination, Lincoln's spirit celebrated the occasion by once again rationalizing his death as God's need to have the man in the spirit land. It was a pleasant experience and, contrary to what most assumed, he felt more invigorated and alive than ever.[47]

Even so, Lincoln's spirit recognized the trouble and turmoil left behind and offered comforting words "to those near and dear to me, who have struggled with the dark side of fortune.... I would say persevere, struggle on, be faithful in the things of this life, overcome all evil with good, and your happiness is sure in the life to come."

A clarion call reminded the President that the spirit world beckoned for him to return, but before doing so he affirmed his conviction that

Spiritualism was more than a fad and that he had found in the afterlife the reality of its teachings. Such assurances surely resonated and reinforced the faithful's certainty in a blissful life after death.

Spiritualists considered messages from the famous and infamous as solemn, incontrovertible evidence of a two-way street linking earthly existence with its ethereal counterpart. For the true believers it was the dawn of a new age that threw off the shackles placed on the minds of the populace by traditional religions eager to maintain their spiritual hegemony. Mediums were passive receivers amplifying the messages transmitted by immortals, and they completed a spiritual circuit for the benefit of eager and usually grieving patrons.

Booth's regular attendance at séances showed sinners what they could expect. It was not a punitive state of eternal damnation but a cleansing of the soul as spiritual revelations washed wickedness away. It was a favorable fate that awaited even the most heinous villains such as John Wilkes Booth.

Booth's evolving contrition dominated another séance at the *Banner of Light* when his spirit blithely admitted that "his earnest purpose was to overcome the power of darkness that surrounded him in this life, and he believes he has done it … he put forth all his effort to 'ascend the ladder of progress' that he might become satisfied with himself, the world, and God." The message was clear that even a man who murdered a President could realize redemption through hard work. Spiritualism did not demand earthly perfection, but it did propose salvation in the spirit world, a pathway corroborated by Booth's intercommunications.[48]

If so inclined a grieving mother could rejoice in an emotional reunion brokered by a sympathetic medium. Mediums banked on these tender moments, and reports of various Lincoln spirits reaching out to Mrs. Lincoln could be viewed as both poignant and problematic. Spiritualists accepted the touching get-together as a factual benefit of their faith, while skeptics could see nothing but a cruel corruption.

Tad Lincoln reached out to his mother on April 8, 1872, beseeching the woman to set aside her immobilizing grief and seek serenity in the certain knowledge that all was well in the spirit world. Imagine the impact when Tad stated, "I am here to send a brief message to my mother. I have to say that my father, brother and myself desire that my mother should settle down where she can be most happy…. For myself, I can say she is the one being nearest my heart."[49]

Whether Mrs. Lincoln ever learned about this appeal is unknown, but for readers of the *Banner of Light* it probably strengthened their conviction that mercy and goodwill pervaded the spirit world and traversed a porous boundary separating the living from the dead. Perhaps it also

Five—Assassination, Resurrection and Exploitation 109

vicariously softened a spiritualist's loss of a loved one by mitigating mourning with the celestial construction of the afterlife.

All the tragedies Mary Lincoln suffered would have unnerved almost anyone and may have contributed to her subsequent insanity. Theories abound regarding the circumstances and causes that led a court to declare her insane in 1875; all of these must be understood in terms of nineteenth-century medicine and an even more rudimentary understanding of emotional disorders.[50]

Mary Lincoln began her court-ordered confinement on May 20, 1875, at Bellevue Place, a private asylum located roughly 50 miles due west of Chicago, Illinois. Her stay was relatively brief. After about four months she engineered a release. Roughly one year later, a second court hearing declared Mrs. Lincoln sane.[51]

During the early weeks of Mrs. Lincoln's treatment at Bellevue Place she maintained a low public profile and shunned curious reporters and visitors intent on gaining a glimpse of the woman's condition. All of this changed when Mrs. Lincoln unexpectedly granted the rarest interview to a correspondent from the *Chicago Post*.[52]

Richard J. Patterson, the physician in charge of Bellevue Place, led the gratified newspaper reporter to Mrs. Lincoln's suite on the second floor of the building. As he scanned the room the reporter noted the simple, plain furnishings as his hostess expectantly rose from her chair and greeted the arrival with a warm handshake. What struck the reporter most was that "she looked worn and ill and her hands ringless and uncared for, were never at rest. I could plainly see in her lusterless eyes and in the forced composure of her manner evidence of a shattered mind." During their brief encounter Mary Lincoln inquired about friends and spoke fondly of her husband.

After a cordial departure the reporter's thoughts and writing turned toward Spiritualism and its influence on Mrs. Lincoln's life. His musings conceded that conversations with the spirits of her children and husband were probably comforting but possibly also mentally corrosive. According to the story, Mary had spent several months in St. Charles, Illinois, with spiritualists.

As was her custom, in 1871 Mrs. Lincoln stayed at the Howard House Hotel in St. Charles under the assumed name of Mrs. May. While there, Caroline Howard and her older daughter Sarah held regular séances during which it is presumed that Mary found comfort in a spiritual reunion with her lost loved ones.[53]

The *Chicago Post* reporter's story did not demonize Spiritualism but instead took a sympathetic tone by recognizing the woman's suffering and accepting the consolation the faith proffered, but a nagging doubt led the reporter to tentatively concede that "it will never be definitively known how much their influence had to do with her eclipse of reason."[54]

Rumors were rife in Washington, D.C., alleging that White House occupants dabbled in Spiritualism. While some insinuations included the President, the main suspect was Mary Lincoln, somewhat sympathetically exonerated because "after the death of Willie Lincoln Mrs. Lincoln took a good deal of interest in the doctrines of spiritualism."[55]

Another account seemingly corroborated President Lincoln's meetings with Charles Colchester. Colchester was a famous medium who made frequent trips to the nation's capital, and during these visits a steady stream of invitations from prominent politicians kept the man quite busy. Even so, the gallivanting reporter who made the rounds in Washington, D.C., observing Colchester's tricks did not believe the President saw anything in it besides entertainment.[56]

Lincoln's supposed dabbling with Spiritualism was mostly revealed by spiritualists claiming firsthand knowledge of the President's attendance at séances and his general interest in supernatural phenomena. One of the earliest such disclosures came from Samuel P. Kase, a successful entrepreneur, inventor, and passionate spiritualist.

Kase was born in 1814 and passed his youth in central Pennsylvania. With approaching adulthood, Kase turned his mechanical and business acumen to the agricultural needs of the rich farmlands by building and selling threshing machines. In the following years Kase centered his activities in the environs surrounding Danville, Pennsylvania, and built iron foundries and mills which substantially supported the local economy. His expertise in iron manufacturing gravitated toward the burgeoning needs of an ever-growing northeastern rail network, which occupied his time and attention during the Civil War era.[57]

George Benson was a close friend of Kase and revealed the connection between the railroad man, President Lincoln, and spiritualism in a letter written by Kase and obligingly published in a St. Louis newspaper along with a disclaimer warning that the account was "a story the reader may believe or not."[58]

Kase's letter began innocuously enough by recollecting the business venture that had brought him to Washington, D.C., in 1862. As an inveterate entrepreneur he was always looking to expand his fledgling interest, which offered a boundless energy that prompted his nephew to seek the man's advice on a floundering railroad venture. Kase's nephew was president of the Reading and Columbia Railroad, a short line in Pennsylvania that was on the verge of bankruptcy.

Mired in dire straits, Kase boldly proposed a visit to Washington to plead for funding. To his nephew it seemed a fool's errand, in view of the ongoing war and the enormous expenses devoted to its prosecution. Kase countered with a wartime argument. The only railroad running between New York and the nation's capital ran along the eastern seaboard and was a tempting, vulnerable target subject to Confederate capture, which would place Washington in serious jeopardy.

Kase proposed expanding the Reading and Columbia Railroad between New York and Washington, which would provide a second and more protected interior passage between the two cities. His skeptical nephew lacked conviction and but tepidly supported his uncle carrying the fight to Washington.

As he strolled the streets of Washington, D.C., Kase recalled his last visit in 1850 and the boardinghouse where he had lived, now neatly lettered with the name J.B. Conkling. As he meandered past his former residence an ethereal voice urged Kase to "Go see him; he is in the same room you occupied."

Startled but not frightened, he did as the voice directed and ascended the stairs. A totally nonplussed Conkling apparently expected his unannounced visitor and immediately requested his service in delivering a letter to President Lincoln. Whatever reservations Kase had were overcome when once again a mysterious voice urged his compliance, an arrangement that the railroad man insisted must include Conkling's attendance.

The pair promptly set off for the White House, and after a brief interval Kase met with the President while Conkling waited outside. After some introductory comments Kase handed Conkling's letter to Lincoln, who thoughtfully read, "I have been sent from the city of N. York by spiritual influence to confer with you pertaining to the interest of the nation; I cannot return until I have an interview." According to Kase, the President issued a written invitation to Conkling, after which Kase considered the case closed.

Over the next month Kase turned his attention to lobbying legislators, hoping to secure congressional funding for his railroad venture. Toward the end of that month, during a Senate session devoted to the subject, a woman approached Kase and handed him a small card that was an invitation to a local spiritual gathering.

Kase accepted the woman's impromptu invitation the same night, perhaps driven by a curiosity that he was determined to satisfy. Of all the enigmatic events Kase described while in Washington, nothing could match what happened when he arrived at Mrs. Margret Laurie's home in Georgetown. It was around eight o'clock in the evening when he entered the house and after crossing the threshold he almost instantly recognized President Lincoln, his wife, and a small security entourage.

After recovering from his momentary shock, Kase exchanged pleasantries with Lincoln. With everyone now seated, a young entranced girl approached the President and for the next 90 minutes lectured Lincoln on the war and the imperative need to abolish slavery. For the duration of the monologue the girl's eyes were closed as she delivered the supposedly spirit-inspired appeal.

At the conclusion of her lengthy speech the spell was broken and the girl, seemingly embarrassed by the attentive audience, fled the room, which set the stage for the next scene. The host's young daughter quietly strode to the room's large piano and with her eyes closed began playing the instrument. It was a musical treat accompanied by the joyful piano rising several inches off the ground. A few nights later the same group reassembled for an encore performance, after which Kase returned to Pennsylvania, firmly convinced that Lincoln's Emancipation Proclamation one month later was directly attributable to the young girl's impassioned phantom-led plea.

Standing somewhat in the shadow of Kase's story was J.B. Conkling, a perplexing psychic who somehow seemingly managed to attract Lincoln's interest from a crowded field of mediums jockeying to do the same and in doing so netted the sobriquet "the President's Medium," awarded by some historians.[59]

Best evidence would suggest that J.B. Conkling was actually John Benjamin Conklin, with the surname's spelling a common victim during this time period. He was probably born in 1820 and most likely in New York City after his father moved to that area. Sketchy details would suggest that Conklin spent a number of years sailing the seas before forsaking that life, possibly motivated by the ever-present risks associated with seafaring.

Conklin's first supernatural encounter occurred in 1845 while visiting his sister in Philadelphia, Pennsylvania. It was a light-hearted family affair with Conklin amusing everyone with magic tricks, after which he went to bed. He placed a lamp near the door with the expectation that his sister would soon retrieve it. As he lay quietly in the darkened room, a woman entered and removed the lamp, placing it on the nearby mantle. The next morning Conklin was surprised to discover that neither his sister nor any other resident admitted moving the lamp, a mystery only resolved when he "became better acquainted with this being, who represents that she was murdered in the room I occupied."[60]

The means by which Conklin discovered the nature of his nighttime visitor was a mystery in itself, but it left an indelible impression that launched the man's lifetime interest in the occult. Not too long after this first encounter, Conklin made a pilgrimage around 1852 to a séance hosted by Leah Brown, one of the Fox sisters, who further cemented his belief in

Five—Assassination, Resurrection and Exploitation 113

J.B. Conklin (Thomas Low Nichols, Mary Sargeant Gove Nichols, *Nichols' Monthly: A Magazine of Social Science, and Progressive Literature*, Volumes 2–3, 1856).

the supernatural when she made contact with the spirit of his mother-in-law, and Conklin verified the authenticity of the communication through the questions and answers that followed. Toward the end of the visit the spirit urged Conklin to start forming his own circles, which he dutifully obeyed.[61]

Conklin first experimented with the help of his wife and child. His first effort was a bit disappointing when the rappings from beyond failed to materialize, although the spirits teased the novice by elevating the table the threesome occupied. His later efforts were more successful, when the spirits started rapping and tapping as expected.

Through a series of fits and starts, Conklin got to the point where he began holding in New York City free public séances that were followed by private meetings with paying patrons. As might be expected, the newcomer swiftly built bridges with more established psychics in a bid to further his range and respect. Like others, he also started traveling the nation and advertised his presence to a supposedly receptive public.

His first visit to Washington, D.C., may have been as early as 1854, at a public séance held with a small group of other spiritualists during which Conklin channeled the spirit of Henry Clay, who provided political pontification. A year later he returned and through his advertisements proclaimed his skill as a test medium, apparently ensuring a steady parade of patrons eager to communicate with spirits. Conklin claimed in the early spring of 1861 that he met on several occasions with a man whom he believed was Lincoln. The anonymous man supposedly betrayed this identification based on his posture and peculiar presence.

Kase capitalized on his celebrity and became a darling of the spiritual community, even snagging an appointment later in life as the president of a mediums' open-air meeting in a lonely wooded area near Philadelphia in 1879. Over the next few days, attendance peaked around 800, with visitors and spiritualists intermingling and sharing spiritual insights.[62]

Kase could not eclipse the young girl who supposedly enchanted President Lincoln on the night of their chance encounter at Mrs. Laurie's home. From her bed, a then feeble and debilitated Nettie Colburn Maynard reconstructed the events from decades earlier in a book altruistically aiming to provide an historical footnote to President's Lincoln's life. She did this good deed based on memories validated by the book's publisher, who obtained numerous affidavits attesting to her respectable character, but still left the reader to answer the question, *"Abraham Lincoln Was a Spiritualist?"*[63]

Nettie's introduction to the spirit world followed a familiar pattern. It was 1845 in Bolton, Connecticut, and family members were sitting around the kitchen table engaged in light conversation when a loud banging noise shook the upstairs door. Before they could investigate, and as if to convince everyone that an intelligent force directed the sound, it was repeated two more times. As might be expected, a close scrutiny of the stairway gave no suggestion as to what caused the banging.

Years later, Nettie recalled the clock striking eight o'clock that night shortly after the banging ceased, which by itself seemed of little importance, but a few days later the young girl learned that a family member had died at the exact moment, a serendipitous sequence interpreted as the lost loved one signaling their presence from the spirit world.

Over the next 10 years, as Nettie matured a few sporadic mysterious events kept her in contact with the spirit world, but an encounter in 1855 ushered in a more permanent relationship. While once again seated at a table her father related a wondrous personal observation about a young man named Thomas Cook who possessed a remarkable talent moving the heaviest furniture by merely touching the objects.

Nettie's father had been duly impressed and invited Cook home to spend an evening demonstrating the levitation. The invitation was accepted, and a few nights later Cook and the family members placed their hands lightly on the dining-room table, which responded by jumping about almost as if irritated by their presence. In an even more bizarre turn, Cook began talking to the table, which replied in the spirits' universal rapping language and eventually revealed itself as Nettie's grandfather. The night's emanations were especially strong and clear, a situation Cook associated with the presence of other harmonious spirit receivers. He believed Nettie had a particularly strong resonance with the spirit world and her mother less so.

Nettie began perfecting her psychic skills, not with her mother but

Five—Assassination, Resurrection and Exploitation

through another chance encounter with Eunice, a similarly aged young girl who also professed latent supernatural abilities. Together the pair spent many frustrating hours in failed attempts at table tipping, with Nettie finally issuing an ultimatum that she would no longer accept the spirits' intransigence. Seemingly cowed by the girl's demand, the spirits responded at their next séance with a rapping serenade that thoroughly scared the young mediums, but Nettie's mother calmed the situation and without evidencing any misgivings encouraged the girls to continue their contacts with the spirit world.

News of Nettie's prowess spread far and wide, and soon nearly every evening was spent with eager visitors sitting around a table and reminiscing with lost loved ones. Nettie progressed from receiving rappings to automatic writing and finally delivered lengthy monologues while thoroughly spellbound. Each enchantment left the young girl drained and remembering nothing that had transpired. Her fame quickly led to public lectures before captivated audiences.

Nettie was on a public lecture tour when the Civil War began, and she distinctly recalled receiving a question after the North's disastrous loss at the First Battle of Bull Run in 1861 that nervously asked how long the war would last. Her reply from beyond surely distressed the inquirer when the spirits prophetically proclaimed "that it would continue four years, and that it would require five practically to end it."

A year later, Nettie's father and three brothers joined the ranks of the Union Army and a farewell séance assured all assembled that the recruits would pass the war's travails uninjured. It was a reassurance that did not include sickness, which was the conflict's greatest threat.

Nettie's youngest brother, Private Amasa S. Colburn, Company F, 16th Connecticut Regiment, fell gravely ill and plaintively hoped his sister would come to his aid. The young man lay enfeebled along with an untold number of similarly weak and wasting soldiers among a vast sea of tents erected in Alexandria, Virginia. What the others didn't have was a young girl determined to rescue her brother.

Nettie wasted no time making travel arrangements to visit her brother and, turning to her spiritual friends, sought the name of a local spiritualist who could aid her mission. Her friends recommended Thomas Gale Foster, a well-known medium and clerk at the War Department. Foster was a man possessing both spiritual and political connections. It was an inspired choice, as Nettie was about to confront the vast military bureaucracy, a frustrating mélange of indifference, incompetence, and occasional sparks of compassion that energized Nettie's ceaseless efforts.

Nettie accepted Foster's hospitality and boarded with his family, at a convenient location where she launched her crusade. Initially her goal was simply to visit her brother, which the scrappy girl accomplished, and sitting with him in a tent Nettie listened as her brother pensively pursued an elusive medical furlough. Despite his many efforts the military surgeons never reviewed his case, and with each successive rebuff his mood darkened. Nettie shared her brother's despondency but not his doubts, and with her distress guiding her steps she sought advice from her benefactor, Thomas Foster.

With his knowledge of the Department of War, Foster suggested Nettie contact John Tucker, the Assistant Secretary. It was a fruitful meeting, with Nettie obtaining a letter directing the military surgeon responsible for Colburn's care to take immediate steps to address his plight. Once again braving the journey alone, she attempted to deliver the letter, but her optimism faded when she learned the camp was moving and the surgeon would conduct no further medical evaluations.

Tucker's letter opened doors but did not unlock the bureaucracy's intransigent grip on dawdling, distemper, and disdain, which forced Nettie to relentlessly reengage a mostly disinterested group of military officials. Nettie's persistence paid off and she finally secured the coveted furlough, but it proved to be a short-lived victory forfeited when her brother lost the precious document.

Dazed and disheartened, an exhausted Nettie felt better when the spirits proclaimed the setback a necessary step in the unfolding drama. A short time later, Cranston Laurie arrived at Foster's home and excitedly asked if Nettie could come to his house, and without further explanation the girl accepted the invitation. Cranston's wife Margret was a well-known medium, and perhaps Nettie assumed that a hastily assembled séance was in the making.

A short trip brought Nettie to the Cranston's home, but it was the elegant, ornate coach that conveyed her to the Georgetown residence that kindled in the girl's imagination the notion that she would soon meet an important person who could favorably finish her brother's quest. Nettie's coach-driven fancy soon gave way to reality upon arrival at her destination, when the surprise of her life greeted the young girl on the threshold of the Cranston's home.

It was Mrs. Lincoln who warmly greeted Nettie and introduced her to a small but distinguished group assembled to attend a séance hosted by Mrs. Cranston and her daughter. Preparations for the night's event included a request for a trance medium, and during the discussion Nettie's name rose to the surface and culminated in Mrs. Lincoln's decision to send her coach to fetch the young girl.

Reflecting back over the years, Nettie remembered Mrs. Lincoln with a deprecatory touch as "a prepossessing woman, apparently about thirty years old, possibly older ... and under any circumstances would be pronounced a handsome woman.... In manner she was occasionally quick and excitable, and would, while under excitement or adverse circumstances, completely give way to her feelings. In short, she was lacking in the general control, demeanor, and suavity of manner which we naturally expect from one in high and exalted position."

Despite this somewhat inimical recollection, Nettie appreciated Mrs. Lincoln's later assistance wrenching her brother's furlough free from

Nettie Colburn Maynard meets with President Lincoln (Nettie Colburn Maynard, *Was Abraham Lincoln a Spiritualist?: Or, Curious Revelations from the Life of a Trance Medium*, 1891).

crotchety, rusty regulators. There was a quid pro quo that Nettie might not have realized at the time, but Mrs. Lincoln wanted the young medium to remain in Washington and meet with the President, and such a meeting supposedly took place shortly after her brother departed for home.

Mrs. Lincoln purportedly requested Nettie's attendance at the White House by extending the invitation through the Lauries, who promptly complied. The Lauries' enchanted daughter inaugurated the evening's enigmatic events with a booming piano recital that brought the instrument off the floor and preceded the entrance of Abraham Lincoln.

According to Nettie's account, the President thoroughly charmed the bashful and embarrassed girl, who after exchanging pleasantries with Lincoln lapsed into a dreamy, prodromal state of semiconsciousness signaling her connection with the spirit world. Over the next hour she channeled political advice from beyond with the strongest and most urgent transmission involving "the forthcoming Emancipation Proclamation ... he was assured that it was to be the crowning event of his Administration and his life."

Not surprisingly, Nettie's White House connection cemented her role in the Nation's spiritual community, and with her fame she drew some of the City's elite to witness her clairvoyance. Yet none could equal the subsequent séances attended by the President and his wife, during which times the spirits offered political and military guidance.

Nettie avoided the inevitable scandal of Lincoln's attendance at séances through secrecy and silence, which were only broken many year's after his death. Her revelations did not fully satisfy a public eager to know whether Lincoln was a spiritualist, with her memoirs ambiguously declaring "that question is left open for general judgement.... I do know that he held communication with numerous mediums ... [and] if he had not faith in Spiritualism, he would not have connected himself with it."

The *Banner of Light*, a periodical devoted to Spiritualism, illuminated more details about Nettie Colburn Maynard's childhood memoirs regarding the Lincoln White House through a rendition tinted by the newspaper's bias and probable embellishment. Painting a picture of pathos, the newspaper portrayed the elderly, bedridden woman as singularly focused on resurrecting memories of séances held between 1863 and 1865 from "her home in the White House, where she gave the President séances almost daily."[64]

Contemporaneous notes and frequent contacts with Lincoln's spirit and other mediums enhanced Nettie's recollections, but while the last admission boosted believers, it simultaneously undermined her credibility among skeptics. Even so, the *Banner of Light*'s audience was composed of the faithful, and the newspaper clearly kept this in mind with each story.

A séance held in Nettie's home in White Plains, New York, in 1891 under the mediumship of Mrs. M.E. Williams amazed a veteran reporter for the *Banner*. Williams conjured up from her improvised cabinet 23 spirits, all of whom took their turn filling in gaps in Nettie's memory. Among the parade of spirit guides, politicians, and soldiers, none could outdo when "the shade of Lincoln, tall, stern, dark and sad-looking, appeared for a few moments, gave Mrs. Maynard assurances as to some details in her story."

Maynard's publisher promoted her book with an advertising blitz dually designed to attract interest from spiritualists and nonbelievers. The publisher assured readers that Maynard's account was perfectly credible and relied in great part on the plethora of eyewitness accounts of séances conducted at the White House that "breathes forgotten whispers, which the rust of time had almost covered." Curiously, the advertisements made no mention of confirmation from Lincoln's spirit.[65]

Much of the controversy immediately following the book's publication involved Maynard's supposed role in spiritually influencing Lincoln's Emancipation Proclamation. Maynard reacted to an article in the *New York Sun* that asserted such by angrily declaring, "I wish it distinctly understood that I was never in any way connected with the Emancipation Proclamation, for I never met Mr. Lincoln until the December after it was made public." In the same denunciation she also denied living at the White House, discrediting the idea of a psychic courtesan at the beck and call of Lincoln.[66]

Maynard's declaration upset the spiritual community, which had long accepted her role in guiding the nation toward a more humane path. The *Banner of Light* gingerly criticized the woman by taking exception to her fresh recantation and softly implied that she had unintentionally misled spiritualists for years. Despite its light touch, Maynard felt criticized and responded with another letter to the *Banner*.

The *Banner of Light* dutifully published Maynard's rebuttal, more out of a sense of devotion to the woman than out of conviction. Maynard's second letter was another effort to set the record straight, denouncing an unattributed 1876 claim in the "Mind and Matter (a spiritual paper published in Philadelphia) ... that the Emancipation Proclamation was dictated by the spirits through me."

As her second letter explained, Maynard wrote to the editor of the *Mind and Matter* disavowing the story and patiently waited for her letter's publication, which never occurred. She then authored a similar missive to the *Banner of Light*, which the newspaper contended it never received. Bowing to Maynard's insistence, the *Banner* veered in another direction, attributing through speculation that the intervention involving the Emancipation Proclamation might have occurred through the mediumship of J.B. Conklin and stubbornly defending Spiritualism's role by stating that "the fact remains that Mr. Lincoln did have sittings with various mediums during the war period, and without doubt received the impulse to bring out the great Charter of Freedom for the slave through some one of these sensitive instruments."[67]

M.P. Turner, the *New York Sun* reporter who chronicled the séance held at Nettie's home, took careful notes of the event and mingled with the other attendees before writing his account of the night's activities, which included multiple validated comments claiming Maynard's role influencing Lincoln's issuance of the Emancipation Proclamation. The reporter even extended the courtesy of letting Williams read the article to Maynard prior to publication, and after receiving no corrections he moved forward.[68]

Beyond the brouhaha about the Emancipation Proclamation, a brief but intense flurry of criticism and commendation followed publication of Maynard's *Was Abraham Lincoln a Spiritualist?* Dragged into the debate was the book's publisher Rufus C. Hartranft, whose reputation hung in the balance and consequently provoked a high-spirited defense "that I would not for one moment place my imprint upon a work that belittled or falsified or misrepresented the greatest man of modern times."[69]

Hartranft suffered the penalties of publishing Maynard's book with a raft of negative newspaper editorials. As might be expected, supporters of Mrs. Maynard and Spiritualism rushed to support both the publisher and the author by embracing both in heroic terms. For supporters, Hartranft's secular views and ultimate decision to publish Maynard's book after investigating her claims only served to strengthen their acceptance of the author's work.[70]

Others savaged the work. Among her many critics, the *Chicago Tribune* seemed to have the most fervent animosity and in furtherance of that opinion brought forth the comments of John G. Nicolay, President Lincoln's private secretary: "In any event I can say, without the slightest qualification, that a séance never occurred at the White House."[71]

It was a bold declaration from a man with intimate contact with Lincoln and from a perch without peer, or so it seemed. The *Banner* assailed the *Tribune*'s broadside, lamenting the attack on Maynard and Spiritualism and returning fire. Maynard supplied the ammunition in the form of a letter directly addressed to Nicolay, which the *Banner* gleefully used to shoot down its opposition. Maynard spared no vitriol piercing her antagonist: "The main fact that is sought to be established by this article is, however, that you Mr. Nicolay, did not even know that Mr. Lincoln attended séances, and that he not only attended séances of mediums, but also had them hold meetings in the White House.... It is also true Mr. Nicolay, that the proofs of the statements which you saw fit to deny are plainly set forth in my book."[72]

For all the dust it raised, in the end *Was Abraham Lincoln a Spiritualist?* was more like a tempest in a teapot and changed few minds after the storm passed. Maynard died a few months after her scathing response to Nicolay, and the *Banner* marked the passing with a solemn, respectful obituary that in part revived the greatest controversy: "This lady did not claim to have given the Emancipation Proclamation in so many words to the President ... [that] emanated from Mr. Lincoln's own mind but the grand spirits who controlled Miss Colburn at the time, and held personal interviews with the President ... encouraged him to put forth his proclamation."[73]

Many well-known spiritualists, including Cora Hatch, attended the funeral and through prayer and poems paid their last respects to Maynard. Shortly after interment, the famous medium's ghost made contact with several mediums and offered words of solace for her husband and friends.

Maynard's passing did not quell or settle the question posed by her book, and in some respects it emboldened others to come forward and share their thoughts on the matter. John Francis Whitney, the grandson of Eli Whitney of cotton gin fame, was among those compelled to authenticate her book. Whitney had no doubts that Lincoln was a believer, based on a personal interview with the President and similar discussions with J.B Conklin, but the most persuasive evidence came from Mary Todd Lincoln.[74]

Whitney's letter to the *Banner of Light* recalled a week-long visit in 1874 by Mrs. Lincoln to his home in St. Augustine, Florida, during the course of which she "often referred to many wonderful manifestations which Mr. Lincoln and herself had witnessed, and said he was a believer in the Spiritual Phenomena." Whitney and his wife held frequent séances, suggesting their keen interest in the subject, but even more astonishing was a reference to Mrs. Lincoln "having strong mediumistic powers."

Dismissing Whitney as a crank was difficult, given his lineage and lifelong accomplishments that included his financial backing of Northern newspapers such as the *Boston Herald* and his role as a real estate promoter and newspaper publisher in St. Augustine, Florida.[75] His support of the Union effort to preserve the Nation was clearly evidenced in the early days of the Civil War, when he wrote a brief letter to President Lincoln announcing his intention "of publishing a weekly war journal, the entire profits of which I shall appropriate to the fund for the maintenance ... of the wives and families of our brave and loyal volunteers."[76]

Whitney confirmed the visit of Mrs. Lincoln in a family record, but little is known of what transpired during that visit, aside from his letter to the *Banner*. Mrs. Lincoln reminisced about her Florida sojourn in a letter written to Mrs. Bradwell that made no mention of psychic phenomena but instead focused on the trip to the Southern city in a journey marked by the wild, enchanting landscape and a raging fever that incapacitated the woman for the first three days after her arrival at the Whitneys' home.[77]

Professor A.B. Severance, writing to the *Banner* from Milwaukee, Wisconsin, also rushed to support Nettie Maynard by recalling a visit to his psychic studio from a heavily veiled woman shortly after the death of President Lincoln. As the sitting unfolded, the recently deceased President made an appearance and tenderly touched the woman he called his wife. The widow's son Tad also offered words of comfort toward the end of the séance, after which the woman now revealed as Mary Todd Lincoln spoke at length with the medium. Severance "asked her if, about the time of the war, the President consulted mediums. She then told me about consulting Miss Nettie Colburn."[78]

Severance offered a wide range of psychic services both in person and for those who could not or would not travel to his office, by encouraging his patrons to "send by letter a lock of hair, or hand writing, or a photograph" for a character assessment, physical diagnosis, and, for an additional fee, a spirit-prescribed course of treatment.[79] Severance published a short article reading like a fortune cookie, titled "psychometric delineation of a lock of hair," which informed the recipient that "in looking into your future, I see that your success will be gradual, and will gain a powerful influence in this world of work."[80]

Robert Lincoln, a surviving son of the late President took issue with Maynard's recollections and the subject of Spiritualism more broadly by flatly emphasizing, "there is not a word of truth in the story ... that Abraham Lincoln ...was a spiritualist... nor any foundation for the accompanying assertion that Mr. Lincoln had a medium living in the White House."[81] Just three days after this denunciation appeared in print, the *Banner* published an authoritative-sounding letter from W.H. Burr, protesting in part that "the knowledge of séances at the White house was carefully guarded from publicity. Young Robert Lincoln was not likely to know anything about them."[82]

Spiritualism stimulated charlatans, satire, sarcasm, seriousness, and scientific inquiry as it spread throughout society in nineteenth-century America. For some it was an amusing form of entertainment, an opportunity to satisfy their curiosity or attack the performer's credibility. Believers in traditional religion blasted the faith as heretical, but much like the mythical Sirens who lured sailors to an untimely demise, Spiritualism

Five—Assassination, Resurrection and Exploitation 123

seductively snared sad, spiritless citizens with a sanguine system eliminating the boundary between life and death. Death need not be feared, and from the spiritualist viewpoint, death progressively cleansed a sinful soul, but even more enticing was a medium giving voice to lost loved ones.

Spiritualism stepped into a crisis of faith created by America's Civil War and the legions of sorrowful survivors that were dissatisfied, discouraged, and depressed with traditional religion. Spiritualism tapped into a basic human desire to reestablish the broken link with departed family and friends. Meeting this demand were mediums of ever-increasing abilities in towns large and small, amplified by public venue presentations and spiritual periodicals. Leading the list of the latter was the *Banner of Light*, a newspaper that published a weekly column reporting the results of public séances ministered by a resident medium, and from the outset of the Civil War the newspaper contacted hundreds of supposedly dead soldiers in an apparent bid to comfort survivors and prove the merits of the faith.

Six

Spreading the Faith

The prevalence and influence of Spiritualism during the Civil War era are impossible to determine with accuracy. The best that can be achieved are estimates based on accounts gleaned from books and newspapers published throughout the mid to late nineteenth century that parallel the rise and fall of American Spiritualism. Sifting through this mountain of material still leaves precious little evidence establishing reliable data, which in itself raises questions as to why so little verifiable data exists.

Answering that question is a matter of speculation, but several possibilities exist. The proliferation of books published during this time points to a commercial interest in the subject, as summarized in the 1871 edition of *The American Bookseller's Guide*. Looking back 25 years, *The Guide* began its review with Andrew Jackson Davis's first book, followed by the momentum given the subject by the Fox sisters, and the subsequent propagation by mediums, scientists, and the burgeoning ranks of faith busters. Emma Hardinge Britten's *History of Modern American Spiritualism*, published in 1870, sold 5,000 copies, which was an enviable number, suggesting a fairly broad public interest in a work chronicling the history of the movement.[1]

The *American Bookseller's Guide* was a monthly publication dedicated to providing booksellers with timely sales numbers and specific suggestions to increase their business prospects. By 1871, "the entire annual sale of Spiritual and Progressive Books, including pamphlets, averages about one hundred thousand volumes. The sale of bound volumes is about fifty thousand, and of pamphlets fifty thousand. The sale of these books is as steady as of books in any other department of the trade, and they should not be overlooked by the bookseller."

Not surprisingly, *The Spiritual Magazine* reported the sales numbers provided by *The American Booksellers' Guide* to its faithful readers.[2] A decade later, anecdotal accounts decried the premature death of spiritual publications, declaring that "there is a prevalent impression that

Spiritualism is on the decline, but proof to the contrary exists in the fact that no class of books commands such rapid and extensive sales as those which narrate Spiritualistic experiences and Spiritualistic phenomena."[3]

An even earlier 1857 tally by the *Advent Review and Sabbath Herald* enthusiastically reported the growth of Spiritualism, which it tied in part to the movement's embrace of free love. Though free love was morally scandalous to many, it did throw off the shackles of restraint imposed by traditional religious teachings. An estimate of the number of spiritualists in 1857 pegged the number around 1 million, with the greatest concentration in New York with 300,000 adherents, followed by 120,000 each for Ohio and Indiana, 90,000 in Massachusetts, 80,000 in Illinois, and 70,000 in Pennsylvania. Southern states added smaller numbers to the total, with Texas and Tennessee both contributing 15,000.[4]

The estimate reported by the *Advent Review and Sabbath Herald* of a million spiritualists in America, along with an unknown number of simply curious citizens, incentivized authors, as reflected by "over one hundred distinct publications on the subject of Spiritualism." Judge Edmonds's book sold 10,000 copies and Andrew Jackson Davis's more popular books exceeded 8,000. As further evidence of Spiritualism's early growth, an admittedly incomplete list identified 16 periodicals devoted to the subject.

Nineteenth-century periodicals devoted to Spiritualism probably offer the best clues regarding the scope and influence of the faith. Their proliferation in terms of sheer numbers provides some evidence of societal interest in the subject, but the evanescence of many titles and their physical loss over time makes their collection a daunting task.

In spite of these obstacles, a few modern researchers have undertaken a painstaking data-driven analysis. One of the most important was *News from the Spirit World: A Checklist of American Spiritualist Periodicals 1847–1900*, which carefully catalogued 214 publications along with their longevities.[5]

According to the *Checklist* there were 13 Spiritualism periodicals available to readers during the Civil War, only three of which were in existence throughout the conflict's duration: *Banner of Light*, *Rising Tide*, and *World's Paper*. The *Banner of Light* presented a mixture of literature, advocacy, and romance and had the longest run and widest audience of any spiritualist publication. Mrs. M.M. Daniel published the *Rising Tide* from Independence, Iowa, from 1860 to 1865, while the *World's Paper* was a Vermont publication that ran from 1857 to 1866.

The number of new periodicals increased sharply after the Civil War, with 51 publications initiated from 1866 to 1876. In the next decade, from 1877 to 1887, there were 43 new publications. The 12-year interval from 1888 to 1900 witnessed only 27 new titles, with the remaining publications mentioned in the *Checklist* preceding the Civil War. As further noted in the *Checklist*, the majority of all new publications had a very short lifespan, with only 31 surviving for five years, and from that small number 12 lasted for 10 years or longer and a mere five had a publication life span that reached at least 20 years.

In the broadest sense, spiritual publications reflected the maturity of the faith and the expanding umbrella covering divergent social interests united by the belief that mortals could communicate with the departed. Antebellum periodicals introduced the concepts of Spiritualism by promoting its religious independence, utopian vision, core beliefs, and testimonials from mediums. The postbellum period experienced a resurgence of new publications after the dearth of attention during the Civil War, with the two decades following contributing nearly equal numbers before falling toward the end of the nineteenth century. In addition to promoting the general philosophy of Spiritualism, the postbellum publications also addressed the presumed scientific nature of the faith, female equality, temperance, antislavery, free love, socialism, and of course occultism. Only the *Banner of Light* provided a continuous record that covered the Civil War era before, during, and after the conflict ended. The *Banner of Light* also offered the best resource to understand the intersection between the Civil War years from 1861 to 1865 and Spiritualism.

Another measure of Spiritualism's influence is based on the frequency of advertisements for public meetings and lectures as extracted from the *Banner of Light* and the *Spiritual Telegraph* from 1854 to 1873. Based on this research, the number of advertisements for Spiritualists after the Civil War more than doubled the pace seen during the war.[6]

Meeting activity was principally concentrated in seven states: Massachusetts, New York, Ohio, Maine, Illinois, Connecticut, and Michigan. In the years after the Civil War, the cities with the highest level of meeting activity in descending order included Boston, Massachusetts; Baltimore, Maryland; New York City; Brooklyn, New York; Portland, Maine; Salem, Massachusetts; Lowell, Massachusetts; Worcester, Massachusetts; Philadelphia, Pennsylvania; and Chicago, Illinois.

In summarizing the data, the author concluded that "the trends reported here are consistent with the claim that Spiritualism burgeoned when concern with the dead increased and the consoling power of traditional religion diminished." The fling with the new faith was short-lived, as its credibility suffered from an onslaught of attacks and as the emotional pain of the war's losses faded with time.

Aside from word of mouth, periodicals were the only means to publicize events, goods, and services in a timely manner. Periodicals accepted an enormous array of advertisements, for items ranging from the common staples of daily living to patent medicines. Specialty publications such as newspapers and journals devoted to Spiritualism targeted their readers with announcements of forthcoming lectures, meetings, mediums plying their trade, and spirit-formulated patent medicines. Advertisements filled lecture halls, brought the faithful, curious, and skeptical to public meetings, generated traffic for mediums, and generated profits for patent medicine makers.

Periodicals also provided a communal purpose, like a nineteenth-century version of social media that both informed and linked the loosely organized group together. Spiritualists published books, journals, and newspapers with passion and promptness that created an outsized presence that "substitutes the press for the pulpit, and the household for the cathedral."[7]

Periodicals offer the best opportunity to understand the vicissitudes of Spiritualism as it adapted to its environment and catered to its practitioners. In the antebellum period, periodicals generally concentrated on explaining the faith and offering psychic manifestations as proof of contact with spirits, and while the postbellum period featured the same, it also added more social themes such as active support of the women's suffrage movement. The paucity of periodicals during the Civil War makes it more difficult to track the association between Spiritualism and the carnage on the battlefields, a seemingly obvious relationship that only the *Banner of Light* can begin to illuminate. While a dozen other periodicals were available during the war, none could match the readership of the *Banner*, given its circulation numbers, weekly publication, and longevity.

A runner up in terms of publication longevity during the Civil War was Andrew Jackson Davis's *Herald of Progress*, which contributed copy from 1860 to 1864. As a source clarifying Spiritualism's role during the Civil War, Davis's publication was less preoccupied with the supernatural and more focused on progressive political and philosophical articles.[8]

The *Herald of Progress* espoused Davis's abolitionist feelings and passionate support for universal human equality, and it regularly published, debated, and defended these positions in editorials and letters. As an example, a reader from Massachusetts saw his letter in print after lamenting that state's failure to appoint "Rev. Leonard A. Grimes, a colored minister, and for seventeen years pastor of a colored church in Boston ... as a worthy candidate for the chaplaincy of the Massachusetts Legislature."[9]

Davis's egalitarianism naturally included support for women seeking social reforms that were entirely consistent with the libertine principles of Spiritualism. During the war years, the *Herald of Progress* often enshrined women's contributions facilitating the care and comfort of sick, wounded, and dying soldiers and indirectly equated their valor to the soldiers' battlefield courage.[10]

The *Herald of Progress* also chronicled the war with a decidedly pro-Union, antislavery stance infused with a pacifist tint. Shortly after the war began, the periodical proclaimed that "a war was never so endorsed by so large a proportion of conscientious peace men as the present ... including Quakers, Spiritualists, and Reformers."[11]

From a more pragmatic point, Davis offered medical advice to readers and in some cases even received letters from soldiers. His replies suggested remedies for the many ills connected to the unsanitary camp conditions. Soldiers' letters provided some limited indication of their reading proclivities, but they also might suggest a shunning of the Civil War surgeons' nostrums.

P.R. Eves, "a grateful soldier in the Union Army," had nothing but words of praise for Davis, thanking the man for prescribing an unnamed medicine. It was a strong tonic that initially weakened the writer but with continued use completely cured him. As a token of appreciation, Eves freely remitted five hard-earned dollars and became a lifelong convert.[12]

Another soldier stationed at Old Point Comfort in southern Virginia plaintively asked Davis, "Can you find something ... that a soldier can carry in his haversack, to prevent the water from giving him dysentery?" Davis's response to the beleaguered soldier answered a concern shared by many on the battlefield and was both thoughtful and insightful. In eschewing traditional medical approaches that might have included the use of opium, Davis actually offered sound advice. His first and best remedy was to boil the water, but recognizing that battlefield realties often precluded that approach he suggested instead "a few drops of the essence of winter green in every tumbler of water.... Or chew the leaves of pennyroyal, or catnip, or spearmint, occasionally."

A Confederate soldier was among the avid readers of the *Herald of Progress* and sent a note to the periodical confessing that "four days ago I resolved to quit the habit of smoking, and to devote the money the tobacco would cost me to the purchase of books and papers." The first recipient of the soldier's generosity benefited the work of the *Herald of Progress*.[13]

Although it was not among the publication's most prominent features, the *Herald of Progress* did not ignore the core of Spiritualism and at the outset of the war sought to reassure readers that "there are hundreds of philanthropic celestial visitors to every camp; and there are ten helpers for every man whose spirit is dislodged by war." As a predominately pacifist philosophy, Spiritualism consoled the grieving with the belief that death was merely a transition, albeit through a nonmaterial transformation, to a more exalted existence that included the capacity to communicate through sensitive mediums with mortals left behind.[14]

In a sign of the evenhandedness extended from beyond, a reader reminded the *Herald* that "the upper world does not neglect the soldiers of either army," a proposition favored by the egalitarian spiritualist but probably at odds with the political passions motivating the soldiers and citizenry of the opposing sides, which left Spiritualism and its converts even more isolated.[15]

As the toll of the war grew, the *Herald* responded by publishing short missives from soldiers in Summer Land, a euphemism for the spiritualist's vision of heaven. It was a peaceful picture preceded by a painless transition, "after falling dead by rifle or cannon fire.... They relate how they intuitively or spiritually ... realized the nature of the accident ... but they did not feel anything like pain being only disposed to sleep very profoundly."[16]

The *Herald*'s description of death removed the fear and replaced it with a sense of dissociation, which was a mind-numbing experience that created no memory traces of the antecedent trauma. The immortal metamorphosis took place while the victim was in a suspended state of animation resembling deep sleep. Upon awakening, the spirit's eyes opened and beheld the wonders of Summer Land. This was a serene passage that lifted both the survivors' and victims' spirits.

Spirit escorts from Summer Land assisted the soldier's transition, and like guardian angels they tranquilly hovered above the dead and with a compassionate touch led the victim to the Promised Land. This additional detail meant that no one died alone even in a distant military hospital far from home, as when "a young soldier's spirit took its flight to heaven. Many of his comrades who had 'gone before' assembled over the hospital and received him into their midst."[17]

A particularly emotional message came from a soldier killed at the "Battle of Sharpsburg" in a disclosure that betrayed his Southern loyalty. His return from the grave was specifically motivated by a desire to relieve his mother's deep sorrow. The *Herald*'s report from the unnamed soldier and his equally cloaked medium consoled his mother by describing his death as painless and peaceful and with a heart-rending finish plaintively noted, "I wish you were here with me. But you must not think of it. Your interests shall be in my thoughts day and night."[18]

Messages from spirits extolling the virtues of Heaven and the seamless transition that permitted continued contact with loves ones carried risks that, intentionally or not, the Sharpsburg soldier seemed to understand. Immediately after wishing his mother could join him, which surely touched the woman and the *Herald*'s readers, the spirit walked the suggestion back, perhaps sensing that the tug from beyond might precipitate the mother's suicide.

Sometimes the wires got crossed when mediums reached out to the occupants of the spirit world, and they left confusing and contradictory messages that left the recipients at best puzzled and perhaps worse off, when leaving the encounter frustrated, disappointed, or disillusioned. An apologetic medium conceded, "It is very likely that the spirit communicating was right in facts, but erred as to the relation of the deceased soldier to you ... they err as men do."[19] Carrying such foibles and myopia to the spirit world helped the medium explain or perhaps obfuscate the error.

Ebenezer V. Wilson was a test medium traveling the country holding séances and seemed to have a penchant for contacting soldiers, one account of which he chronicled in a letter to the *Herald* dated July 23, 1863. With a precision meant to enhance credibility Wilson recalled an unannounced bedroom visit from a soldier spirit from the Army of the Potomac on April 27, 1863, at 2 p.m. For a war-weary nation the soldier had good news that supposedly foretold how "the rebels would invade the union ... threatening Washington, Baltimore, and Pittsburg. Neither of these places would be attacked, but there would be a great battle on free soil, our army would be victorious, the rebels defeated."[20]

Nothing more was heard from the itinerant soldier spirit until July 3, 1863, when he again made his presence known and reassured Wilson in what would come to be known as the Battle of Gettysburg, Pennsylvania, "Do not be uneasy; all is going on well. Lee will be defeated but will get back into Virginia." Over the next several weeks the same spirit predicted that a great battle would soon decimate the Rebels and peace would follow shortly thereafter. The prescient phantom apparently did not envision the Civil War continuing for almost another two years.

Wilson was an early convert to Spiritualism and, like many of his kind, began his career interpreting spirit rappings. As a self-styled seer from Chicago he soon began the lecture and séance circuit, eventually adding to his trade with animal magnetism and clairvoyance. From his memoirs, Wilson offered a torrent of testimonials, many from unnamed soldier spirits, as evidence of Spiritualism.[21]

Spiritualists with second sight weighed in on the war and frequently predicted the course in terms favorable to the Union. From her home in Buffalo, New York, E.A. Maynard held regular séances under the guidance of medium C.H. Reed, and on January 23, 1864, a séance offered a disturbing vision of the war.[22]

Breaking from the traditional hand-holding séance, the medium dreamily described a recent vision: "I see armed soldiers near a fort; its name is Wagner. Oh! There is a soldier blind folded—they are going to shoot him—I can see his name now, it is Giles Bennet—he stands by his coffin ... there! they have shot him." With terror spreading across his countenance, the affected medium's vision continued with the slain soldier lowered into his grave.

The *Herald of Progress* skirted around reporting detailed, direct contacts with soldier spirits and usually omitted identifying characteristics, which prevented even the most basic validation of the claims. Readers were left vouchsafing the credibility of communications based on the medium's reputation and perhaps the *Herald*'s publication of the reports, which lent some authority. Another periodical took a different approach and throughout the Civil War routinely presented readers with far more comprehensive accounts of soldier spirits, including their names, locations of death, descriptions of the spirit world, and amusing anecdotes.

The *Banner of Light* was the most influential and longest running newspaper devoted to Spiritualism. It was a weekly publication from 1857 to 1907 a nd presented an eclectic mix of romance stories, poems, spiritual philosophy, the comings and goings of mediums, political commentary, reports of manifestations, and advertisements that informed readers about new books, coming lectures, contacting the broad array of practicing psychics, magnetizers, and healers, and spirit-formulated or -approved patent medicines. The *Banner* principally owed its success to Luther Colby, who was joined in that endeavor by William Berry and Frances Conant.[23]

Luther Colby was born in 1814 in Amesbury, Massachusetts, and spent his early years with his mother and seafaring father. At the age of fourteen he traveled to an Exeter, New Hampshire, printing office to begin learning the trade as an apprentice. After successfully completing this training he moved to Massachusetts and over a twenty year career at the *Boston Post* successively assumed more prominent positions before retiring, citing fatigue as the precipitating factor.

Colby's career took precedence over his personal religious views until

Banner of Light masthead (*Banner of Light*, January 16, 1864).

his retirement, at which time his independent nature gravitated toward Spiritualism in a conversion aided by his attendance in 1856 at a séance that included the presence of Frances Conant, who would eventually join with Colby in ministering the *Banner of Light*. Conant profoundly influenced Colby's spiritual life through weekly séances that steadily moved the man's faith toward conviction.

Conant's clairvoyance predicted the Colby, Berry, and Conant triumvirate that would publish revelations from the spirit world through a newspaper dedicated to that purpose. It was a spirit-informed message that became reality with the *Banner of Light*'s inaugural printing on April 11, 1857. The newspaper's standard was "not the organization of a new sect, nor the special separation of its believers from the rest of the world by party lines but rather ... illumination taking the place of gloom as the result."

According to the *Banner*'s cryptic mission, gloom was a multifaceted consequence of the straightjacket imposed on the free thinking nontraditional beliefs espoused by Colby and the legions of like-minded individuals who rejected the ways and means of established religions. Spiritualism enshrined individualism by unshackling rigid moral restraints. Another dysphoric element common to traditional thinking involved the communication barrier between life and death, which was neatly resolved by psychic mediums gaining access to the spirit world and reuniting the dead with their living friends and family.

The *Banner of Light* boasted of a worldwide readership and, perhaps blinded by its success, failed to see the looming clouds of the Civil War and its impact on the newspaper. Even so, the greatest blow came with the death of William Berry, who was killed in action supporting the Union cause at Antietam, Maryland. His loss was magnified by the *Banner*'s perilous financial condition during the Civil War, which forced the newspaper into bankruptcy, but like the phoenix of Greek mythology it arose from the ashes as a revitalized business venture through the assistance of William White. A decade later, ashes were all that was left after a devastating Boston fire in 1872 destroyed the building housing the *Banner*, but once again the resilient periodical was resurrected as sums large and small financed the newspaper's rebirth.

As Colby's spiritual growth expanded, he became an accomplished clairvoyant and medium, eventually partnering with Frances Conant at the paper's inception by offering free public séances, which were held on a regular basis in Boston. During these séances, Civil War soldiers became regular and more frequent visitors as the conflict lingered on.

Until his untimely death, William Berry was a driving force behind the *Banner*'s early development. Less is known of this man who co-founded spiritualists' main medium of communication, but his determination and energy was indispensable in launching the fledgling publication. Described as temperamental and choleric, Berry's hot nature vacillated with his intelligence. He was a motive force overcoming the resistance that a new project like the *Banner* needed. His introduction to Spiritualism came about through a psychic relative of his second wife and led to a lifelong conversion. Once a week thereafter, Berry and his relative hosted well-attended séances in Boston. The arrangement ended when the 37-year-old Berry died at the Battle of Antietam on September 17, 1862, facilitating Frances Conant's ascension.[24]

Frances Conant was born April 28, 1831, the daughter of parents of modest means in Portsmouth, New Hampshire. Illness and death dominated her earliest years, ultimately shaping a life focused on overcoming personal losses. Her first brush with fate was accompanied by a severe fever that prostrated the young seven-year-old child and burdened her mother with concerns about her child's survival. With an inflamed brain and a child's imagination, Frances struggled to understand her mother's perpetual bedside presence and soft-spoken appeal to some invisible agency. It was later explained by her vigilant attendant as prayers to guardian angels hovering nearby. This was the child's introduction to and naive acceptance of looming sympathetic spirits.[25]

Two years later, Frances's mother was stricken with a severe life-threatening illness, scaring the child, but it fell to her to fetch a local doctor while other family members held a fretful vigil. Frances got lost after excitedly running a short distance, and while overwhelmed with emotion "suddenly she fell, and, as she supposed fainted away—but after-experience has shown that she passed into the state of trance." After Frances awakened from the stuporous state she observed a man quietly standing nearby, whom

Frances Ann Conant (Theodore Parker, *Biography of Mrs. J.H. Conant, the World's Medium of the Nineteenth Century: Being a History of Her Mediumship from Childhood to the Present Time*, William White and Company, Boston, 1873).

she later interpreted as a guardian angel named Epimenides who appeared in response to her prayers and then guided the girl to the doctor.

Frances's mother survived, and later the pair traded roles when the 10-year-old girl suffered seizure-like activity followed by a prolonged obtunded state. Puzzled doctors could not explain or treat the condition, but Frances channeled advice from the spirit world and provided prescriptions that the baffled physicians supposedly prepared.

With remission from that mysterious nervous malady, Frances suffered another blow a year later when her mother died. It was a painful process for Frances to watch her mother's lingering death, albeit mitigated by a series of fantastic events immediately following the last breath. At that moment, raps resounded through the death chamber. Frances became entranced, and observed a white, faint form arise from her mother's mortal remains. It was a comforting vision confirming her mother's transition to an immortal state and ascent to a higher plane of existence.

Around her 20th birthday, Frances, then living with her husband John Conant in Boston, was again stricken with illness. It was a dire situation made worse when a local physician prescribed too much morphine. As she sank into respiratory depression her alarmed physician feared a fatal outcome and certainly did not reckon that relief would come from the spirit world. With a series of tremors, the stuporous woman seemed to awaken herself but was instead controlled by a deceased doctor who came to her aid and prescribed a naturopathic remedy that restored her vitality. During her period of insensibility Frances made contact with her mother, who insisted she return to the mortal realm and continue her life's psychic work.

Her recovery was short, punctuated a few months later by a deep descent into a malady described as "consumption of the blood." Her condition was fully resistant to conventional medical ministrations and surely left the woman despairing of remission. It was during this time that a friend suggested the debilitated woman seek counsel with a medium, which Frances reluctantly and pessimistically agreed to.

Anna Richardson was a teenage medium in Boston who had already achieved local fame as a skilled and sensitive medium, and when she and Frances met, Anna became entranced and controlled by John Fisher, a spirit doctor. By means unknown, the dead doctor diagnosed Frances's condition and, contrary to her mortal mentors, assured a recovery if, and only if, the patient made a specific payment. Naturally, Frances assumed this to be monetary, but the spirit doctor needed no currency and instead, after assessing her inherent power as a prospective medium, pronounced his quid pro quo: his medical cure in exchange for her commitment as a public medium.

Fisher made good on his end of the bargain, and a thoroughly rejuvenated Frances began fulfilling hers under the tutelage of the spirit doctor. As might be expected, the arrangement permitted the spirit doctor to extend his skill through Frances to an increasing swath of patients with maladies both major and minor. Satisfied clients spread the word of the spirit doctor's medical largesse and soon Mrs. Conant was besieged with aspiring patients.

One such patient suffered a severe leg injury and apparently bypassed traditional emergency treatments by instead hastily seeking Mrs. Conant's spirit doctor. Mrs. Conant immediately became entranced and Dr. Fisher took control. The spirit examined the injury and, through the physical means provided by the medium, carefully set the broken bone. A member of the patient's family took exception to the spirit doctor and after the procedure was completed demanded that a regular doctor be summoned, a request granted by the medium and the spirit doctor. After a brief examination the consulting physician deemed the intervention provided by the spirit doctor to be complete and thorough.

In addition to medical treatments, Mrs. Conant held séances accompanied by the usual table tippings, manifestations, and predictions. Her prominence eventually attracted the interest of Luther Colby, who attended a séance she mediated and left the circle deeply impressed with the woman's abilities. The *Banner*'s triad was completed when Colby referred Mrs. Conant to William Berry, who was likewise impressed.

Berry's fiery, intransigent nature soon clashed with Conant's less impulsive personality, particularly in matters relating to the *Banner*'s operation. Both turned to their respective spirit guides for assistance, with Berry's urging restraint and negotiation. Berry dismissively rejected Conant's suggestions, leaving the tensions between the pair unresolved until his death terminated the conflict.

One area of dispute between the pair involved the séances conducted as part of the *Banner*'s mission. Berry wanted private séances, while Conant and Colby agreed that public meetings with larger groups were a better strategy. Berry lost the battle but faithfully continued to transcribe Conant's contacts with the spirits for publication in the *Banner*.

In the beginning, Conant held daily public séances lasting several hours, but the strain became unbearable and forced a reduction to one hour on three days each week. All of this served to prepare Conant for the onslaught liberated by the Civil War, when "spirits from both armies who had passed from their bodies amid the roar of battle … crowded to this avenue of communion," facilitated by the *Banner*'s in-house medium.

Seven

Phantoms of War

The *Banner of Light* became a favorite haunt for spirits during the Civil War, with their supposed visits providing an interesting glimpse into the afterlife as relayed through Frances Conant. No other period publication offered such an extensive array of spirits commenting on the war, with combatants from both sides reaching out to the *Banner*'s resident medium, along with deceased loved ones yearning for communion with their survivors.

Through the Message Department, which was a regular feature in the *Banner of Light*, the newspaper reported spirit messages. The *Banner* solicited donations to fund the effort, claiming that "each Message in this Department of the *Banner* we claim was spoken by the spirit whose name it bears, through Mrs. J.H. Conant, while in a condition called Trance.... We are full aware that much good to the cause has been accomplished by our Free Circles, persons who first attended them as skeptics, now believe in the Spiritual Philosophy, and are made happy in mind thereby."[1]

It seems reasonable to speculate that Frances Conant, along with her counterparts at the *Banner* and their faithful readers, accepted the spirit messages at face value, a gratuity or gullibility not seen among skeptics. For the unbelievers, the spirit communications from dead soldiers might have seemed at best as fraudulent or at worst a cruel deception, designed to do nothing more than anchor the *Banner*'s role as the preeminent spiritualist periodical. This criticism was not without merit, given that most of the soldiers' messages were soothing, comforting visions of death and its afterlife, which surely consoled those with emotional wounds left by their losses. In other cases the spirits brought closure to their demise during a time when news of a soldier's death was often delayed or, even more sadly, never known.

An exclusive focus on the question of authenticity of the soldiers' messages is a polarizing debate without resolution and obscures an understanding of how Spiritualism contended with America's Civil War. As a pacifist, Universalist philosophy, the faith was challenged by the war to respond, and one way it did was through spirit messages. The *Banner of Light* accomplished this through Frances Conant's mediumship, which extended a warm, inviting, welcome mat that encouraged soldiers from both armies to share their experiences. It was a bold step for a newspaper published in a Northern state that was suffering dreadful losses from Southern soldiers.

Spirits of colored soldiers, slaves, and repentant slaveholders showcased Spiritualism's support of emancipation and at the same time painted an egalitarian afterlife free of prejudice. This was an interesting dichotomy that shed the immortal's prior racial prejudice but retained religious bigotry, with numerous spirits bemoaning established faiths and Catholicism in particular, which resonated with Spiritualism's antipathy toward traditional religion's doctrinaire behavior.

In almost every case, the spirits remembered the fatal incident that heralded their demise, an event followed by a brief period of confusion or bewilderment but rarely accompanied by physical discomfort, since spiritualists considered the conversion a normal transfiguration analogous in some respects to caterpillars transforming into moths and flying heavenward after their metamorphosis.

William Berry meticulously transcribed the soldiers' messages as transmitted through Frances Conant, which was an arduous task complicated by Southern dialects, euphemisms, and colloquialisms, all of which were tediously copied verbatim for the *Banner*'s readers. The process lent an air of authenticity to the spirit messages in a manner that seemed as if the immortal soldier was speaking directly to an attentive audience.

In the broadest sense, the spirit messages were hopeful, uplifting communiqués connecting a dead soldier with a spouse or family member. Sometimes the spirit made a request, such as requesting a family member visit a medium or insisting that material support be provided to the spirit's destitute spouse. A few spirits, perhaps bent on revenge, criticized negligent medical care that directly contributed to their death.

As the war progressed, the *Banner*'s Message Department became increasingly dominated by soldiers seeking out Frances Conant. Their revelations were like diary entries, often very personal and at times rough and unapologetically caustic. Patriotism migrated into the spirit world, and soldiers of both sides often contended their fight was right and just. There were some dissenters, and these were always soldiers from the south who regretted their role in the conflict and who, through the spiritual cleansing occasioned by death, renounced their previous enmity.

Not every spirit visiting the *Banner*'s public séances was a soldier, and some of the more heart-wrenching stories came from depressed wives who died without knowing their husband's fate. These pitiable women stretched their ghostly arms from the grave, hoping to once again embrace their husbands. In a few other cases spirits discussed and denied their suicide.

Atrocities in prisoner-of-war camps across the battlefield inflamed tensions on both sides of the conflict, and concretized hatred and fanned flagging public morale as the war dragged on. The *Banner of Light* contributed to the emotional tragedy, with soldier spirits declaiming the disgrace.

Freedom from their mortal remains liberated some spirits to admit their inclinations toward Spiritualism while alive, but fearing the social consequences they acknowledged their timidity in doing so. Others took the occasion of their death as an opportunity to return in ghostly form and convince the naysayers. Such admissions served at least two purposes, by advancing the idea that the number of Spiritualists was far greater than imagined and by demonstrating Heaven's liberality and acceptance of their beliefs.

Spiritualists probably accepted the soldiers' communications as consistent with their faith through a credit strengthened by the variety of spirits descending on Frances Conant's public séances. Officers and enlisted soldiers breached military protocol and commiserated together, spirits from a wide swath of regiments both Union and Confederate passed by, and ghosts from nearly every major battle sent representatives to populate the *Banner*'s weekly Message Department.

Camp followers rifling the dead (*Frank Leslie's Illustrated News*, **October 11, 1862**).

Seven—Phantoms of War

While the actual number of spirits attending the *Banner*'s séances was small, this was a consistent weekly affair that closely tracked the Civil War clashes that killed so many soldiers. As news of these key battles seeped into public life, readers of the *Banner of Light* received firsthand accounts from the decedents, which were usually accompanied by salient details describing each one's mortal blow and then variously comprehensive critiques of the war and their new afterlife.

The weekly dirge of dead soldiers and their family members affected by the war offered a unique perspective of the Civil War that was clearly colored by ardent advocates of an emergent faith leveraging the conflict to explain and advance their ideology. As the only newspaper devoted to Spiritualism that could legitimately claim a national audience, albeit small, the *Banner of Light* nonetheless took its mission of spreading the gospel seriously, and with the helpful assistance of spirits it did just that.

In total, 498 soldiers and family members contributed to the *Banner*'s Message Department, with the first stopping by on June 8, 1861. The ghostly gleanings gathered for this study extended through December 31, 1865. The 55-month period covered the battle years and included the typical lag time between a soldier's supposed death and subsequent reappearance at Frances Conant's séance. Admittedly, these numbers are a tiny fraction of the Civil War's overall casualties, but nonetheless they constitute a steady stream of spirits that offered a unique perspective on Spiritualism's role during the conflict.

Soldiers accounted for 395 messages or 79 percent of the 55-month total, with 14 of 24 (58 percent) in the truncated first year of the war coming from soldiers. In the following years the total number of spirit messages remained rather steady, while the proportion of soldier spirits increasingly dominated the *Banner*'s Message Department with 70 soldiers (71 percent) accounting for the 99 total messages in 1862, 99 soldiers (85 percent) out of 116 total messages in 1863, 105 (77 percent) soldier messages out of 137 in 1864, and 107 (88 percent) soldier messages out of a total 122 throughout 1865.

Looked at another way, it seemed as if all the spirits adhered to a monthly quota. Throughout the entire time period studied, the monthly spirit messages had a surprising consistency. In successive Januaries from 1861 to 1865, The *Banner of Light*'s Message Department reported communications from 46 spirits, 39 in February months, 40 in March months, 33 in April months, 41 in May months, 34 in June months, 40 in July months, 43 in August months, 45 in September months, 51 in October months, 42 in November months, and 44 in December months. Perhaps not unexpectedly, the favorite month for ghostly visits was in October.

The spirits had a slight preference for appearing during the cooler months of the year, with the *Banner*'s Message Department reporting 129 winter visits, 114 in spring, 117 in the summer, and 138 during the autumn months. Combining the cooler months from September through February netted 267 messages, as compared to the 231 messages received during the warmer months from March through August.

On average, each weekly edition of the *Banner of Light* during the 55-month period presented readers with nine spirit messages. As noted, even the month by month tallies were fairly consistent, with just a slight increase in the combined autumn and winter period.

If the *Banner of Light* wanted to present a generalizable sample of the universe of Civil War soldiers and their families through the Message Department, then its weekly publication of spirit communications was a step in that direction but by itself not enough. A statistically valid sample needed a cross section of combatants collected over time and in different battles to approach this condition. Whether intentional or not, The *Banner of Light* moved in that manner, and as the events of the Civil War unfolded during the 55 months studied, willing spirits shared their stories.

Spiritualism exemplified equanimity by not ostracizing soldiers from the South when they made overtures to Frances Conant at her public séances, providing a hospitable welcome accepted by 94 Confederates (24 percent) among all of the soldier visits. In a similar manner, Conant raised no bar preventing officers and enlisted soldiers from attending her séances, as demonstrated by 60 officers, a full 15 percent, who shared their experiences of death and life in the hereafter.

As a temporal measure, the *Banner*'s Message Department closely tracked the great battles roiling the country. Not every soldier identified the specific conflict where he died, but 158, or 40 percent, provided that information, which spanned 46 battles throughout the war's duration. Not surprisingly, some of the bloodiest battles seemed to produce the largest number of spirit soldiers attending one of Conant's séances, as evidenced by 14 soldiers who died at the Battle of Antietam, 12 at the Battle of Seven Pines or Fair Oaks, 11 at the Second Battle of Bull Run, nine at the Battle of Gettysburg, nine from the Battle of Fredericksburg, nine at the Battle of Shiloh or Pittsburg Landing, nine from the First Battle of Bull Run, eight at the Battle of Richmond, and eight from the battles around Petersburg.

Spirit soldiers were sometimes reluctant to identify their unit affiliations, but 196, or 50 percent, provided at least their state and regiment. In all, 27 states furnished soldier representatives for the *Banner*'s Message Department over the 55 months studied. Perhaps the *Banner of Light*'s Boston location facilitated visits by soldiers from Massachusetts, for which 52 spirits or 13 percent of the total soldier visits from 24 different regiments comprised the largest military group attending the séances. New York was a distant second with 26 spirits from 24 different regiments, 12 soldiers from seven different Pennsylvania regiments, 10 soldiers from six different Indiana regiments, nine soldiers from six different Maine regiments, and eight soldiers from five different Ohio regiments.

Confederate spirits came from eight states: Georgia, South Carolina, Virginia, Alabama, Louisiana, North Carolina, Tennessee, and Florida. Virginia had 13 spirits from eight different regiments; Georgia supplied nine soldier spirits from eight different regiments; there were seven spirits from six different South Carolina regiments; five soldier spirits came from four different Alabama regiments; and one spirit each came from the remaining states.

The vast majority of the soldier spirits died from battlefield wounds, although 33 met their fate through illness, which they mostly described as various incapacitating fevers. Military authorities executed two soldiers whose spirits subsequently spoke of the events surrounding their deaths. Another two soldiers were murdered by unnamed assailants. Among all of the spirits that left messages were three individuals, including a soldier's wife, who committed suicide. There were also three physician spirits.

Even though most of the spirits provided personal information such as their names, military units, and details of their death, only 24 soldiers' identities could be confirmed with certainty when matched with records maintained by the National Park Service's Soldiers and Sailors Database based on records that "have been transcribed from the National Archives' original documents; alternate names and/or misspellings are recorded as initially documented."[2] As an additional crosscheck, names and regiments were also cross-referenced with historical military records maintained by Fold3.[3] Confirmation resulted when a soldier's name, regiment, and company matched entries in the databases.

Of the 24 confirmed soldiers, 17, or 71 percent, came from the Boston *Banner of Light*'s home state of Massachusetts. Only two Confederate spirits supplied enough information for verification. New York, Indiana, Minnesota, Ohio, and New Hampshire each supplied one Federal spirit that completed the list.

The principle reason so few soldiers could be matched with historical military service databases was due to the spirits providing incomplete information, with their military units most commonly absent. In nearly half the cases the spirits did not mention their regiment, and when they did their assigned company was not mentioned. In addition, many of the spirits' names were very common, which further prohibited validation. The use of aliases also compromised the analysis.

During the Civil War the means to authoritatively question the authenticity of any particular soldier spirit would have been a difficult task.

Readers of the *Banner of Light* and their followers probably had little inclination to do so, and skeptics probably had little interest or wherewithal to positively refute Conant's claims. As a matter of speculation, perhaps this explains why the vast majority of confirmed soldiers came from Massachusetts, which might have been the *Banner of Light*'s effort to avoiding embarrassing revelations in its back yard or, perhaps more benignly, reflected simply the ease of acquiring factual information.

A closer examination of these data revealed that some military units were particularly fond of attending the *Banner*'s public séances. Once again, spirits from Civil War regiments in Massachusetts led the list, with seven former soldiers from the 54th Regiment Massachusetts Volunteer Infantry sending the largest single contingent from all states to the *Banner*'s séances. The 35th Regiment Massachusetts Volunteer Infantry sent five spirits; the 15th and 16th Regiments Massachusetts Volunteer Infantry each sent four; and the 2nd Regiment Massachusetts Volunteer Infantry, 9th Regiment Massachusetts Volunteer Infantry, 20th Regiment Massachusetts Volunteer Infantry, and the 3rd Massachusetts Volunteer Cavalry Regiment each had three spirits attend a séance.

Robert Morriston was the first supposed casualty of the Civil War to appear at a *Banner of Light* séance. His spirit arrived about a month after his death, and the results of his death were subsequently published one month after that. Robert's spirit conceded that the novelty involved in converting to the spirit world was confusing, but said that his familiarity with Spiritualism while alive made the transition a bit easier.[4]

Robert's monologue began with a brief introduction that would become typical for spirits attending a *Banner of Light* séance. He was born in Philadelphia in 1823, the son of Robert and Elizabeth Morriston, and was the only surviving sibling from a family of seven children. Robert's death left his 80-year-old father the last living member of the lineage.

At some point his parents moved to Norfolk, Virginia, inculcating the Southern sympathies that led the man to support South Carolina's secession. Robert's spirit claimed, "I was at Fort Moultrie, and at the second shot from Sumter, I was wounded slightly, and at the fourth shot was killed outright, with seventeen others, as I have been informed." His spirit message assured his father and friends that his death was painless and his only memories were the smell of gunpowder and the thunderous boom of cannons.

Robert probably did not expect to die, since "Our commander told us there was no need of fear on our part, for Anderson's force was so few we should silence them all in death at the first shot." The spirit harbored no grudges, in spite of wondering whether his commander deliberately misled his men. Death also moderated his political convictions: "I am

Seven—Phantoms of War 143

not sorry I went, for I then believed I was doing right. I do not feel so now."

The *Banner of Light*'s Message Department presented to readers an "eyewitness" account of the first shots fired in the Civil War from a Southern defender at Fort Moultrie. His message excluded the battle's outcome, but the loss of 18 men hinted at a devastating defeat, and in an interesting confession Robert's spirit reversed his previous support of the looming war.

Historical records do not support the *Banner of Light*'s version of the events at Ft. Moultrie. There were no Federal forces killed during the bombardment of Fort Sumter.[5] When considering Southern casualties, one opinion suggested that "Anderson could not hurt the Confederates. All his guns were smoothbores firing round shot; the enemy was beyond his effective range."[6] Contrast that position with Abner Doubleday, second-in-command at Fort Sumter at the time of the shelling. In his memoirs, Doubleday reported rumors of numerous Confederates killed and wounded at Fort Moultrie, but he ended that speculation by averring that "men holding high official position on the other side, that no one was killed or injured, would seem to leave little room for doubt."[7] Taken as a whole, it seems most unlikely that 18 Confederates died at Fort Moultrie.

Two soldier spirits returned from the grave after suffering their ultimate fate through a military execution. One case involved an authen-

Federal evacuation and destruction of cannon at Fort Moultrie (*Frank Leslie's Illustrated News*, January 5, 1861).

ticated Union soldier, and the other a Confederate soldier's story relying solely on the *Banner of Light*'s report. Both were executed for desertion.

The unauthenticated execution involved Theodore Guild. He supposedly died in the service of the rebellion but returned in spirit form to assert a different allegiance: "I'm from Poolesville, Maryland. I-I-I'm Union—understand that; but I was chucked into the rebel service, and deserted, but was retaken and shot." Guild spent the greater part of his visit explaining the series of unfortunate events that triggered his execution.[8]

Times were tough for Guild out West, and after considering the alternatives he moved south hoping his bad luck would improve. His travels ended in Poolesville, where, along with his wife Susan, he began the new phase of his life. It seemed things were not much better for the transplanted Westerner, and with the South's dire need for manpower, Guild was compelled to join the fight. The reluctant warrior was in a no-win situation: "It's there you can shoulder a musket and fight for their side, or you can die. So I entered the rebel service, thinking all the while I'd clear out as soon as I got a chance to; and I did, but I was retaken again." Guild was 45 years old when a volley of musket fire "in the outskirts of Yorktown" terminated his tortured military service. Beyond that, his spirit offered no details.

Guild implored the *Banner of Light* to communicate the news of his death to Susan and make sure she understood that forces beyond his control compelled his military service. "She don't know that I'm dead, and I don't want her to stay in that infernal hole, hoping that I shall turn up some day; but I shan't in that way." Before departing, Guild's spirit gushed, "Well, I'm right glad to get here," and having found the way, promised to attend a future séance.

William E. Ormsby suffered the same fate as Theodore Guild with one major difference: historical records document this man's execution. Ormsby was another soldier from the prolific Massachusetts regiments that supplied the *Banner*'s Message Department with new spirits. His sad journey began in San Francisco on February 15, 1863, when the 20-year-old man enlisted for three years with the 2nd Regiment, Massachusetts Cavalry, Company E. Military records described Ormsby as standing 5 feet, 3½ inches tall, with a fair complexion, blue eyes, brown hair, and born somewhere in New York.[9]

The fate of Private Ormsby was inseparably linked with the recruiting efforts of Captain Charles S. Eigenbrodt and the discipline of Colonel Charles Russell Lowell. His ill-fated rendezvous with the two men began out West. Ormsby joined the Union war effort while living in San Francisco. Although military records describe the man hailing from New York, Ormsby's presence in California was a matter of speculation. Eigenbrodt was also in California during the height of the gold rush, but the shiny metal and its fortunes eluded the prospector, forcing a reassessment of goals, which eventually led to his interest in recruiting soldiers for the war effort.[10]

California newspapers helped entice men to enlist for "three years of the war, under the Massachusetts Quota." Charles Eigenbrodt became a prolific recruiter and his efforts resulted in a promotion on March 19, 1863, as a company commander. The newly minted officer's contingent consisted of 103 men and two subordinate officers. Four days after accepting command, Eigenbrodt's troops boarded a steamship for the long trip back East and eventually arrived at Camp Meigs in Readville, Massachusetts, where the California recruits joined forces with the 2nd Massachusetts Cavalry under the command of Colonel Lowell.

Men from the 2nd Massachusetts Cavalry joined forces with soldiers from New York and Illinois regiments in a campaign to eliminate the guerrilla operations of Major John Mosby. Also known as "Mosby's Raiders," this particular Confederate cavalry unit operated with seeming impunity in the Virginia environs near Washington, D.C.[11]

Little is known of Ormsby's day-to-day existence with the 2nd Massachusetts Cavalry, although as a soldier with the regiment he deployed in the summer of 1863 along with the other troops to begin hunting the elusive Mosby's Raiders. Perhaps it was Ormsby's overall unhappiness with military life that led to his unauthorized absence from the regiment on November 27, 1863, an event that preceded a more serious charge a few months later.[12]

Private Ormsby made a fateful decision to desert Company E on January 24, 1864, taking advantage of his camp security assignment to escape unnoticed. Ormsby started his five-hour security detail at 8 p.m. on January 24, 1864, at the conclusion of which he reported that "all is quiet" and promptly disappeared. About an hour later and for unknown reasons, First Lieutenant A.W. Stone, Company M, 2nd Massachusetts Cavalry, who had prepared the duty roster that assigned Private Ormsby to the camp patrol, went looking for the soldier, but by then he was nowhere to be found.

About a week after Ormby's desertion, Colonel Lowell ordered Captain J. Sewall Reed, 2nd Massachusetts Cavalry, to comb the area near Middleburg, Virginia, in an effort to locate and capture the soldier. Reed organized his unit with a main column and a rear guard under the command of Sergeant B.F. Partridge, Company E, 2nd Massachusetts Cavalry.

A few days after beginning their search, Sergeant Partridge spotted eight Rebels advancing against his rear guard on February 5, 1864.

Two Confederate soldiers, one of whom the sergeant identified as Private Ormsby, led the enemy soldiers straight toward Partridge's rear guard. Ormsby was leading the small Rebel unit and upon seeing the imminent threat fired several shots at Partridge before fleeing the area. Captain Reed heard the volley and immediately "came around with the command ... saw the prisoner [Ormsby] turn in the saddle and fire in the direction of our party." In a desperate bid to avoid capture, Ormsby "jumped his horse into a creek," and while hastily escaping the area fired a few more shots. Partridge returned fire, rapidly sending 11 rounds in the deserter's direction, but all missed their mark. At this point Ormsby probably realized that his arrest was inevitable, as Partridge swiftly crossed the stream and cornered his prey.[13]

One day after Ormsby's arrest, Colonel Lowell convened a drumhead court-martial. The trial started promptly at 5 p.m. on Saturday, February 6, 1864, at the Headquarters of the Cavalry Camp located near Vienna, Virginia. The judge advocate read the criminal charge, "Desertion to the enemy ... dressed in the Rebel uniform and armed and in the act of using his arms against the United States."

The court-martial moved quickly after Ormsby plead not guilty. Four prosecution witnesses refuted he prisoner's innocence, and each in turn briefly described the events leading to his arrest. Without a doubt, the

A DRUM-HEAD COURT-MARTIAL.

Political cartoon of a drumhead court-martial (no known copyright. Special Collections and College Archives, Musselman Library, Gettysburg College).

most damaging testimony came from Sergeant Partridge, who unequivocally identified Ormsby as the leader of the small Rebel unit.

In the concluding moments of the military trial, Private Ormsby, "having no testimony to offer in defense," stood before the drumhead court-martial and made a rambling statement. He began with the admission that "I deserted from here to go home and see my parents." Ormsby hoped to fund his travel to Boston after selling the two cavalry horses taken when he deserted. Unfortunately, Mosby's Raiders captured the deserter and unceremoniously took the horses, after which "I were taken ... up above Middleburg and left with a widow lady.... I was acquainted down there with some ladies."

Before meeting the "ladies," a "young man named Davis" suggested they "get some liquor." It was a tempting offer "and I got drunk." Ormsby resumed his journey toward Aldie, Virginia, presumably to meet the "ladies," and before arriving there met an unnamed man inquiring about Yankees in the area. Soon afterward a large party of men showed up, with Ormsby lamely admitting, "I knew two of them."

Ormsby's explanation of the events surrounding his desertion sounded hollow, but the prisoner, no doubt sensing his impending conviction, related that the group of men surrounding him spotted a Union detachment and attacked. In response, Ormsby admitted, "I drew my revolver then and cocked it and it went off." Perhaps recognizing the incriminating comment went too far, Ormsby tried walking it back by adding, "I was so drunk that I couldn't see nothing at all and I turned down and tried to jump a creek but my horse couldn't jump and I got off on foot. I could scarcely stand I was so intoxicated." Ormsby concluded his defense with an apology. "I know I done wrong and I'm sorry for it and I think I was always counted a sober man." For the prisoner the outcome was a foregone conclusion following the court-martial, where the members after "mature deliberation upon the evidence" found the prisoner guilty of desertion and that for his punishment he "be shot to death."

Colonel Lowell ordered Ormsby's execution the day following the drumhead court-martial. The execution took place at noon on a cold, windy day near Vienna, Virginia, on February 7, 1864. The condemned man sat glumly on top of his coffin and somberly addressed the assembled troops. "Comrades! I want to acknowledge that I am guilty and that my punishment is just. But I want also that you should know that I did not desert because I lost faith in our cause.... Boys I hope you fire well." The firing squad did just that and mercifully ended Ormsby's life.[14]

Ormsby confounded his executioners and returned from the grave by taking advantage of a rendezvous sponsored by the *Banner of Light*'s public séances. His homily was philosophic and forgiving, without a trace of animosity directed toward his executioners It was a placid mental state resulting from a loss of conviction in the war effort, issued by an unhappy former soldier.[15]

Just prior to deserting, the soldier's spirit regretted that his command rejected his request for a health-related military discharge. After concluding that no honorable options were left, Ormsby impetuously decided that desertion was the only path to escape a miserable military life. Acting out what seemed a passive suicidal impulse, the soldier's spirit exclaimed, "I might as well release myself by desertion, even if I am shot, as to die there.... My God! I had rather be shot as a deserter than do it under the conditions that existed around me."

Ormsby's spirit was magnanimous in death by releasing his captors and executioners from any guilt. "I do not return sir, with a spirit of revenge against my superior officers who ordered that I be sent higher so early in the morning.... They did what was right to them; and I deserted because I was heartily tired of that way of living, and sick, besides. I knew I should die, anyway, and I said to myself, I might just as well die as a deserter, as to linger out a miserable existence."

Even though Ormsby's spirit exonerated the members of his military command, he had thoughtful advice for the public at large. Asking but not expecting a compassionate verdict, the spirit continued, "I'm well aware that the deserter is looked upon with cold eyes and a still colder heart, by the greater part of humanity; and I am aware, also, that had humanity the power to read human hearts, they might be led to exercise more sympathy and less censure. But as they have not the power, I suppose we must take whatever they see fit to offer us."

The *Banner*'s portrayal of William Ormsby contrasted sharply with official records. Aside from a fondness for alcohol, the official records do not document any health issues motivating the soldier's desertion, nor does the newspaper's story make any mention of his apparent Confederate conversion. Ormsby's spirit message also omitted any reference to the gunfire aimed at his former unit members and the harrowing escape attempted and thwarted.

The *Banner of Light* printed a sympathetic version of a man executed for desertion to the enemy, although the rush to judgment and the harsh sentence quickly imposed by the Massachusetts Cavalry unit could be viewed as depriving the soldier of a fuller, fairer hearing. None of this surfaced at the séance. Ormsby instead chastised an insensitive society unwilling to look beyond a label and consider the person's thoughts and feelings. It sounded a lot like the public's contemptuous disregard of Spiritualism: a condemnation without contemplation. In that sense, Ormsby's spirit message resonated with spiritualists, as both were victims of an imperfect human morality that would only be perfected in the afterlife. A case could also be made that the *Banner of Light* was humanizing desertion and indirectly advocating for its less severe punishment.

Fourteen soldiers killed at the Battle of Antietam returned as spirits, with some arriving just a few months after the battle and the remainder coming periodically throughout the Civil War. Interestingly, the November 15, 1862, edition of the *Banner of Light* first reported the communications from Confederates Colonel Alexander Harris and Lieutenant Jacob Buckingham, who were supposed casualties of the battle, but neither has historical record confirmation.[16]

Alexander Harris's precognition of death weighed on his mortal mind, and sensing that a fatal future was inevitable, he reassured his friends and family that he would return. His embryonic belief in Spiritualism gave birth to his spirit's awkward séance, during which he tepidly wondered whether a Confederate officer would be welcomed. The spirit's soliloquy ensued after gaining Mrs. Conant's assurances of a fair hearing.[17]

Colonel Harris was 42 years old when his spirit life began. His brief autobiography included a stint as a printer in New Orleans, followed by unspecified business in Kentucky, from which point he joined the Rebel cause. At the Battle of Antietam the officer described grievous wounds to his left arm and shoulder that necessitated an amputation, while adding a dispassionate footnote that prompt medical attention would have spared his life.

For some inexplicable reason the spirit needed to pledge his personal identity. Speaking to Mrs. Conant, the soldier said, "I have a favor to ask. It is this: that you will ask the friends to whom I come, to forward you, if they can, something that shall give you proof that I am the person I say I am." It seemed an odd request because Mrs. Conant expressed no doubts and sought no such reassurances. On the other hand, maybe the *Banner of Light* posted the spirit's request in an effort to forestall accusations of deception.

Lieutenant Jacob Buckingham was the other hesitant Confederate officer propelled to tell his friends and family about his demise. Buckingham hailed from Charleston, South Carolina, and counted his wife, two children, father, and three brothers among his surviving family members. None knew of his death, and through the séance the spirit wanted to convey this outcome.[18]

Buckingham arose from the dead two weeks after being "wounded first in the shoulder, and subsequently shot through the head, and died quietly, without much suffering," at the Battle of Antietam. Before the séance, the only news that had filtered back to his family suggested that he was a prisoner of war, an ambiguous fate that left open the possibility of a mortal reunification. Death closed that door, but his spirit proposed an alternative: "Inform them of my ability to return and commune with them, and my desire to do so." His only caveat was to avoid any political discussions "and lay aside all enmity."

The *Banner of Light* published spirit messages from seven dead soldiers killed at the Battle of Antietam in 1863. None of the seven names could be confirmed with existing historical records.

Joseph Whittier was a 19-year-old soldier supposedly killed at the Battle of Antietam on September 17, 1863, while fighting with the "35th Regiment, Massachusetts Infantry, Company E."[19] Historical records do not associate that name with the 35th Regiment, Massachusetts Infantry, Company E, although there is a match with the 34th Regiment, Massachusetts Infantry, Company E.[20] According to historical records, Joseph H. Whittier, 34th Regiment, Massachusetts Infantry, Company E, mustered out of service on June 16, 1865.[21]

Whittier's family knew of his death, but that did not stop the spirit from reaching out to them through a medium. Prior to entering the army the former soldier was a boiler maker in training and made friends in that trade that he also hoped to visit with. Apparently, soldiers' spirits were lining up to meet with mediums, forcing each to wait his turn, and a "good many of the boys say they've been, and most of them say they've got to send for a pass from this place to their friends ... it's a good deal harder to get a pass home from here than in the army."[22]

One of the officers among the spirit class of 1863 was Lieutenant Walter Hillyard, a 28-year-old man from Greensboro, Alabama. Hillyard was wounded at the First Battle of Bull Run when a bullet passed through his arm, an injury he subsequently recovered from, only to lose his life the following year at the Battle of Antietam.[23]

Somehow Hillyard made his way to Boston and joined Mrs. Conant's séance, but in speaking of his wish to meet with friends and family he seemed uncertain whether such arrangements could be made in Alabama. Conant gave a half-hearted reassurance reasoning that there must be mediums in the Southern state but the first step was publicizing his message in the *Banner of Light*, which seemed to offer a sort of advertisement that might attract a local medium's interest.

Hillyard's ascension to heaven created a growing influence on his political views. He still remained implacably opposed to the Union war machine, indignantly proclaiming that "I am fully satisfied with the course I pursued while here on earth. You doubtless believe you are doing right, and you will, I suppose, at least give us credit of thinking the same way.... I believe the war spirit was born with you at the North."

News from Earth kept the spirits involved with their mortal brethren, as suggested by Hillyard's recognition "that your President has issued a Proclamation declaring the slaves in all disloyal states free." The soldier's spirit did not fully endorse the move, but in a sign that his morality was adapting to the liberal spirit world he admitted that "I am not entirely antagonistic to Liberty or Freedom in any or all of its forms."

Hillyard desperately wanted a private meeting with Benjamin Hillyard, an uncle serving with "Stuart's Cavalry." It seemed unlikely that a message would reach him since Hillyard could not provide the specific location that Mrs. Conant requested. Nonetheless, Hillyard hinted at the message's subject by declaring that "most of the systems of religion belonging to the earth are good for very little" and obliquely indicated that his evolving views on slavery would be discussed.

The Civil War not only fractured the nation but also ruptured family relations, as witnessed by Levi H. Griswold. Griswold's father was a staunch Union man residing in Maryland and warned his son against taking up arms for the Confederacy, which turned out to be sensible but ignored advice. The son traveled south to Montgomery, Alabama, and although initially hesitant to become a soldier finally succumbed to the pressure brought to bear by friends and neighbors.[24]

Griswold was 28 years old when he died at the Battle of Antietam, leaving behind an impoverished wife and two children. His avowed purpose in visiting Mrs. Conant's séance was to mend fences with his father, which he attempted with two confessions. With an emotional appeal, Griswold first wanted to make it clear that his wife had no influence on his political views and that he fervently trusted his father would support his surviving family and not hold her responsible for his actions.

Perhaps his father's abolitionist stance spurred Griswold's spirit to admit, "I felt at heart that I was doing my duty when I took up arms against the North, and I feel that in one sense I did right in fighting for slavery. Were I on earth again, in my own body, I certainly would not hold slaves, for I now see that there is a better highway upon which to travel." Whether this new-found sentiment resulted in Griswold's father forgiving his son's rebellion and supporting his family was unknown.

Spiritualism's appeal in the South was less notable than in the North, but Thomas Ormsby suggested that the faith had followers. Ormsby returned nine weeks after a mortal wound ended his life at the Battle of Antietam. He was 39 years old at the time and was born in Troy, New York, but moved south and for the 17 years before his death he lived in Louisiana and Alabama. He was solidly behind the Confederate cause not because of slavery "but because I see no possible chance for North and South to remain together, or to be at peace with each other. They differ in climate, soil, thought and feeling."[25]

Ormsby wanted to share his political thoughts with his brother, "who is in office under the Confederate Government," not through Mrs. Conant's intervention but wanting instead to speak through a local medium. After a moment's reflection the soldier's spirit recalled that his brother "some two or three years since, he visited a place—I believe they styled it a circle—somewhere in New Orleans." With that memory, Ormsby's spirit was optimistic that a reunion could take place near his former Southern abode.

Rambunctious mortals seemed to settle down in the afterlife and focus on mending misdeeds perpetrated while alive, and Sidney. T. Graves was among that collection. He was a boisterous, egotistical spirit who "always knew I was better than some folks when on the earth," an assertion that earned a rebuke from Mrs. Conant, who sternly added that "we have no right to judge others."[26]

Graves's spirit was unflappable despite the criticism, and under the insistence of his host he still provided only the most parsimonious details of a military career that ended at the Battle of Antietam. He identified no battle units, but from his home in Pennsylvania Graves joined the Federal army and made the ultimate sacrifice when 32 years old.

Mrs. Conant asked the spirit to provide more details of his life to prove his authenticity and help relatives identify him. Graves's spirit obliged the *Banner*'s medium by comparing his rowdy life to that of his pious brother. During his mortal existence Graves was part scoundrel and part gambler. At the age of 19 he stole an uncle's horse and only his relative's good-natured dismissal of the crime kept Graves out of jail. Prior to his enlistment, Graves was a gambler and apparently not very lucky, which may have been the factor motivating his interest in joining the army and providing a more stable income for his wife.

After leaving home, Graves was comforted by his brother the pastor's promise to support his wife. All seemed to go well until the soldier died at Antietam, after which the pastor's beneficence ended. In a darkly veiled threat, Graves asked Mrs. Conant to help relay a message to the petty preacher: "Be kind enough to inform him that I aint dead." The spirit's story exposed his brother's pious hypocrisy and suggested that death did not prevent retribution.

One of the great tragedies of the Civil War happened all too often when family and friends did not know the fate of a soldier. Lieutenant William Conway had two important messages for his father John T. Conway, who still lived at the family home in Montgomery, Alabama. The Confederate soldier's spirit clarified "that I believe my father understood that I was wounded at Antietam, and was taken prisoner by you. I was not taken prisoner, but died on the field of my wounds, and was buried there."[27] Even more heartbreaking was the spirit's disclosure about his mother. Shortly after arriving in the spirit world, Conway apparently met his mother, who died from fretful apprehensions wondering about her son's fate. It was an outcome that could have been avoidable had she known about his death and come to terms with the loss while still earthbound. The spirit's message seemed clear enough in suggesting that timely communications with a medium could moderate a serious, suffering suspense.

Montgomery, Alabama, sent another former soldier to meet with Mrs. Conant, and like the others this spirit had a message for his family. Thomas Christian fought for the Confederacy and died at Antietam, but "they have never been able even to recover my body since death ... my folks felt very bad because they were deprived of that they held so dear."[28]

Christian was 40 years old when he died at the Battle of Antietam. Prior to his death Christian was a dry goods merchant in Montgomery, which supported his wife, two sons, and a daughter. The soldier's spirit remained loyal to the Rebel cause, although hinting that his views might

Bodies of Confederate artillerymen near Dunker Church (Library of Congress, Prints and Photographs Division, Washington, D.C.).

change with the afterlife's enlightenment. He reassured his family that he was happy and looked forward to an Alabama medium arranging further contacts.

The *Banner of Light* reported messages in 1864 from three soldiers killed at the Battle of Antietam. As for others, there was not an exact match with historical records. William H. Smith came closest being "of the Thirty-Fifth Massachusetts, Company A."[29] William H. Smith was a common name among Massachusetts soldiers, but despite the shared sobriquets, none precisely matched the spirit's statement. A soldier by that name served with the 35th Regiment, Massachusetts Infantry, Company D, but was still alive after the Battle of Antietam.[30]

Smith was a genial spirit who quickly admitted that it took a long time to return, but having done so he wanted to inform his brother Henry about his death. It was a fairly graphic account that began when "I was wounded in the arm. I stood that pretty well, until I got shot through the shoulder. I didn't cave in then, neither. The next thing I knew, my head was in one place and the rest of my body in another."

It was a traumatic injury, with the soldier's spirit recalling that "the sensation was something like two worlds coming together with a crash. I didn't think I was killed, at first. I had an idea that something or somebody was, yet it didn't seem as though it was me. But then I examined my body a few hours afterwards, I ascertained it was minus the head, so I came to the conclusion that I must have gone out, I suppose head first."

Smith downplayed death, telling the *Banner of Light*'s readers that the transition was not a dreadful event and they need not fear it. After all, his spirit could still communicate with the living and with an oblique compliment to Mrs. Conant indicated that all he needed was "a first-rate talking machine."

The Battle of Antietam cost the brave and resolute soldiers of the Andrew Sharpshooters dearly, with that one campaign accounting for 25 percent of desertions, 52 percent of mortal wounds, and 72 percent of battlefield deaths suffered by this unit throughout its distinguished record of military service during the Civil War.[31] In one of the briefest of messages published by the *Banner of Light*, a probably fictional Jerry Deering "of the Andrew Sharpshooters, killed on the 17th of September, at Antietam, would be glad to talk with his friends."[32]

Jim Paige, also claiming service with the Andrew Sharpshooters, was a more talkative spirit. Like his supposed comrade, the 22-year-old Paige died at the Battle of Antietam and used Mrs. Conant's séance to send a message to his mother. A former lieutenant from the battle unit who apparently believed in Spiritualism while alive helped arrange Paige's séance.[33]

Paige was a reckless youth and religion played little role in his life, despite a mother who was "one of those good people who believes in baptism, church, creed, sacrament, and such things ... she's feeling pretty bad, because she thinks I'm suffering sorry for deeds done in the body. But it aint so; so she need't feel bad about me, for I'm just as well off as I deserve to be in the spirit world." It was a comforting message for the mother, but it also alluded to the folly of embracing traditional religious practices.

On the second anniversary of the Battle of Antietam, the *Banner of Light* published a message from Richard S. Andrews on September 17, 1864. His spirit helped address the sometimes quite lengthy time span between death and subsequent reemergence at a séance. As Andrews noted, "I was killed at Antietam. I suppose you'll say that was a good while ago, for one who promised to come back to earth within twenty-four hours. Well, I've no apology to make.... I did the best I could to fulfill my promise, but somehow there was always a crowd before me."[34]

Andrews was a medium during his days on earth, and shortly after joining the "Pennsylvania Reserves" he made a compact with fellow soldiers Charley Allen, Philander Yulee, and Jake Porter that he would return from the spirit world if he died on the battlefield. From that trio, Porter was the least inclined to believe in Spiritualism, and as a testament to his authenticity Andrews reminded him of the two-year-old conversation during which the promise to return was made.

Allen was more in tune with Spiritualism, based on his sisters, whose routine practice of receiving communications from beyond made him receptive to the faith. Andrews did not elaborate about Yulee's beliefs, but his inclusion among the group suggested he at least leaned in that direction.

After explaining his tardiness in returning from the grave, the soldier's spirit commented on the seesaw nature of the Civil War. His spirit expounded specifically on the Union army's failure to decisively defeat the enemy and end the rebellion. Andrews assigned the blame to irresolute, apathetic, and unreliable soldiers and warned, "Oh, God help 'em when they come on the other side, for it's whipping enough they'll get there."

Circling back to Spiritualism, Andrews concluded his visit with Mrs. Conant by proudly proclaiming his four-year history as a medium skilled in "speaking, and pretty well for physical manifestations." Now forever residing in the spirit world, Andrews encouraged his earthbound friends to find a medium so he could "convince them that there is a life after death, and that we can cross the river and come back and speak."

The war was over when the *Banner of Light* published the message from Robert Reidelberg, a soldier born in Hanover, Germany, who moved to Pennsylvania and from there joined the "9 Reserve Corps." Reidelberg's spirit was foggy on details such as how long he had been dead, but he remembered falling at the Battle of Antietam after "I was shot in five or six places before I found it was time for me to lay down me musket and go to the spirit-land."[35]

Reidelberg's spirit repeatedly heard the plaintive cries of his wife wistfully wishing for his return, but the former soldier knew his wife Charlotte would be scared to death if he appeared as a ghost. With this in mind the soldier's spirit was determined to send a message through a medium to his wife, but was continually bumped by others presumably ahead of him in a very long queue awaiting their turn. Apparently, patience was a virtue that rewarded both earthlings and their heavenly counterparts.

The *Banner of Light* published 20 spirit messages from the two Battles of Bull Run, with 11 from the Second Battle of Bull Run appearing at a séance. None of the spirits have historical records precisely documenting their authenticity as soldiers.

Among this group of 20, the first spirit's message came from William Chamberlain just a few weeks after the Union army suffered a dramatic loss at the First Battle of Bull Run.[36]

Chamberlain was a volunteer with the "Second Maine Regiment, Co. A" and died in the hospital after receiving a shoulder wound. Before

Visiting the battlefield at Antietam (*Frank Leslie's Illustrated News*, October 18, 1862).

joining the army, the former carpenter lived in Portland, Maine, and was presumably consumed with patriotic fervor, as suggested by his spirit communicating deep disappointment at his quick death, which robbed the soldier of future glory.

The soldier's spirit directly attributed his death and the humiliating battlefield loss to poor leadership and alluded to a consensus in the spirit world: "I don't speak for myself, I suppose you all know; but it's high time somebody did. If you ever expect to conquer the South, you must send out better officers ... you don't know what you are doing, when you send out boys in command, who know nothing of military science, and still less of what belongs to humanity."

Confederates were always welcomed at a *Banner of Light* séance, and their musings were supposedly enlightened glimpses of how the enemy fared after death. For most spirits, animosities stayed on earth, and any remnants seemed to lighten with the afterlife's illumination. Joseph Stillings was a jeweler from Montgomery, Alabama, who died at the First Battle of Bull Run, and even after nine months in the spirit world he had not completely reconciled his suspicions of Northerners when complaining to Mrs. Conant, "Excuse me, but you Yankees are in the habit of carrying two faces."[37]

Stillings was on a mission to speak with his son, and that overruled his doubts and dislikes. It was part business and part pep talk, but the soldier's spirit seemed resigned to not connecting with his son through a medium in his home town. He recognized the South's wartime peril, too: "We are much dispirited at home, because the Yankees seem determined to place more than half their feet on ground not their own."

Forgiving human transgressions was especially difficult for Nathaniel Jackman, a 25-year-old Union soldier from Corliss, Indiana, who was wounded at the First Battle of Bull Run and subsequently imprisoned "in Richmond, one of the meanest holes you ever saw. Yes, I've been there, between heaven/hell and earth,—living sometimes on a crust of bread, sometimes without it."

The terrible ordeal left a bitter taste in Jackman's mouth that could only be removed through revenge. Spirit life only seemed to harden his resolve. It was a sentiment he justified, even though "I know it's a revengeful feeling to have, stranger, but I died with it, and I can't help it." Jackman implored his family to avenge his death, but with little prospect of that happening, he left the séance with Mrs. Conant's fond farewell.[38]

Jack Woodbury was a 23-year-old soldier with the "New York Zouaves" who died at the First Battle of Bull Run but still had plenty of fight left in him. His spirit demanded that Mrs. Conant "Tell the boys to fight like the devil, and tell them I'll be there pretty soon. Come, I'll thrash you if you aint quicker. I want a uniform. Trot off and get me a uniform-come, be lively; I don't want to be here all day."[39]

Despite numerous imperious requests for a uniform, it soon dawned on Woodbury's spirit that he could only talk through the *Banner*'s medium since his ethereal remains would not support a uniform. A sober spirit thought for a moment and suggested a substitute: "Well, if you haint got a uniform for me, give me a drink, then—give me a punch."

Certain rules governed the interactions between a spirit and a medium, but the means by which they were declared was often unclear. Robert Collins received some basic instructions from somewhere but he tried to push the boundaries. Collins died on the battlefield and "I went out slick as an eel. I's in the battle out there at Bull Run.... They don't wait for you to finish up your business, there."[40]

Like most soldiers, Collins considered the prospect of death as quite remote; as a consequence, he made no arrangements for his loved ones or the management of his store. The main reason for Collins's appearance at the séance was the disposition of several thousand dollars, which the worried spirit hoped Mrs. Conant would convey to his brother Dick. His final wishes included a sizeable sum for Louisa Gannett and the remainder for his brother.

Almost instantly, Collins reconsidered his request, seemingly motivated by distrust of his brother's fidelity in the arrangement. The apprehensive spirit proposed an alternate solution and asked Mrs. Conant if he could borrow her body for a few days, travel home, and through her, personally distribute the money. Collins interpreted her silence as a refusal, glumly concluding, "I don't know what will become of three or four thousand dollars in three or four weeks."

War had its terrible moments, and Charlie Hiland of "the New York Zouaves" had such a story. Hiland died at the First Battle of Bull Run and was uncertain whether it was a bullet or sword that terminated his military service. At the time of his demise, Hiland "was twenty-two years ... somewhere about five feet, six inches in height ... sandy complexion ... hair rather inclined to curl ... [and] under my left eye was a scar, received in a little muss about two years ago."[41]

Hiland's wife Jane nervously awaited details of her husband's death, which proved to be fairly gruesome. The soldier's uneasy spirit was still upset, not with his battlefield death, but because "I was buried four days after my death took place, and nine days after I was dug up, and a sort of dissecting process was gone through with, the result was my thick skull was carried into Virginia as a trophy of rebel victory over the Federals."

Hiland implored his wife to shed no tears over his death and desecration, claiming that her melancholy would only inflame his anger and his appetite for revenge. For readers of the *Banner of Light* his message portrayed the Rebels as a reprehensible, heathen lot, but perhaps in an effort to defuse incitement, the spirit cautioned against reprisals.

Not every soldier had the good fortune to die on the battlefield, according to Joseph L. Sawyer, whose death came from a lingering week-long fever after a minor foot injury. Sawyer died in a Rebel hospital after being captured by Confederate forces at the First Battle of Bull Run, but the soldier's spirit did not blame his captors for the medical care that resulted in his eventual demise.[42]

Sawyer's spirit quizzed Mrs. Conant: "They say you publish some kind of a magazine, or book, in which you print our letters to our friends. Is it so?" The *Banner of Light*'s resident medium responded favorably to the question, but not before the soldier's spirit expressed annoyance with the "mighty sight of truck and rubbish you have to clear out before you get here." Without further elaboration, whatever aggravating factors stood in the way of the spirit's return had delayed his return by nearly 18 months after the First Battle of Bull Run.

The former 38-year-old soldier finally got his turn to send a message to friends and family after patiently clearing the hurdles that prevented a timely return. His wife and children still lived in Perrysville, Wisconsin, and the soldier's spirit wanted the *Banner of Light* to publish his message inviting them to a séance near their home.

Sawyer had several topics to disclose. He met his father in the spirit land and was pleased that the man no longer abused alcohol, in a reformation that resulted from his ghostly transfiguration. Even more surprising was the absence of a punishing underworld, which totally upended a lifetime of religious teaching. With the supposed authority of an eyewitness, the spirit confessed, "It seems to me if there was such a place as hell ... that I should have gone there, for I never could believe in religion." The spirit's sacrilege was surely a comforting allowance for wayward, irreligious mortals.

Two spirits from the First Battle of Bull Run sent messages in 1864. James L. Smyth, "from the 9th Michigan," died at the First Battle of Bull Run and bucked the conventional assessment of the afterlife, frankly disclosing that "I don't like the spirit-world, sir, as well, sir as some of 'em do; don't like it to live in as well as this world.... No sir, I don't like it; haven't liked it all the time I've been in it." Unsettling the spirit was a premature death that prevented him from routing the Rebels.[43]

Thomas Woodbridge took his time returning, too, but faulted only the complex task of learning the ways of the spirit world. Woodbridge was 19 years old and a newly minted soldier with the "Seventh Vermont, Company A" when death claimed another victim at the First Battle of Bull

Run. His story was full of compassion for an enemy soldier who tenderly carried the wounded man to a hospital, but death was imminent despite the Rebel's ministrations. In a seemingly incongruous conversation, his Confederate caretaker commented, "My dear boy.... I'll tell you truly what I think, and that is that Death will be the first one to claim you."[44]

Now firmly ensconced in the afterworld, Woodbridge hoped to speak with his mother and share insights gleaned from his new abode. He could talk about reuniting with his father, sisters, and friends, all of which would surely bring some sunshine to the woman's melancholy life. At the same time, the spirit admitted, "I've had to turn my attention to something to keep off the blues. We have 'em on our sides sometimes, when our folks think we are a good ways off."

The *Banner of Light* published 12 spirit messages from soldiers who died at the Second Battle of Bull Run, with the first three just a few months after the conflict ended. Henry T. Sanderson was the first to return. The 22-year-old Confederate soldier from Enterprise, Kentucky, died at the Second Battle of Bull Run while supporting the "Virginia Riflemen." His demise was guaranteed after "I received eleven wounds, any one of which have proved mortal. I lived I can't tell how many hours; it's my opinion something like eight or ten."[45]

In those final hours Sanderson's pain was excruciating and his suffering stamped a stubborn mark on his soul that death could not erase. In an effort to forget the agony, his spirit avoided any contact with the living and only reached out to provide advice and to console his mother. His mother was a widow and destitute, as the ravages of war took a toll. With a sense of sadness, Sanderson urged his mother to travel north and live with welcoming relatives in Philadelphia. In parting from the séance, the spirit told Mrs. Conant, "I am anxious for her welfare, and if I was not, my God! I'd not come here. I thank you for all your kind intentions."

Sixteen-year-old Richard Aldrich had the approval of his father, a physician in Montgomery, Alabama, to join forces with the "Montgomery Rifles." He died at the Second Battle of Bull Run, and though every effort to recover his body was made, in the end his mortal remains was not found. Mrs. Conant urged the former young soldier to provide any details that would help his family identify him. As proof, Aldrich recalled a prescient, poignant letter he wrote his mother: "I cannot but feel I am fated; and should I return no more, you will consider that I lost my life in a good cause, and so not regret me." After disclosing that intimate letter, Aldrich's spirit wanted to reassure his parents that his death was painless and he was happy in the spirit world.[46]

Henry A. Kingsbury left behind an invalid sister and a grieving mother, both of whom depended on him for support. When the 21-year-old joined the "10th Ohio Regiment" it probably never occurred to him that he would be killed at the Second Battle of Bull Run, but after being severely wounded and lying on the battlefield for many hours his spirit finally fled his physical body. Kingsbury's sole motivation in speaking at the *Banner of Light*'s séance was to publicize the details of his death and allay any anxieties about his current situation. "I want to say to my mother and sister that I'm dead, as folks say here on the earth, and alive, as they say in the spirit land."[47]

Death did not come easily or quickly for Benjamin Creggan, who lay on the Bull Run battlefield for days after suffering multiple gunshot wounds. The agony was unbearable. "I was wounded in four or five places—I don't know where, but so bad I could only move my head and left arm, and not a drop of water all that time! I thought I could blow out my brains with my pistol, but I couldn't navigate with my left hand at all. I got out my knife and tried to cut my throat, but I couldn't do that."[48]

Creggan's pitiful death spawned an introspective reflection in the 36-year-old former native of Vermont, much of which centered on the failings of organized religion. His elderly mother was a regular churchgoer and she tried to instill that piety in her son, but to no avail. As it turned out, Creggan's impiety was not a factor hindering his afterlife: "I've seen plenty in the spirit land who died with their prayer-books under their head, and the chaplains praying over them, who are no better off than I am, and some of them are not so well off." His spirit espoused no animosity toward chaplains on earth but no one needed their preaching in the

Agony of a wounded soldier (*Frank Leslie's Illustrated News*, **March 15, 1862**).

afterlife. Creggan also wanted to reassure his mother that his rebellious youth did not prevent him from achieving happiness in the afterlife.

Try as he might, Billy Thornton had a hard time coming back because he found "plenty of wires, but the operators are infernal scarce; that's the reason I haven't kept my word." Thornton's "word" was a pledge to speak with his friends after death and prove to them the reality and value of Spiritualism while also sharing the beauty of the spirit world. He hastily mentioned an agonizing death, lying for two days on the bloody fields at the Second Battle of Bull Run before an eternal peace ended his misery.[49]

Thornton's spirit worried that his friends had forgotten his pledge to return and he earnestly requested Conant's assistance for a future séance. "Now give me a coach in New York, and if I don't come, it will be because you don't give me a good one; and I object to riding a bad one." During the requested get-together Thornton planned to advise his friends "to leave off smoking, chewing, and drinking rum ... if they want to be happy when they get on this side."

James Monroe Granby vaguely recalled being "shot through the heart" at the Second Battle of Bull Run, a quick death for the 22-year-old former cigar maker from Hartford, Connecticut. The mortal injury left his spirit confused and hesitant to share much. Granby's only purpose in overcoming his reticence was to inform his mother that her husband was alive and well in the California gold fields, and with that announcement the meek spook quietly departed.[50]

Like many spirits, Peter Connety worried about his family and used the séance to send a message. He wanted to provide material support for his forlorn wife, but that was impossible without a physical body and Mrs. Conant would not provide hers. A frustrated but not discouraged spirit settled for sending a comforting message. His wife Mary Ann apparently lived in Columbia Court, New York, "very near the Bowery," but when pressed for the house number the flustered spirit exclaimed "Faith ... but I've not got the number straight in me head, and I'm afraid to give it, for fear I give that is not right."[51]

Connety was in the "New Jersey 10th, Company C," and before joining that unit was a tailor. Patriotism led the Irishman to gallantly take up arms for his new country, but his military service ended at the Second Battle of Bull Run. Somewhat comically, his spirit conceded that "I think I could handle the needle and a goose better than the musket; though I got pretty well drilled while I was at war; however, of the two, I'd take the needle and the goose, I think."

Many Irish spirits attended a séance, and among them was Michael Kelly, which was a very common name for Union soldiers. This spirit "belonged to the One Hundred and forty-third New York Regiment,

Company I." Historical records document a Michael Kelly in the 143rd New York Infantry Regiment but the company affiliation is missing.[52]

Kelly provided a short biography to prove his identity, which began with his birth in Belfast, Ireland, in 1829. As a youngster around the age of eight years he contracted smallpox, which left both physical and emotional scars. Kelly left Ireland around his 21st birthday and first settled in New Jersey before moving to New York. Kelly married twice, with his first failing: "I had been married about four or five months, my wife tells me she don't like me any more ... so she leaves. I applies papers for desertion ... and I got it, too."[53]

A foot injury incapacitated the soldier at the Second Battle of Bull Run and eventually resulted in his capture by Confederate soldiers. Kelly died at the infamous Libby Prison in Richmond, Virginia; he did not use the séance to castigate the conditions but boasted instead that "I was wounded, that's how I came to be taken. Faith, I don't think I'd have been taken if I hadn't been."

Kelly wanted to meet with his wife as quickly as possible, but his spirit soon learned, "It's all hurly-burly, and all want to come first; but I find it's by law we all come back here, so there's no use in one's trying to get back before another." It was another message from beyond explaining the delay between death and return, which once again suggested that patience was a virtue rewarding both spirits and mortals.

Abram Torrey, supposedly from the "16 Pennsylvania, Company A," was 41 years old when he died at the Second Battle of Bull Run. Many months had now passed, but Torrey's spirit worried about his body. "Part of it is above ground now, waiting for some kind hand to put it under ground." Mrs. Conant assured Torrey that he no longer needed his body and encouraged him to stop fretting about the burial. Torrey conceded that his ex-wife probably did not care about his remains, but when thinking about his mother the spirit disagreed, because "I suppose the old lady'll feel pretty bad because it aint buried."[54]

In classic mythology Keres were death spirits that hovered about battlefields and claimed dying soldiers as victims.[55] Perhaps Moses Adams was familiar with Greek legends, since the soldier's story bore some resemblance to the Keres, albeit totally benign when compared to those evil demons.

Moses Adams was 19 years old and supposedly with the "Eleventh Ohio, Company C," when he died at the Second Battle of Bull Run. He fought tenaciously and continued to fire his revolver even after receiving a dreadful bullet wound to his ear that eventually led to his death. From the spirit world, Adams wanted to reassure his mother that "I'm here, safe and sound, without a body—yes, I've got a body, but it's not like my old one; it's a first rate one, bullet proof.... I've been on the battle-field with it, and the balls whizzed right through it, and didn't hurt me at all." Adam's disclosure suggested that phantoms of war haunted battlefields just like the Keres, but with no ostensible purpose besides adapting to their new bodies.[56]

Doubt drove William Connors, supposedly with the "17th Massachusetts, Company D," to post a message just after the Civil War ended. He died at the Second Battle of Bull Run and complained about his belated appearance at the séance: "I just got here today, after more than five hundred thousand promises. Well, maybe I've stretched it a little. I suppose I have, but then I was promised so many times that I should come."[57]

Just before he died, Connors entrusted Tim Kelley with a sum of money destined for his family, but the spirit was suspicious that if "they ain't got the money, why then it's stopped in Tim Kelley's pocket, that's certain." His spirit had an ominous warning for Kelley: "Now if he should come on the other side, and I knew he didn't give the folks the money, if it's a thousand years in the future, expecting I can feel right toward him ... he'll be very much mistaken." Despite the menacing note, Connors did not seek revenge and was hopeful that his message in the *Banner of Light* would resolve the apparent injustice.

Nine soldiers' spirits returned from the battlefields at Gettysburg; five of these were Confederates, and among that group were four Rebel officers. While others spirits chafed at the seemingly innumerable impediments precluding their timely return, Colonel Thomas Weld went to the head of the line and met with Mrs. Conant just a few days after his death.[58]

Weld's sudden death bewildered his spirit, who was still confused and unhappy because "I have friends, very dear friends, at home, and I believe heaven will never seem heaven to me until I can commune with them." The timorous Virginia native's spirit opened up after Mrs. Conant's assurance that "You are as welcome here as if you had been a friend to us." Her calming comment exemplified Spiritualism's tolerance, which resonated with the faithful and surely appalled its disbelievers.

Colonel Weld's brother was a Confederate lieutenant who was severely wounded and recovering in a hospital. Weld wished his brother well and looked forward to the pair communicating through a medium, during which time his anxious spirit would seek support for his long-suffering family. After learning that "Lee's army had been beaten" at Gettysburg, the sagacious spirit matter-of-factly accepted the eventual capitulation of the Confederate cause.

Colonel Moses Delano followed in the footsteps of his fellow officer and appeared at a *Banner of Light* séance a few months after his death. The 44-year-old officer was wounded at the Battle of Gettysburg and died soon after. His spirit remained loyal to the army he fought and died for, but his passions were now solely focused on holding a séance with his wife in attendance. With a jaunty air, Delano's spirit ask Mrs. Conant to send a message to his wife: "That is what I pray for. Well, cast it out upon the waters. Direct it to Evelyn Delano, Richmond, Virginia, perhaps she'll get it."[59]

Spirits often described their death and what the transition was like. John Grant was a 33-year-old private in the "7th Indiana" who died at the Battle of Gettysburg. Grant analogized his death to a dream-like state: "I—I slept; yes I did; can't say I was dead, for really I don't feel dead at all. I went to sleep after the battle of Gettysburg, and I—I woke up shortly, to find myself in the company with folks I knew had gone to the other world before me."[60]

After collecting his thoughts, Grant's spirit realized he was dead and soon made his way to the *Banner of Light*'s séance, hoping to send a message to his family. He knew his family was terrified of ghosts and wanted to spare them a materialization, opting instead for an Indiana medium who could open a channel between the two worlds and allow unfettered, but presumably less frightful, communications.

Horace Jenning came to Mrs. Conant's séance "with a flag of truce," expecting a less than hospitable reception for a Confederate soldier. The *Banner*'s resident medium swept those concerns aside and was subsequently pleased to hear that the Southern soldier was familiar with Spiritualism, although he quickly added that he was a nonbeliever while still alive.[61]

Jenning's primary reason for attending the séance was to clarify a misconception. "Now my parents think I was taken prisoner, and don't know whether I'm killed or not. But I was killed at Gettysburg, dead killed, shot outright, wasn't taken prisoner at all, and I want my folks to know of my death." All that remained was for the *Banner of Light* to publish the 19-year-old's death notice, which, in homage to the spirit's last request, was done.

Chivalry existed in the spirit world, much to the annoyance of Joe Brown. "By golly, they're always ahead! I never see a woman yet that didn't manage to get ahead of a man.... Well, I thought I was going to get the first chance here, today. I've waited long enough to get it, at any rate, but I didn't get it. Now, you see, I was booked for first chance, but, fortunately for the lady it's a gentleman that has charge of this thing, so he let her come first."[62]

Brown was disappointed with the delay, but once in the séance he turned his attention to requesting a medium in Wisconsin to discuss private business matters. For purposes of identification, the spirit mentioned that he was a private in the "5th Wisconsin" and married just two weeks. To his grieving widow Adelia, the former soldier offered soothing thoughts: "Let her know that I'm not dead, but can come back and talk. I didn't suffer much—didn't have a chance to."

America's Civil War sometimes pitted family members against each other, as Lieutenant Hamilton Burgess, "5th Alabama, Company G," learned shortly after his death at the Battle of Gettysburg. After entering the spirit world, the Confederate officer learned that his surviving brother-in-law was also at Gettysburg, and that revelation left the officer exclaiming that it was "A pretty state of things!"[63]

Despite their different loyalties, Burgess was anxious to speak with his sister Sarah in Buffalo, New York, and inform her of his death on the battlefield. Death had not dissuaded him from backing the South, as he conveyed in a message to Sarah "that I am just as well persuaded as I was before death, that our cause is as near right as yours."

Captain Paul Higgins, "Company E, 18th Virginia," never contemplated his death on the battlefield, but the Gettysburg campaign claimed the Confederate officer's life. In the spirit world, Higgins was astonished to learn that Spiritualism was conquering the heavens. "The last time I was at the North, I heard considerable talk about your Spiritual Philosophy, but I never learned aught of it myself. But I find that there is such a great flood tending this way, that, in coming, one has to fight against wind and tide. The great flood gates seem to be thrown wide open, that all who wish to may come."[64]

Before joining the "10th New Hampshire," Charles Williams was a carriage maker in Concord. His spirit painfully recalled, "The battle of Gettysburg was pretty rough.... I suppose there was a good many that came out with whole heads, but a good many that was left there sure. I laid a long time on the field, and the last few hours I suffered a good deal."[65]

Williams wanted to speak with his brother, who was a sailor onboard the "gunboat Wyandotte." He cryptically hinted at learning about life and death since entering the spirit world and urgently wanted to pass the insights along to his brother. His cheerful closing comments confirmed Spiritualism's rapturous concept of death: "Tell the folks I'm happy, well, and a soldier in the army of the Lord."

The *Banner of Light* published a very short message from a reticent spirit in 1865. The pithy obituary simply stated, "Will you say that Charles A. Graves, of the Florida Invincibles, died shortly after the battle of Gettysburg, and does not live a prisoner, as reported at home?" As usual, the spirit hoped he could reunite with his friends on earth.[66]

The spirits represented in the *Banner of Light* contained two broad types of messages. Roughly half simply confirmed their death, described the afterlife, and wanted to speak with family and friends. The other half's messages were filled with pathos, politics, and philosophic presumptions.

Eight

Pathos, Politics and Presumptions

A few weeks after President Lincoln issued the Emancipation Proclamation, Secretary of War Edwin Stanton promulgated an order on January 26, 1863, declaring "that Governor Andrew of Massachusetts is authorized, until further orders, to raise such numbers of volunteers ... and may include persons of African descent." Governor John A. Andrew needed little prodding, having long supported and vigorously advocated recruiting African Americans for the Union's war effort.[1]

Governor Andrew wasted no time setting his vision in motion, extending command of what would become the first African American military unit assembled in the Northern states to Robert G. Shaw, an ardent abolitionist. Andrew extended a similar offer to Norwood P. Hallowell, and both men, captains at the time, accepted the challenge and the promotions, for Shaw to Colonel and for Hallowell to Lieutenant Colonel.

Shaw and Hallowell spared no effort in selecting the remaining officers of the newly minted 54th Regiment Massachusetts Volunteer Infantry and then turned their attention to filling the ranks, buffeted by "a strong prejudice [that] existed against arming the blacks and those who dared to command them."

Massachusetts could not supply sufficient numbers of African American recruits to populate the 54th Regiment Massachusetts Volunteer Infantry, so recruiting was expanded beyond the regiment's home state. It was an arduous undertaking, beset with persistent public prejudice, but a steadfast organization composed of liberal-minded citizens soon succeeded in raising money and recruits, finally fulfilling Governor Andrew's dream.

In February 1863, recruits began arriving at Ft. Meigs, Readville, Massachusetts, located just outside Boston, for initial medical processing and subsequent military training. Recruiting continued over the following months, as the steady stream soon swelled to 21 officers and 400 enlisted soldiers by April 1863. By the end of May 1863 the unit was ready to join the war.

Early on the morning of May 28, 1863, the 54th Regiment Massachusetts Volunteer Infantry boarded trains for a short trip to Boston. After departing the cars several hours later, the unit marched in triumphant procession through Boston's many streets before arriving at the wharf and embarking on a steamship bound for action against Confederate forces in South Carolina.

On July 8, 1863, the 54th Regiment Massachusetts Volunteer Infantry received orders to join in the assault against Morris Island, South Carolina, a heavily defended Confederate position. Both armies maneuvered for the coming clash, and on July 16, 1863, the 54th began skirmishing with Confederate forces on James Island, which was a vulnerable vantage point from which Union troops could threaten Charleston, South Carolina. General Alfred H. Terry, Colonel Shaw's commanding officer, praised the conduct of the 54th Regiment Massachusetts Volunteer Infantry in the fighting that followed for bearing the brunt of the attack after a brief engagement that left the unit with 14 dead soldiers, 18 wounded, and 13 missing.

Following their first combat engagement, Shaw received orders "to report the regiment to General Strong at Morris Island without delay." It was a short, miserable, rain-soaked boat trip that positioned the soldiers for the assault on the Confederate stronghold stationed at Morris Island's Fort Wagner.

As a gauge of Confederate resolve, 1,700 Southern soldiers stood ready to defend Fort Wagner in what an observer of the day considered "the strongest single earthwork known in the history of warfare." Menacing canon, rifle trenches, and efficient use of the landscape confronted the Union attack, which began with a naval bombardment on July 18, 1863, an assault briskly answered in turn by the occupants of Fort Wagner. Toward the end of the day the Confederate defenders could no longer be seen, and along with an absence of cannon and rifle fire it seemed as if the Southern soldiers had abandoned Fort Wagner, prompting a Union decision to capture the long-sought-after prize.

Colonel Shaw's regiment meantime had completed its grueling movement, and with his tired and hungry troops Shaw reported to General Strong. The brief encounter resulted in Shaw accepting the general's offer that Shaw lead his troops in the attack on Fort Wagner. It was early evening when Shaw's 600-man force received the order to advance. A few desultory shots from Fort Wagner contradicted the enemies' supposed retreat.

Eight—Pathos, Politics and Presumptions 169

Descending darkness cloaked the 54th Regiment's advance across a perilous stretch of nearly one mile of hostile, open terrain, with Colonel Shaw leading the way. Fort Wagner's defenders responded with a withering barrage from their rifles and cannon, which decimated the determined ranks of the 54th Regiment. Undaunted survivors of the fusillade quickened their step, traversed a water-filled trench, and finally breached the fort's ramparts. Colonel Shaw "stood there for a moment with uplifted sword, shouting, 'Forward, Fifty-fourth!' and then fell dead, shot through the heart."

A brief, intense period of close combat followed, but the 54th Regiment was outnumbered by the determined Confederate force, and Union efforts to mobilize another assault on Fort Wagner faltered. The 54th Regiment suffered grievous losses that day, but the regiment's bravery was officially cited. In the battles that followed throughout the 54th Regiment's 26-month tenure, nearly 40 percent were killed, wounded, or reported as missing.

Seven soldiers from the 54th Regiment Massachusetts Volunteer Infantry, all killed in the attack on Fort Wagner, purportedly attended a séance hosted by Frances Conant, the results of which were subsequently

The gallant charge of the Fifty-Fourth Massachusetts Colored Regiment on the rebel works at Fort Wagner, July 18, 1863 (Library of Congress, Prints and Photographs Division, Washington, D.C.).

published in the *Banner of Light*'s Message Department. The list of soldiers included James Peer, William Sowie, Archibald Lewis, William Culnuigh, William Sampson, William Andrews, and William Briggs.

William Briggs was the only name that exactly matched historical records based on the reported regiment and company as published in the *Banner of Light*. William M. Briggs was 21 years old when he enrolled at Readville, Massachusetts, on March 29, 1863, as a private in Company E, 54th Regiment Massachusetts Volunteer Infantry, and was subsequently mustered into service on April 23, 1863, for a three-year enlistment. Briggs was born in Albany, New York, and prior to his enlistment worked as a waiter. In the assault on Fort Wagner he suffered a mortal gunshot wound on July 18, 1863, and died two days later at Hospital Number 6 in Beaufort, South Carolina, leaving behind nothing more than his military accoutrements.[2]

The *Banner of Light* resurrected William Briggs in its Message Department on December 5, 1863. Briggs began his monologue through his entranced medium by acknowledging his death as a member of the 54th Massachusetts Regiment, Company E, at Morris Island as part of the Federal campaign at Fort Wagner. "I got a pretty tough wound at Wagner ... that was altogether too much for me ... so about the second week in July I began to live—I began to *live*—that's the better word. I didn't die."[3]

There may have been a nagging question among the readership of the *Banner of Light* as to why some soldiers' spirits returned and others did not. The newspaper seemed to approximate an answer when Briggs's spirit claimed permission from an unknown entity to return in his ethereal form and reassure his family that all was well. "Folks here in Boston, that is my folks don't know that I'm alive, and can come back.... I can get words through a white skin as well as I could through my own black one."

Having explained how he arrived in the spirit world, Briggs went on to discuss what it was like: "Some things is very much different in this new world, from what they were when I was on earth. Then it was colored folks admitted only to the gallery; now it's colored folks occupying the chief seats. There's the difference between God's law and man's law. For my part, I like the God law best.... I've got the best seat in the crowd."

Briggs ended his visit by extending a phantom hand of friendship and mentorship to "white folks." His arrival to the spirit world marked the transition to an eternal life where remembrance of previous grievances remained but equanimity in relationships prevailed. This fit perfectly with Spiritualism's denouncement of slavery and the vindication of its immorality and consequent rectification of the practice in the afterlife. In another sense it also indirectly rebuked traditional clerics who twisted traditional religious teaching to politically support slavery in a misguided approach that its adherents would find rebuked by God's Law after death.

James Peer was another soldier purportedly from the 54th Regiment Massachusetts Volunteer Infantry who attended a Conant séance. Unfortunately, James Peer's name is not associated with the regiment, although a John Peer of Company B did appear on the muster roles. John Peer was a 21-year-old private who died August 5, 1863, from dysentery while stationed at Morris Island.[4]

Fittingly enough, the story of James Peer, a supposedly late member of the 54th Massachusetts Regiment, appeared in the 1863 Halloween edition of the *Banner of Light*. Peer provided no details about his death or further military information to corroborate his association with the Massachusetts unit.[5]

Frances Conant received messages from spirits while entranced. This was a semiconscious state that did not impair the medium's ability to interrogate her subjects. Her coaxing of James Peer seemingly helped the reluctant spirit share his innermost thoughts, which both paralleled and extended those of William Briggs.

In a similar manner to Briggs, Peer ambiguously explained his presence at the séance as simply being on a heavenly list expected to speak with a medium. After joining the séance, Peer hoped the medium would convey a message to his mother and sister but doubted that outcome, since "I know you don't think much of helping colored folks." Conant interrupted her messenger with a spirited defense asking him not to prematurely judge her motives, a plea countered by Peer, who plaintively noted, "I don't know how it is now, but when I was here I was always treated so. It was the white man first, and black one next."

Peer and Conant quarreled briefly, with the medium insisting that spiritualists harbored no racial prejudice and the soldier's spirit recalling a much different mortal life: "You know I've been brought up so all my life, and it's hard to get over it." Setting their contretemps aside, Peer once again requested that the medium make contact with his mother and sister. Conant agreed to send a letter to Sarah Peer, his sister, who would in turn relay its contents to his mother. James Peer appreciated Conant's offer: "Well, I'll be obliged to you if you do what you can for me."

Peer and Conant's mildly contentious exchange cast the spiritualist as a defender of racial equality by doing her utmost to convince a wary spirit through her words and deeds. It also suggested that shedding a physical body did not heal the emotional wounds suffered in life, adding yet another indictment of slavery and the lingering harms it created even after death.

As was the case with James Peer, the exact names of William Sowie,

Archibald Lewis, William Culnuigh, and William Sampson are all absent from historical records associated with the 54th Regiment Massachusetts Volunteer Infantry, although the *Banner of Light* reported that each attended a Conant séance.

At the séance, William Sowie announced his death, which was the result of a mortal wound received attacking Fort Wagner as a member of the 54th Regiment Massachusetts Volunteer Infantry. Sowie was proud of his military service, only lamenting that "I'm kind of sorry I lost my body at the time I did. I'd like to fight a little longer, for I'd just got into the spirit of it." According to his recollection, he was ascending a berm as part of a frontal assault on Fort Wagner when a Confederate bullet killed him instantly. Looking back on his death, Sowie preferred the quick transition as opposed to being wounded: "I was killed outright…. I didn't stay to have any of my limbs cut off. That's a good thing, you know."[6]

Sowie was 22 years old, supposedly hailed from Pittsfield, Massachusetts, and left behind a sister, Celia, and a brother, both of whom he wanted to speak with. The soldier spirit worried that his family would be too scared to meet with a medium and openly questioned Conant in this regard. The *Banner*'s medium offered no specifics but reassured Sowie that "we have full faith that you will." Sowie ended his brief visit will a gallant, "Well, sir, good-day."

An 1864 séance began with an introduction: "Would you be kind enough to say that Archibald Lewis, of the 54th Massachusetts, who fell at Wagner, would be glad to meet his friends?" Lewis quickly reassured the *Banner*'s readers that his death was trouble-free, aided by the frenzied fighting, which acted like a shield and immunized his physical body from the piercing bullets just as he gained Fort Wagner's parapet.[7]

After his death, Lewis was pleasantly surprised by the reception: "In my spiritual home I am not oppressed by color, caste or station. I am respected for what I *am*, not for what I *seem* to be. There's no division there, such as there is on earth." It was a joyous message that the soldier spirit earnestly hoped Mrs. Conant would convey to his sister Rebecca.

Historical records do not connect an Archibald Lewis with the 54th Massachusetts Regiment, which, as previously mentioned, may be due to many factors, including fabrication. His message nonetheless supported Spiritualism's core belief that death corrected social injustices perpetrated in life.

Another unsubstantiated soldier visitor attending one of Conant's séances declared, "I was a member of the 54th Massachusetts, and died from my wound at Morris Island. My name was William Culnuigh." Culnuigh's motivation for speaking echoed others in wishing to get to his surviving family members the message that he was happy and could talk with

Eight—Pathos, Politics and Presumptions   173

them. After arriving in the spirit world, Culnuigh met his father, in an admission that surely tugged at the heartstrings of the *Banner*'s audience members, who naturally ached for a blissful reunion with their departed loved ones.[8]

Culnuigh's conscience troubled him, and before leaving the séance he shared an unrelenting uneasiness. It seemed that some earthly debts were not alleviated by death but continued to haunt the spirit, and so it was with William Culnuigh: "Oh! one more word: tell Mr. Jacobs—he's a second-hand clothes dealer—that I haven't forgotten him, and I'll pay for that coat when he comes on the other side."

According to the spirit message published in the *Banner of Light*, William Andrews "was a private in the 54th Massachusetts, and fell at Wagner." William Andrews was a common name with multiple entries in historical records, but none were associated with the 54th Regiment Massachusetts Volunteer Infantry.[9] Boston-born Andrews was only 18 years old when he entered the spirit world, with the exact cause of his death not noted. Unknown heavenly sources apparently persuaded the young spirit to contact Mrs. Conant and through her to urge his mother "to go to some medium like this, so I could talk."[10]

The last supposed soldier from the 54th Massachusetts to attend one of the *Banner*'s séances was William Sampson, a particularly loquacious spirit. Samson died at Fort Wagner while witnessing the bravery of Colonel Shaw as he stormed the fortification's parapet, a feat he was unable to duplicate owing to orders purportedly received. Unlike others, Sampson did not die immediately and alluded to festering, agonizing wounds that delayed his death.[11]

Prior to his enlistment, the self-admitted private from the 54th Massachusetts Regiment lived on Washington Street in Cambridgeport, Massachusetts, along with his wife Susan, a child, and his mother-in-law. As was typical for returning spirits, Sampson was reaching out to his family. Colonel Shaw apparently nudged the soldier to contact Mrs. Conant. As the meeting progressed, Sampson shared his concerns, hoping that "they aint starved to death ... hope they aint in the almshouse." Conant offered to ferry his message to a grocer who knew the family, implying that the man's generosity would relieve any suffering.

In his closing moments at the séance the soldier spirit inquired about the war and in a twist shared an insight gleaned from his new home: "Old Uncle Abraham is going in, they say, for the next four years. Oh, the most of 'em in the spirit-world are in for it. Yes, sir, he's bound to go in."

Sampson's monologue was notable for its political commentary that offered an unmistakable endorsement for President Lincoln's reelection from the spirit world. Wavering spiritualists considering otherwise had to reconcile spirits' stumping for Lincoln versus their earth-based choice. The outcomes of those personal deliberations will never be known with certainty, but the *Banner of Light* surely sought to tilt the balance in the President's favor with a helping hand from beyond.

The *Banner of Light*'s adamant antislavery advocacy seemingly crossed the great barrier between life and death, motivating slaves and repentant Southern slaveholders to share their thoughts. None of the spirits' mortal bodies could be verified with historical records.

Without a doubt, the most poignant plea came from Alice Burnap. Alice was the 19-year-old daughter of Oliver Burnap, whose outrage and sadness brought the girl back from the spirit world after two and half years of silent repose. The anguished spirit implored her father "to cease, oh, cease at once his murderous work. He has shot, this day, eleven of his slaves and they have come to me full of revenge."[12]

At the séance, Alice needed Mrs. Conant's help in getting a message to her father. That message asked her father to find a medium in Conway, North Carolina, where Alice could make a spirited appeal to him "to cease his murderous work." Oliver's father was a minister and would join with Alice at the séance, hoping to avert the slaveholder's seemingly inevitable descent to hell.

Colonel Thomas Jones did not escape the fate that awaited Oliver Burnap but somehow managed to momentarily wrest himself free from the Devil's clutches to attend a séance. Among his many sins were fighting for the Confederacy, which led to the abject impoverishment of his family as the tides of war turned against the South. He made the wrong choice with a decision not shared by his wife and two sons, who remained loyal to the Union but still lived in Georgetown, South Carolina.[13]

Jones's return was an attempted expiation for not liberating his slaves. The soldier's spirit addressed the issue delicately and obliquely, lamenting that "certain members of my household believe that they are free, that they were free at my death; that I left papers granting them their freedom. I promised to do this, but I put Death off too far, for I never had a thought that I should be killed in battle, and so I neglected doing my duty."

Apparently the soldier died at the February 1862 Battle of Roanoke Island but had to wait nearly a year before he could attend a séance. Making amends meant reaching out from the underworld, and fortunately for Jones one of his sons was a medium-in-waiting. The soldier's spirit eagerly anticipated the opportunity to kindle his son's psychic gift. To achieve this, Jones only needed his son "to take a seat at a table, on which is paper and pencil, and to sit quietly and as passive as possible, in order to receive spirit influence." Once the son was mesmerized, the soldier's spirit would provide all necessary instructions to free the slaves.

Eight—Pathos, Politics and Presumptions 175

Jones's message was stark and clearly conveyed the condemnation waiting Southern slaveholders. For this spirit there seemed to be no pathway for redemption, only an eternal punishment seemingly at odds with Spiritualism's belief in a benevolent afterlife. After making his appeal, Jones presumably returned to the underworld, leaving his fate and penance unknown.

Philip Mason surely earned an abolitionist's ultimate contempt as an unrepentant profiteering slaveholder. Mason supposedly died shortly after losing a leg during the 1863 Battle of Chancellorsville and was upset that dying declarations made to friends went unheeded.[14]

The soldier's spirit recalled his birth in Massachusetts and later life in Kentucky, where he bought and sold slaves, but "after awhile I got quite rich and abandoned that business, and went into Louisiana, bought me a plantation and settled down." At the outbreak of the war, the new plantation owner joined forces with the Confederacy and was later killed in action.

Mason's reason for returning was to speak with his brother-in-law, now in charge of his former estate. The soldier's spirit would not elaborate on his concerns but in requesting Mrs. Conant's help brashly admitted that "I did fight against you when here, I'm not sorry for it, for I'm not sorry for anything." Interestingly, an uncowed Mason somehow avoided the punishment meted out to Colonel Thomas Jones even though his wrongdoings were arguably greater.

Maryland had its share of Southern sympathizers during the Civil War, which greatly troubled Steven T. Dustin, who supposedly "belonged to the 26th Pennsylvania, Company I, and lost my life out here at Murfreesboro." Although light on details, Dustin apparently moved to Pennsylvania, leaving his mother and sisters in Bel Air, Maryland, a small town north of Baltimore and near the state line.[15]

At his séance Dustin exhorted his mother and sisters to renounce their Southern sympathies based on states' rights as the compelling factor causing the conflict unfolding on bloody battlefields, by arguing instead that "I believe that slavery is a curse—that this rebellion was the result of the existence of slavery." Having made his case, Dustin warned his mother to make the right decision: "If she takes my advice, she will do well; if she don't take it, she won't do quite as well."

It would seem that some Confederates were reluctant warriors goaded into Rebel service, which was a claim made by Hugh Fitzwilliam at a séance hosted by Mrs. Conant just after the Civil War ended. In their mortal life Southern soldier spirits seemed well off, often living on plantations, and Fitzwilliam fit that narrative with a spacious spread near Albany, Georgia. From that point, his story became morose and sympathetic.[16]

When the war started Fitzwilliam did not rush to join the effort, apparently content with sitting the conflict out. His liberal views and lukewarm support of the Confederate cause earned enemies, particularly when "I said something like this; I believe that slavery is the cause of all this misunderstanding; and, for my part, I hope that it will be wiped out before we lay down our arms."

For *Banner* readers, perhaps this cast a different light on Southern soldiers, suggesting that their support of the Confederacy was compelled. It was an admission that somewhat lessened their moral burden. Fitzwilliam's less than ardent support of the war cost him dearly and converted the man into a victim.

Fitzwilliam's audacious thoughts about the war roused his less sensitive neighbors, who interpreted his traitorous comments as a call to action and "declared their intention to deal harshly with me unless I raised the rebel flag, and, what is more, shoulder the musket." Standing bravely, the beleaguered man rebuffed the threats, hoping his principled stance would quell the dispute. Unfortunately, his determined neighbors had other ideas in mind.

A few nights after the confrontation, a rowdy group gathered outside the plantation, "prepared to act like anything but Christian people toward me." Fitzwilliam began to reconsider his righteous intransigence after surveying the escalating scene and being mindful of his wife and children. Adding to his ethical dilemma was a frightened wife concerned about the crowd's nefarious intentions. In acceding to the mob, Fitzwilliam's spirit explained that his family's safety and not the Southern cause forced his acquiescence.

Fitzwilliam unwillingly surrendered his autonomy, but his lack of conviction made desertion morally acceptable. He never acted on the impulse to flee combat, citing concerns that his family would suffer by the cowardly act, so he plodded on until an unstated illness or injury terminated his military service during the 1865 siege of Richmond, Virginia.

Despite throwing his support to the Confederacy, Fitzwilliam lost everything. His plantation was seized by the Confederate government and used as a military hospital, and his dispossessed family was left in ruins. His spirit now demanded restitution from those neighbors who originally threatened him by demanding that they "seek out my family and give them assistance. So sure as they don't, so sure, some day, vengeance will be visited upon them."

The South's surrender silenced the battlefields but not the long-pent-up acrimony, a painful predicament that Julius Graham hoped to correct. His task was doubly difficult by having to span an interfamilial chasm created by the war and another gap caused by his death. Graham's spirit reached out to Mrs. Conant using her mediumistic powers to bridge those great divides.[17]

Julius Graham picked the wrong side when admitting, "I was captain in the 7th Virginia Infantry, Company K; died while fighting for what I supposed to be Southern rights." His father supported the Union, creating a rift between the two that remained unchanged with the son's death. Further straining their relationship was the son's stubborn insistence that "Yes, I was a dealer in slaves; but allow me to ask who of you are not? The difference is only in the way and manner in which you conduct yourselves toward those who are dependent upon you. But I'm not here to talk about slavery."

Graham's spirit hoped Mrs. Conant would publish his entreaty encouraging his father, his wife, and a friend to overcome their superstitious disbelief in Spiritualism and contact a medium so he could speak with them. For his wife he had business and financial advice, he wanted his friend's help in supporting her, and less confidently he wished for a belated father-and-son rapprochement.

Whether any of this occurred is unknown, since spirits received only one chance to have their visit published in the *Banner of Light*. It would seem that the outcome was unimportant, suggesting instead that Graham's message demonstrated Spiritualism's coming significance in healing the war's emotional wounds. While certainly self-serving, Graham's philosophic analysis of slavery could also be seen as opening a new chapter in Spiritualism's enshrinement of equanimity and individuality.

In a different kind of table tipping, a former slave named George L. Josselyn turned the tables on a mortal nemesis through a display of supreme daring at the Battle of Fort Pillow. Josselyn's spirit provided some background: "I was killed, sir, at Fort Pillow.... I was formerly a slave of Colonel Brown, in Thompsonville, East Tennessee. Later, was owned by a gentleman by the name of Josselyn, in Louisiana, and still later, I owned myself."[18]

The Battle of Fort Pillow turned against the Union defenders, and according to Josselyn's spirit an unnamed Confederate officer demanded their surrender, an ultimatum resolutely refused by Josselyn, who continued the fight until killed. Submission did not come easily to the former slave, particularly when "the officer who ordered me to surrender ... was the son of the owner of the next plantation where I was a slave. He knew me very well, and probably didn't like some things I said, and the way I managed."

Josselyn relished the day when that officer arrived in the spirit world. "I'll order him to surrender, and he'll be sure to do it. He'll get down on his knees to me, and ask me to lead him where it is light." It seemed like Josselyn's restive spirit required retribution as a prerequisite for absolution.

Another slave named Prince attended a *Banner of Light* séance with the specific goal of "sending thoughts to Ms. General Bragg and the General himself. I was a slave of General Bragg; been owned by him about seven years." In the Confederate General's absence, his wife supposedly relied on the slave for the management of their plantation in Thibodaux, Louisiana, but Prince had other ideas: "I had a higher General's commands, and his name was General Liberty; and I thought I should obey him."

Prince apparently harbored no ill will against Mrs. Bragg when he announced his intention to leave and follow his dream of joining the Union army to "fight for the freedom of my race." His visit made no further mention of military service or the cause of his death, but speaking from the spirit world, Prince offered to counsel General Bragg on the subject of slavery: "I may be able to give him some light. He needs it bad enough."[19]

Four Massachusetts soldier spirits vented their displeasure with the Catholic Church; none of these was an exact match to historical records. Michael Smith proudly proclaimed his former affiliation with the 26th Regiment Massachusetts Volunteer Infantry, Company D. No recorded entry for Company D lists the common name of Michael Smith, but the regiment did list that name in Company K.[20] Smith died from unknown causes toward the end of 1864, and after spending nine weeks as a spirit decided to come back with two divergent goals in mind: to comfort and advise his impoverished wife and to warn the world about Catholicism.[21]

Smith was vague in alluding to his wife Mary "getting the money that's due her." Whether this represented back pay or a widow's pension is unclear, but Smith had little confidence in lawyers helping and hoped his family would provide the needed assistance. He also wanted his wife and brother to visit a medium, during which time he could expound on the options available to alleviate his wife's hardship. Smith generously invited all of his family to attend a séance but in doing so clearly set some ground rules: "I want them to pay attention to me when I knock at the door. If they don't, begad, I'll tear the house down over their heads, and then take possession myself."

The Massachusetts soldier's spirit had harsh words for faithful Catholics: "I've seen nobody that knows whether the Catholic religion is any help to one. Now what's the use of all this confessing business here, planking yourself down on your knees and going on with a long string, if it's no use when you die?" In another discouraging revelation it seemed that after death Catholics entered a confusing limbo, uncertain where they were and most certainly not enjoying the shortest path toward heavenly bliss.

An even more caustic attack followed with Smith sparing no venom: "Well sir, now I'd like to tell the priest just what I see there, and how I find

Eight—Pathos, Politics and Presumptions

things. He tells us the Catholic religion will take us to Heaven. It's a lie; 'taint so at all; and how the devil should he know when he's not been on the other side at all?" The spirit's rebuke brought a snickering endorsement from Conant, who couldn't refrain from adding, "and you have" been in the spirit land.

Patrick Walsh still smarted from slights received as a native-born Irishman and was hesitant to join the *Banner*'s séance until Conant offered her warm welcome. With her reassurance, the spirit opened up and briefly mentioned losing his life as a captured prisoner from the 20th Massachusetts.[22]

With introductions completed, the soldier spirit dominated the remaining time excoriating the Catholic Church, ostensibly for the purpose of persuading his family to reconsider their allegiance. He scarcely tendered a kind word to his family, being too consumed castigating the Church. "I should like, sir, to have a fair talk with the priest, if I could. ... it's all the one story they have, and a very bad story it is, too ... and I, for one, would like to say something to the priest about this wholesale lying business.... Ah, there's many a poor soul, like meself, that's been deluded by the priest, and when you get across, you got no priest, got no religion, no nothing, anyway."

Walsh painted a dismal future for Catholics, but speaking through Mrs. Conant he suggested redemption's path was through renouncement of the Church and acceptance of Spiritualism. "Well, I like for you to tell the folks I'm out with the Church.... Maybe I couldn't know anything about the Latin, but I could tell about the English and the Irish, and what I know to be truth." The soldier's spirit ended his assault by apologizing for his brashness and promised to be more composed on his next visit.

John O'Brien was a common name among Union soldiers, and helping illustrate that point were two spirits with the same sobriquet from different military units that attended a *Banner of Light* séance. Neither soldier's historical records matched their supposed military service.

The first John O'Brien, "of the 32nd Massachusetts," had only been dead about 10 days before he returned, attributing his demise to yellow fever.[23] As a further testament to the ubiquity of the name John O'Brien, historical records identify three such members in companies A, H, and G of the 32nd Regiment Massachusetts Volunteer Infantry.[24] Since the soldier spirit did not identify his company, it is not possible to further match his name.

Not long after arriving in the spirit world, O'Brien renewed his acquaintance with Father Rooney. "First thing he says to me was, 'Johnnie, you're all right.' I said, 'I'd like to confess.' 'Not to me, but yourself,' he says; and I couldn't understand him at first, but it came to me naturally that I was accountable to meself; that I didn't have any other God to confess to but meself ... the Church is a kind of hold back upon us; keeps you in the traces, you know."

The other erstwhile John O'Brien claimed service with the "10th Indiana, Company C," and returned to provide the details of his death along with a muted swipe at the Catholic Church. As he recalled, "Well, I suppose I was paralyzed by a shell—a passing shell. There was no wound, no bruise upon me at all; and all at once I was unable to use my musket, and then I found myself on the other side." O'Brien reassured everyone at the séance that his death was not painful.[25]

Like others who entered the spirit world, O'Brien pondered his former mortal life and his religious beliefs in particular. "I was in the Catholic Church when I was here, but I don't know at all whether I am there now.... Ah! It's gone out of my head entirely. I got some kind of an idea about God, but whether it's a Catholic or not, I can't tell."

Patrick Burns, of the "32d Massachusetts," lingered several painful hours in a hospital after suffering mortal wounds to the head and arm. His primary impetus in returning from the grave and seeking the *Banner of Light*'s medium was recognition that his wife and family "are fretting themselves to death because I had no absolution." Burns did not need a priestly confessional to relieve that burden, insisting that "I absolve meself, and that's the very best absolution to have."[26]

Burns reduced his new found irreverence to a few choice words: "Ah, the divil with the Church, what do I care for it now." His liberation from a lifetime of conformity came when the spirit of Father Shaw admitted that Catholicism had no place in the afterlife, and, in an ironic twist, it was the priest who encouraged the soldier spirit to speak through Mrs. Conant. It seemed that death broadened the priest's dogma, resulting in a tacit endorsement of Spiritualism.

Michael Devine was another Irishman, supposedly from the 160th New York Volunteer Infantry Regiment, Company I, who returned after three months in the spirit world to formally invite his wife, child, and friends to speak with him. Devine admitted that death had not stilled his pugnacious behavior, "because the fight's not out of me yet," but without mortal Confederates the spirit's passions turned against the Catholic Church.[27]

Devine was disillusioned. His arrival in the spirit world forced a reconsideration of long-cherished religious beliefs after meeting a spirit priest. It was a wizened 80-year-old priest that deflated Devine. "Well, I met him, and I said like this to him: 'Father Higgins, how is it? Where is there any Catholic church in the spirit land? What about the Catholic religion?' 'Michael,' he says, 'the Catholic religion is all very good when

Eight—Pathos, Politics and Presumptions

you are living on the earth. It's a something that's very much like gold and silver. That's all very well to have on the earth, but you can't take it any further than the grave.'"

Higgins's confession upset Devine, who carefully weighed the priest's words before reaching the conclusion that "the whole world was a humbug." With the priest's revelation, the disturbed soldier's spirit lashed out, hoping to spare his wife the same disappointment from a gratuitous religious fealty.

Further criticism of the Catholic Church came from three spirits who did not identify their military units: Dennis Casey, John Murphy, and Patrick O'Connell. Even though they did not provide that specificity, the spirits wanted two points clearly understood: they were all Irish and soldiers.

Dennis Casey emphatically declared, "I was a soldier, and I died fighting for the Ameriky that was my home ever since I came here." Casey was happy in the spirit world and pleasantly surprised that the rules and rigidity of the Catholic Church did not follow him after death. The enlightened spirit now understood the futility of a mortal life devoted to religion and wistfully remembered a carefree cousin. "He's not bound up in the faith; kind of free and aisy.... He has a tender heart, never likes to see anyone suffer. Now I want him to go to my folks ... and talk this way and explain the whole thing to them."[28]

John Murphy spoke from the spirit world about a month after his death and was so focused on alerting his survivors to the errors of the Catholic Church that he made no mention of his military service. Murphy was a staunch believer in Catholicism, having devoted his life to its teachings, but in the afterlife "it was not in the market, anyway; that was what surprised me. All that was told us when here about heaven and hell wasn't true."[29]

The revelations left Murphy confused and unhappy, drifting without the moral anchor the Church provided in life. With his eyes opened to the truth as revealed in the afterlife, the soldier spirit slowly began accepting that a life of good deeds, and not blind obeisance to religious dogma, earned heavenly tribute. It was an alarming discovery, and Murphy urgently wanted to contact his brother Daniel. Speaking through Mrs. Conant, he declared, "I like to talk with him. I've a great deal to say to him; Oh, so much! But I'll not say it here.... Ah, he's a Catholic, clear round; he's a Catholic as much as I ever was meself."

Murphy used his visit to warn not only his brother but the *Banner of Light*'s readership about the folly of following Catholic doctrine. He also took the opportunity to persuade his supposed brother to attend a séance, subtly proselytizing Spiritualism from the grave.

The first words uttered by Patrick O'Connell lambasted his former religion: "Yes, sir: it's hard for a man who has been educated in the Catholic religion ... and when he come to die, find it's all a nothing, anyway. Oh, it's pretty hard; yes, sir, pretty hard." Aside from a brief reference to fighting in the war, he could not budge from obsessing about the failures of Catholicism.[30]

O'Connell was deeply hurt that his earthbound faith meant nothing in the spirit land, leaving him without any support, or so he thought. His spirit mentors patiently educated the novice, and "I've learned this much, that I can confess can lean upon myself, and it's my own good deeds that are going to make me happy, and the only heaven I can get into-if I get into one at all-will be one of my fashioning."

With his old faith upended, O'Connell's spirit thought of his friends and family and wondered, "How am I going to get the idea, that the Catholic religion don't amount to anything, into their heads." Mrs. Conant reminded her guest that Spiritualism provided a platform to "give the truth, always." It was a prudent, thoughtful phantom that decided the best course of action was to meet mortals at séances individually and determine their receptivity to his message. "I'll tell them what I know about the Catholic religion. If they are soft about it, I'll say nothing about religion, but talk about something else."

Dave Carney, "from the 2nd Michigan," met his fate on the banks of the Chickahominy River, an apparent reference to the 1862 Battle of Gaines Mill in Virginia. It took over three years for Carney's spirit to return, as he patiently waited his turn to speak through a medium, but after finally getting to the head of the line he wanted to reassure his mother that his rambunctious, irreligious life had not resulted in an eternal damnation.[31]

From afar, Carney's spirit heard his mother's mournful prayers, a maternal solicitude born from a fear that her son was perdition bound. The soldier's spirit answered those concerns. "I'm just as well off as I deserve to be. I've plenty to do. I liked to help others along here, and there's plenty of poor cusses that want helping up; and the very ones that want helping up most are those that went across in the boat of some religious dogma. I tell you they're the deepest in the mire. I always say, let go of your religion, and follow me."

Carney's spirit not only dismissed traditional religion but insisted that it caused more harm than good. This was an enlightenment that came with death and rebirth in the afterlife. Even after resurrection, the spirit admitted never seeing God, which seemed an odd state of affairs explained by a long-time denizen who admonished his younger charge, "Don't go around looking for God ... for he's always with you."

Eight—Pathos, Politics and Presumptions 183

The spirits condemning traditional religion shared certain similarities: all were Irish, denounced Catholicism, and made their appearance in 1865. It seemed as if the spirits subscribed to the *Banner of Light* and paid particular attention to articles published that year, such as "Catholicism and Spiritualism: The Opposing Religious Systems of the World." Hudson Tuttle supposedly wrote with input from the spirit world this critical essay, which by its very title presumptuously elevated and equated the two religions.[32]

Hudson Tuttle was an ardent acolyte of Spiritualism, influenced like so many by the mysterious Rochester rappings. At the age of 16, from his home in Berlin, Ohio, he became a local sensation, tipping tables and rapping with the dead, but the spirits had different designs for the boy. Tuttle was a prolific author and credited automatic writing as the sole source for his numerous contributions. His inquisitive mind flirted with phrenology, the evolution of human life, and most consistently with the development of organized religions, which he loathed.[33]

Even at an early age, Tuttle's contrarian nature surfaced in discussions about religion. A story from his boyhood illustrated the point. A traveling preacher spent a night at the Hudson home discussing theology. Noting the boy's apt attention, the preacher suggested that his interest boded well for a similar career, which earned a rebuke from the youngster: "If I do.... I shall preach what you don't."[34]

Tuttle claimed all of his books were divine inspirations transcribed while in contact with the spirit world. In setting forth some of the fundamentals of religion Hudson proposed that "the only possible mediatorship that can exist between man and God is knowledge.... Man is, and must be, his own savior ... a creature of organization, and subject to unchanging laws, man, in the church sense, is not a free agent ... immortality is not bestowed but evolved." The spirits stressed the concept of a decentralized religion that placed on its members no encumbrances such as priests, social illiberality, and intolerance.[35]

The *Banner of Light* published Tuttle's critique of the Catholic Church in 1865, giving the piece particular prominence on the newspaper's front page. Interestingly, all of the soldier spirits attending Conant's séances throughout 1865 echoed the article's major themes, presumably reinforcing its authority.[36]

Tuttle lodged a litany of criticisms against the Catholic Church citing its historical intolerance, opposition to progressive ideas, smothering of curiosity, gilded buildings of worship, devotion to religious relics, and strict hierarchical organization. He reserved special condemnation for "the priest [who] becomes the pardoner of sins, the real power to which to appeal." Placing the priest as the intermediary between God and parishioner was antithetical to Spiritualism, which envisioned a direct channel between the two, with the spiritualist receiving salvation through self-reflection and reformed behavior.

In constructing his argument, Tuttle pitted Spiritualism as the iconoclastic choice, rather than the orthodox Catholic Church stuck in the past and unable to move forward. His harsh comments objected to the Church's "gorgeous trappings calculated to excite the attention of rude natures," a swipe at the lofty cathedrals, luxurious garments, and ostentatious display of silver and gold. But the main theme that Tuttle pounded was how Catholicism "denies the right of reason, ignores the individual."

Spiritualism contrasted sharply with Catholicism in Tuttle's view by "setting the individual free, trampling on the traditions and mythologies of the past, and declaring MAN to be the most sacred object in the universe." It was a radical religious reinterpretation, but the collective observations from soldiers residing in the spirit world fully reinforced the proposition that believers in conventional religion would belatedly discover their error and find truth in Spiritualism.

Suicide presented Spiritualism with a moral challenge. Spiritualists considered the afterlife full of bliss, contentment, and atonement, but most importantly it lifted a ban on communion between spirits and mortals and in doing so created a nirvana that carried the risk of luring the dispossessed and depressed to commit suicide. For some, trading the hardships and heartaches of a mortal life in exchange for an eternal glory might have seemed a reasonable price to pay, particularly when spiritualists muddled death's finality. Ardent believers might have weighed the risks and benefits of suicide tempered by a philosophy that subtly tipped the balance toward considering self-harm. This was a conversation that some spirits brought to the *Banner of Light*'s séances.

Michael Connelly appeared at a séance hosted by Mrs. Conant in 1865 and in addition to his name provided further identifying information. He was 36 years old when he died, just short of six feet tall, born in Ireland, and a proud member of the 69th Regiment, New York Infantry, Company D.[37] Historical records identify a Michael Connelly in the 69th Regiment, New York Infantry, Company A, who was 28 years old and went missing in action in 1862 with no further entries.[38]

Like most other spirits, Connelly wanted to speak with his family and used the séance to arrange a connection between his brother, Daniel, and another medium. Daniel seemed more disposed to the proposed arrangement, and through him Connelly hoped to inform his wife and children about important financial matters. At the same time, most matter-of-factly and without elaboration, the soldier's spirit wanted to tell his wife "that I was taken prisoner down South; and so I was, too, but I never saw a day in a rebel prison; oh, no, I'd committed suicide meself first."[39]

At most séances held by the *Banner of Light*, a nameless spirit congregation usually attended and provided a platform to answer any questions offered by the attendees. Just a few months after the Civil War began, and for some inexplicable reason, the spirit ensemble addressed such a query posed by a member involving "the difference, if any, between the future condition of the spirit of a suicide and that of a soldier who dies by the hand of an enemy?"[40]

The wise spirits answering the question delicately attempted to thread the needle by parsing the distinction between a soldier's battlefield death and the voluntary act of suicide, by claiming both suffered through a violent act. Their premature deaths robbed them of a life full of experiences and "consequently much of that which we call heaven, as he enters into spiritual existence." In other words, the totality of a person's mortal life and natural death shaped their joy in the afterlife.

If that was ambiguous, then the spirit's argument of moral equivalency between a soldier's battlefield death and a less glorious suicide was heretical for mainstream nineteenth-century theologians. As the séance revealed, "We can see no difference. The condition is almost precisely the same. When the soldier dies in battle, or when he goes to battle, he says and feels, in the heat of excitement 'I care not for death.' Indeed, he loses all thought of himself, and forgets the holy law that belongs to self, and rushes madly on, as it were seeking death. So does the suicide."

The wise spirits recognized that their argument transgressed conventional dogma on the subject and airily countered, "It is supposed by some that the suicide trespasses upon a divine junction—the law of God. But does he do this any more than the soldier does who coolly gives his body to the enemy.... Verily, we can see no difference."

Why the *Banner of Light* published the supposed spirit message about suicide, and particularly at the advent of the Civil War, remains a matter of speculation. Perhaps the newspaper expected a rash of suicides as an alternative to a death in combat and through the spirit message sought to assuage the penalty. It also trampled traditional religion's moral repugnance and denunciation of suicide and in some respects even elevated the act by equating it with a soldier's death.

Even a casual analysis finds flaws in the wise spirits' moral equivalency. Soldiers in battles are not searching for bullets or cannonballs to end their life; in fact, it is quite the opposite, as they deliberately assume various defensive and offensive strategies to minimize their injury while maximizing the enemy's losses. On the other hand, a person considering suicide may see it as a voluntary choice liberating them from life's toils and troubles. This seemed to be a decision that the spirits sanctioned.

The wise spirits' moral mitigation apparently did not lighten the stain of suicide, as suggested by restless ghosts determined to prove otherwise. Among that group was Philip Ropes, an inveterate gambler whose life was a constant topsy-turvy, rags-to-riches roller coaster. His small circle of friends mourned a death that by all appearances and known motives was the result of suicide.[41]

Ropes returned from the grave after only nine days in a bid to counter that assessment. "I was no suicide, and I want my friends to distinctly understand that I was not coward enough to take the life of my physical body because I lost four thousand dollars, or all I had. If any one has anything to say about the manner of my death, tell them I've got no regrets about it, and tell them to cherish none." Aside from his denial, Ropes provided no details about his death or what factors led his friends to conclude it was suicide. The spirit quickly pivoted to a broader discussion of an afterlife filled with optimism and contentment in a narrative only marred by an ambiguous death.

Rebecca Thompson had a hard life. After her parents died Rebecca, along with a sister and brother, was left poverty stricken. At the age of 19 Rebecca married and set in motion travels that took the pair to Michigan and Ohio, all of which abruptly ended with her husband's death. One of her two children subsequently died, but the widow at least initially found some solace in marrying Albert Thompson and moving to Salt Lake City, Utah.[42]

Rebecca's spirit castigated Mormonism, and aside from that tirade she provided no details surrounding her death except "they will tell you I committed suicide, and so am classed with the undeveloped and unpurified. Much as I have to regret the act of my last moments, still my accusers have more to regret. They will see that the fate of suicide is not the worst that can be taken upon oneself."

After this admission, Rebecca's spirit again attacked Mormonism with a renewed vigor. Her spirit never directly connected Mormonism with her suicide but through various insinuations, such as "the Mormon sets up a rule of his own, and he is a despot in every sense of the word," she seemed to suggest that her life in Salt Lake City was unhappy.

Rebecca hinted at another possible motive for her suicide as she eagerly awaited her husband's arrival to the afterlife, when "we will talk of wrongs and rights; we will talk of freedom in the spirit-world; for in that world there is no distinction between the soul of a woman and the soul of a man." Equal rights apparently eluded Rebecca, and her spirit seemingly blamed Mormonism and her husband for stifling her independence. Spiritualism vigorously supported gender equality, and Rebecca's message from the grave starkly publicized the sad consequence of her subordination.

Ada was only 10 years old when she moved to the spirit world, but she returned with a reassuring message for Harrison D. Elliot, her father, who was "in the Federal Army. He isn't a rebel; he's an officer." The little girl's spirit wanted to lift a dark cloud that tenaciously darkened her father's life. Harrison believed his mother committed suicide, an inglorious act in the man's eyes that cast long shadows of shame. Ada knew better, and through a *Banner of Light* séance she set the record right.[43]

The little girl met her grandmother in the spirit world and learned that Harrison's "mother didn't hang herself. She wasn't hung. She didn't hang herself, she says. She was found dead in a position that would lead folks to suppose that she hung herself.... Tisn't so; she's often told me about it."

Ada's message from beyond showed the power of spirit communication in that it not only reunited loved ones but could remove indelible stains. Just like guardian angels, spirits in the afterlife could reach out and ease a mortal's life. All it took was faith in Spiritualism and an accommodating medium.

Soldiers accounted for most of the *Banner of Light*'s spirit messages during the 55-month period studied but 103 noncombatants appeared too, although their numbers declined as the war intensified. This was a heterogeneous group comprised of family members such as mothers, fathers, wives, children, and more distant relatives. Child spirits were the largest single category, with 40 messages or 39 percent of the total. Another 10 messages came from spirit wives, who uniformly complained about the war's hardships and were seeking help for their motherless children.

Spirit messages from children and wives were filled with pathos and could be considered the most exploitive by praying on the reader's sympathies. A case in point was eight-year-old Eddie Stevens's message that educated his grieving mother on two points, one exculpatory and the other poignant.[44]

Eddie's mother was "crying all the time since I went away" and her anguish was magnified by guilt. In a clear effort to relieve that burden, the child's spirit insisted, "I should have died if she'd given me the medicine she wished she had. She thinks if she'd given me the medicine she'd have saved my life. She needn't cry about it, because I should have died if I'd taken the medicine, just the same."

Whatever solace came from Eddie's admission was probably erased with his remark that "my father was killed in the war," which was a ca-

A vision in the night (*Frank Leslie's Illustrated News*, January 16, 1864).

lamitous insight the poor woman was unaware of. Again, in an effort to soften the blow Eddie reassured his mother that her husband's spirit would return.

Little Georgia Dodge was only seven years old, but during her seven months in the spirit world she perfected her ability to communicate. In the beginning the young child's spirit rapped her messages, then used a medium to write notes, and later even became proficient at table tipping. It was presumably through these efforts that her mother asked the young spirit to provide updates on her husband's status in the war.[45]

Georgia chose the *Banner of Light*'s séance to announce that Hiram Dodge, her father, "was killed, and he's just got around to the spirit-land, and he don't know—he can't talk himself. He's too weak. As soon as he learns he'll come to." According to Georgia, her father had died a week earlier and news of his death was not yet officially recorded. The little girl's spirit along with the obliging help of the *Banner of Light* apparently provided a public service with the expedited obituary.

Death amplified Johanna Sheenan's anxieties. Her restless spirit could not be calmed, knowing that her children were "in a strange place, and I was told by the folks in the spirit-land I should come back here and make some talk about them." Johanna's husband was in the army and although wounded several times was still alive and well. During his absence

Eight—Pathos, Politics and Presumptions 189

"it was said we had nothing to eat, and was bad off." Perhaps this hardship motivated her spirit to bypass her husband's help and turn instead to Mr. Kennedy.[46]

Kennedy was a casual acquaintance but was available when Johanna's mortal illness began its downward spiral toward death. During the three weeks preceding her death, Kennedy was a comforting influence, but perhaps even more important was his belief in Spiritualism. Johanna was a devout Catholic and dismissed her friend's spirit beliefs as eccentric, but after her death she realized that he was right and through him hoped to find her children. Johanna's impassioned, uneasy spirit had a plan. "I know me children is not well cared for, somehow. Oh, I'm troubled all the time about them ... and I likes to spake to Mr. Kennedy ... and then I'll tell what I likes him to do for me children."

Johanna's plight highlighted the unseen casualties of the Civil War

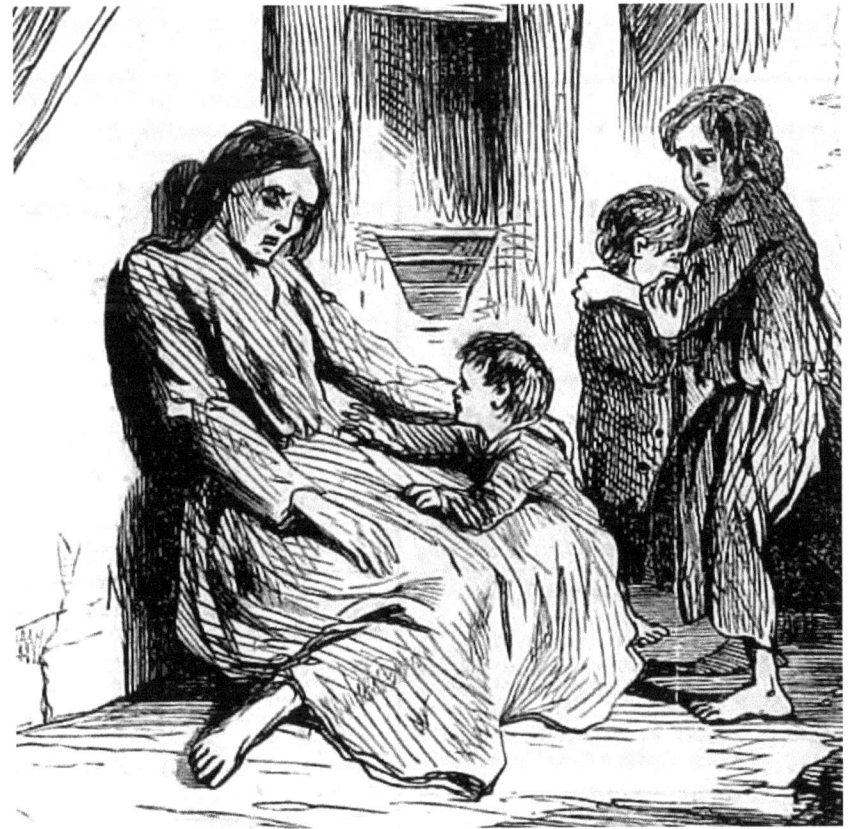

Unseen casualties of the Civil War (*Frank Leslie's Illustrated Weekly*, March 22, 1862).

that represented an inconvenient truth hidden behind fluttering banners, political speeches, vile condemnations, and bloody battles. Through her spirit, the *Banner of Light* demonstrated the war's toll on family life while at the same time it supposedly extended a helping hand through the séance.

Spiritualism was a fiercely independent faith that scorned the hierarchy and authority of traditional religions. It was a conviction confirmed by phantoms of the spirit world. Spiritualists prized their autonomy and self-reliance, but their decentralized organizational structure and their disdain for enshrining physical edifices as places of worship complicated the faith's growth. Traditional religions had soaring church spires, richly clad clerics, pews, and pulpits as tangible evidence proclaiming their dominion. Spiritualists relied on word of mouth, celebrity speakers, an endless parade of evolving, ethereal manifestations, and acceptance by the avant-garde.

This potent mix fueled the initial growth of Spiritualism, but without the robust publicity garnered through a steady stream of publications the faith would have faltered. As a group, spiritualists were ardent publishers of pamphlets, books, and newspapers that passionately represented their presumptions. Mainstream periodicals added to the public's awareness of Spiritualism with a cascade of articles ranging from fawning approval to scornful rejection.

Publications alone cannot explain Spiritualism's nineteenth-century appeal. Other factors included an erosion of trust in traditional religion, the nascent ascent of scientific discoveries such as magnetism and electricity, the marketing of mysterious manifestations as both entertainment and education, the rise of spiritual healers, and endorsements from societies' elite. But without a doubt, Spiritualism's most potent leverage was its claim to communicate with the dead.

Nineteenth-century critics castigated Spiritualism's channeling of dead spirits as fraudulent and exploitive in preying on the sympathies and sensitivities of survivors seeking consolation. The *Banner of Light* went even further than that when using the carnage of the Civil War to proselytize its philosophy.

The newspaper's Message Department devoted most of its space during the Civil War to the spirits of dead soldiers and their families, most of whom probably never existed in reality. Even more curious than this seeming deceit was the spirits' unequivocal support of the policies and politics of Spiritualism. Without fail, the spirits described death as a pain-free transition to a new life where misdeeds and misfortunes gradually gave way to an enlightened renaissance. It was soothing for believers and tempting for others. Spiritualism supported individuality, freedom of expression, and human equality. Not surprisingly, then, the spirits attending a *Banner of Light* séance unequivocally supported these ideals. Spirits denounced slavery just as vigorously as they did the restrictive bonds imposed by organized religion. The spirits even supported the reelection of President Lincoln. Spiritualism leaned heavily on the moral authority of the messages from beyond. It was a fragile crutch that eventually collapsed under the weight of doubt and derision.

Chapter Notes

Preface

1. J. R. W. Smith, *Speeches Concerning Politics and Government During the Civil War Period*, 1864.
2. P. G. T. Beauregard, "The Battles of 1861." *Richmond Daily Dispatch*, February 3, 1862.
3. D. G. Faust, *This Republic of Suffering: Death and the American Civil War*. New York: Vintage Books, 2009.
4. E. H. Britten. *Modern American Spiritualism: A Twenty Years' Record of the Communion Between Earth and the World of Spirits*. New York: The author, 1870.
5. A. P. Andrew, *Statistics for the United States, 1867–1909, Compiled by A. Piatt Andrew*. Washington, D.C.: U.S. Government Printing Office, 1910.
6. John Benedict Buescher, *The Other Side of Salvation: Spiritualism and the Nineteenth-century Religious Experience*. Boston: Skinner House Books, 2004.
7. H. K. Carroll and United States Census Office. *Report on Statistics of Churches in the United States at the Eleventh Census, 1890*. Washington, D.C.: U.S. Government Printing Office, 1894.
8. Christopher Grasso, *Skepticism and American Faith: From the Revolution to the Civil War*. New York: Oxford University Press, 2018.
9. Bridget Bennett, *Transatlantic Spiritualism and Nineteenth-Century American Literature*. New York: Palgrave Macmillan, 2007.
10. Ben Wright and Zachery W. Dresser, Editors, *Apocalypse and the Millennium in the American Civil War Era*. Baton Rouge: Louisiana State University Press, 2013.
11. Cathy Gutierrez, *Plato's Ghost: Spiritualism in the American Renaissance*. New York: Oxford University Press, 2009.

Chapter One

1. D. M. Dewey, *History of the Strange Sounds or Rappings Heard in Rochester and Western New-York*. Rochester, NY: D. M. Dewey, 1850.
2. E. H. Britten, 1870. *Modern American Spiritualism: A Twenty Years' Record of the Communion Between Earth and the World of Spirits*. New York: The author, 1870.
3. "An Hour with the Spirits." *New York Daily Tribune*, June 5, 1850.
4. A. L. Underhill, *The Missing Link in Modern Spiritualism*. New York: Thomas R. Knox & Company, 1885.
5. "The Spiritual Rappings." *The Spirit of the Times*, June 25, 1850.
6. "Wonders of the Nineteenth Century." *The National Era*, August 8, 1850.
7. H. D. Barrett, *Life Work of Mrs. Cora L.V. Richmond*. Chicago: Hack & Anderson, 1895.
8. R. Gregory Lande, *Psychological Consequences of the American Civil War*. Jefferson, NC: McFarland, Incorporated, Publishers, 2017.
9. "Mrs. Cora V.L. Hatch." *Evening Star*, April 15, 1857.
10. "Another Convert to Spiritualism." *Richmond Daily Dispatch*, April 17, 1857.
11. "Spirituality and Mathematics." *Wheeling Daily Intelligencer*, January 11, 1858.
12. Cora L. V. Hatch, *Discourses on Reli-*

gion, Morals, Philosophy and Metaphysics, vol. 1, 2nd ed. New York: B. F. Hatch, 1858.

13. R. B. D. Wells, *A New Illustrated Hand-book of Phrenology, Physiology and Physiognomy*. London: H. Vickers, 1860.

14. Cora L. V. Hatch, *Discourses on Religion, Morals, Philosophy and Metaphysics*, vol. 1, 2nd ed. New York: B. F. Hatch, 1858.

15. "Infatuation, Fantacism, Delusion, Humbug." *New York Herald*, May 26, 1851.

16. "Literature and Logic of 'The Interior.'" *The National Magazine* 1 (1852):353.

17. E. W. Capron, *Modern Spiritualism: Its Facts and Fanaticisms, Its Consistencies and Contradictions. With an Appendix*. Boston: Bela Marsh, 1855.

18. B. E. Carroll, *Spiritualism in Antebellum America*. Bloomington: Indiana University Press, 1997.

19. Joseph Twitchell, "Spiritual Manifestations." *Daily Alta California*, December 28, 1852.

20. Isaiah Hyatt, "Modern Inspiration, at Mountain Cove." *Spiritual Telegraph*, October 16, 1852.

21. "We Copy the Following Good Story." *The North Carolinian*, February 10, 1855.

22. "To Printers." *The Mountain Cove Journal and Spiritual Harbinger*, October 20, 1853.

23. R. S. Fogarty, *All Things New: American Communes and Utopian Movements, 1860–1914*. Lanham, MD: Lexington Books, 2003.

24. L. D. Ingersoll, *The Life of Horace Greeley: Founder of the New York Tribune, with Extended Notices of Many of His Contemporary Statesmen and Journalists*. Chicago: Union Publishing Company, 1873.

25. W. M. Cornell, *The Life and Public Career of Hon. Horace Greeley*. Boston: Lee & Shepard, 1872.

26. "More About The Spirits." *New York Daily Tribune*, January 29, 1851.

27. "The Fish Family." *Northern New York Journal*, January 19, 1853.

28. "A New Development." *The Troy Weekly Times*, July 31, 1858.

29. D. D. Home, *D. D. Home: His Life and Mission*. London: Trubner & Company, 1888.

30. "Hume, the Medium and Rufus Elmer." *Banner of Light*, December 4, 1858.

31. D. D. Home, *Incidents in My Life*, 5th ed. New York City: A.J. Davis and Company, 1864.

32. "The Mysterious Mr. Home." *Evening Star*, July 5, 1908.

33. "The New Fashion in Spiritualism." *New York Times*, February 27, 1921.

34. "Hume, The Medium." *The Spiritual Age*, November 13, 1858.

35. "D.D. Hume and Napoleon III." *Banner of Light*, July 2, 1857.

36. "Affairs in France." *The New York Times*, March 13, 1863.

37. T. L. Nichols, *Supramundane Facts in the Life of Rev. Jesse Babcock Ferguson*. London: F. Pitman, 1865.

38. "Spiritualism in Biography—John Murry Spear." *The Spiritual Magazine*, 8(5) (1864):344–351.

39. J. M. Spear and S.C. Hewitt, *Messages from the Superior State*. Boston: Bela Marsh, 1853.

40. F. Podmore, *Modern Spiritualism: A History and a Criticism*. London: Methuen & Company, 1902.

Chapter Two

1. *Sketch of Robert Hare. Popular Science Monthly*, ed. William Jay Youmans, vol. 42. New York: D. Appleton, 1893.

2. R. Hare, *Experimental Investigation of the Spirit Manifestations, Demonstrating the Existence of Spirits and Their Communion with Mortals*. New York: Partridge & Brittan, 1856.

3. "Obituary—Ex-Judge Edmonds." *New York Times*, April 7, 1874.

4. "Judge Edmonds on Spiritualism." *New York Times*, October 20, 1853.

5. "Letter of Judge Edmonds on Spiritual Manifestations." *New York Herald*, August 6, 1853.

6. John W. Edmonds and George T. Dexter, *Spiritualism*, 4th ed. New York City: Partridge and Brittan, 1853.

7. "Judge Edmonds and the Spirits, Visit of Our Reporter." *New York Herald*, October 30, 1853.

8. "Interesting Interview Between Judge Edmonds and a Reporter." *Sunbury American*, December 3, 1853.

9. "Position and Progress of Spiritualism." *New York Herald*, March 5, 1854.

10. John W. Edmonds and George T.

Dexter, *Spiritualism*, 3rd ed., vol. 2. New York City: Partridge & Brittan, 1855.

11. William H. Ferris, "A Review of Modern Spiritualism." *Ladies' Repository*, January 1856.

12. "Spiritualism in Court." *Brooklyn Daily Eagle*, March 16, 1855.

13. "Spiritual Magnetism." *The Star of the North*, April 19, 1855.

14. "Advertisement for Mr. A.B. Whiting." *Baltimore Sun*, January 29, 1858.

15. "Advertisement Spiritualism." *Baltimore Sun*, February 12, 1858.

16. "Advertisement Mr. Laning." *Baltimore Sun*, February 6, 1858.

17. "The Spiritual Age." *The Spiritual Age*, January 2, 1858.

18. "Advertisements." *The Spiritual Age*, January 1, 1859.

19. "Poughkeppsie Seer and His Revelations." *Fraser's Magazine for Town and Country*. London: James Fraser, February 1848.

20. A. J. Davis and W. Fishbough, *The Principles of Nature, Her Divine Revelations, and a Voice to Mankind*. Boston: Colby & Rich, Banner Publishing House, 1847.

21. "The Herald of Progress." *The New Republic*, July 5, 1862.

22. F. L. Mott, *A History of American Magazines, 1850–1865*. Cambridge, MA: Harvard University Press, 1938.

23. "Mediums and Believers." *The Herald of Progress*, February 4, 1860.

24. Stephen Dudley, "Wonders at Koons' Spirit Room." *Spiritual Telegraph*, December 30, 1854.

25. "Fire-Incendiarism." *Meigs County Telegraph*, December 28, 1852.

26. J. Koons, *The Spirits in Athens County*, ed. S. B. Brittan, vol. 3, *The Spiritual Telegraph*. New York City: Partridge & Brittan, 1853.

27. J. Everett and J. Koons, *A Book for Skeptics*. Columbus, OH: Osgood & Blake, printers, 1853.

28. "Spiritual Machine." *Scientific American* 21 (1855):162

29. R. Hare, *Experimental Investigation of the Spirit Manifestations, Demonstrating the Existence of Spirits and Their Communion with Mortals*. New York: Partridge & Brittan, 1856.

30. "Visit to the Koons Family." *Plymouth Banner*, March 15, 1855.

31. "Powerful Manifestations of Spirits." *The Richmond Palladium*, February 23, 1855.

32. "Spiritual Manifestations." *Richmond Palladium*, March 2, 1855.

33. "Spirit-Rooms at the West." *The Spiritual Telegraph*, March 26, 1859.

34. "Modern Spiritualism." *The New York Herald*, March 7, 1858.

35. "President Mahan on Modern Spiritualism." *Evening Star*, February 25, 1857.

36. "The Cherry Colored Cat Outdone." *The Sun*, October 11, 1858.

37. "A Celebrated Spiritualist." *The Sun* November 1, 1858.

38. "Confession of a Table Mover." *The Geneva Gazette*, December 24, 1858.

39. "Spiritualism." *The Sun*, June 3, 1857.

40. "Mrs. Cora L. V. Hatch in a Trance." *New York Times*, January 8, 1859.

41. "Spiritual Languages." *Brooklyn Daily Eagle*, July 20, 1859.

42. "The End of Spiritualism." *Brooklyn Daily Eagle*, January 28, 1859.

43. "Lecture by Miss M. Johnson." *Brooklyn Daily Eagle*, January 10, 1860.

44. "Another Victim." *Baltimore Sun*, May 29, 1860.

45. "Just Published." *The Sun*, May 10, 1860.

46. "Confessions of a Medium." *The Atlantic Monthly*, December 1860, 699–714.

47. "Magic and Mystery." *Marysville Daily Appeal*, February 11, 1860.

48. B. Taylor, *Confessions of a Medium, Prose Writings of Bayard Taylor*. New York City: G.P. Putnam, 1862.

Chapter Three

1. "A New Colony." *Bradford Reporter*, January 10, 1861.

2. H. W. Wilbur and W. B. Hand. *Illustrated History of the Town of Hammonton; with an Account of Its Soil, Climate and Industries*. Hammonton, NJ: The Mirror Steam Printing House, 1889.

3. "Spiritual Manifestations." *Daily Nashville Patriot*, January 24, 1861.

4. "Spiritualism." *The Evansville Daily Journal*, January 25, 1861.

5. "Mobocracy in Michigan." *Chicago Tribune*, January 31, 1861.

Notes—Chapter Three

6. "Suicide Caused by Spiritualism." *The Sun*, February 9, 1861.
7. "A Wonderful Child." *The Daily Exchange*, March 21, 1861.
8. "Patriotic Woman." *Green Mountain Freeman*, May 1, 1861.
9. A. J. Davis, *The Penetralia; Being Harmonial Answers to Important Questions, Fourth Edition*. Boston: Bela Marsh, 1858.
10. A. J. Davis, *Answers to Ever-Recurring Questions from the People. A Sequel to The Penetralia*. New York: A. J. Davis & Company, 1862.
11. "Should Spiritualists Go to War?". *The Herald of Progress*, May 18, 1861.
12. "Sentiments of a Southern Wife." *The Richmond Daily Dispatch*, June 15, 1861.
13. "The Danger to the South." *The Richmond Daily Dispatch*, June 27, 1861.
14. "No Fighting." *Indiana State Sentinel*, June 26, 1861.
15. "A Word With The Spiritualists." *Watertown Republican*, July 26, 1861.
16. "Madame Victorine Hollard Advertisement." *Cass County Republican*, November 7, 1861.
17. "Astrology." *New York Herald*, November 13, 1861.
18. "The Beauties of Spiritualism." *The Jeffersonian*, November 14, 1861.
19. "Spiritualism in Camp Dennison." *Cincinnati Daily Press*, November 18, 1861.
20. "Concerning Chaplains." *National Republican*, December 28, 1861.
21. "Letter From Brother Peebles." *The Herald of Progress*, March 22, 1862.
22. "Mrs. Cora L.V. Hatch." *New York Herald*, April 13, 1862.
23. "Mrs. Cora L.V. Hatch at Brainard's Hall." *Cleveland Morning Leader*, July 15, 1862.
24. "Mrs. Anderson." *Chicago Tribune*, June 17, 1862.
25. "Hydro-Electric Cure." *Evening Argus*, June 19, 1862.
26. "Spiritualism." *The Sun*, December 17, 1862.
27. "Spiritualist Lecture." *Cleveland Morning Leader*, December 20, 1862.
28. "Dispepsia and Fits." *Nebraska Advertiser*, October 11, 1862.
29. "Renunciation of Spiritualism." *The Sun*, February 10, 1862.
30. "To the Public." *Indiana State Sentinel*, September 1, 1862.
31. G. C. Bartlett, *The Salem Seer: Reminiscences of Charles H. Foster*. New York: United States Book Company, 1891.
32. W. E. Burns, *Witch Hunts in Europe and America: An Encyclopedia*. Westport, CT: Greenwood Press, 2003.
33. "Spiritual Phenomena." *Sangamo Journal*, May 22, 1861.
34. "An Evening with a Spiritual Medium." *Brooklyn Daily Eagle*, April 1, 1862.
35. "A Sad Story." *The Sun*, November 1, 1862.
36. "A Sad Story." *The Caledonian*, November 7, 1862.
37. "It Is Said." *Wood County Reporter*, January 18, 1862.
38. "Whisperings to Correspondents." *Herald of Progress*, 3(45) (1862).
39. "War Meeting in Brooklyn." *New York Herald*, September 4, 1862.
40. "New Light on the Campaign." *Daily Intelligencer*, May 16, 1862.
41. G. J. Rains, P. S. Michie, and H. M. Schiller, *Confederate Torpedoes*. Jefferson, NC: McFarland, 2011.
42. "From Gen. McClellan's Army." *New York Times*, May 8, 1862.
43. "Just So." *Penn-Yan Democrat*, May 16, 1862.
44. A Curious Instance of Spritualism in the Army, *The Herald of Progress*, October 4,1862
45. "Prof. Grimes." *Penn-Yan Democrat*, May 30, 1862.
46. "A Wag Beats Spiritualism." *Penn-Yan Democrat*, January 17, 1862.
47. "The People and the Fast Day." *Richmond Daily Dispatch*, August 11, 1863.
48. "Skeptic." *The Free South*, July 11, 1863.
49. "Wiltsie." *The Ottawa Free Trader*, January 31, 1863.
50. W. Howitt, *The History of the Supernatural*. London: Longman, Green, Longman, Roberts and Green, 1863.
51. "Spiritualism in Bloomington, Illinois." *Banner of Light*, December 12, 1863.
52. "Spiritualism in Grand Rapids, Michigan." *Banner of Light*, December 12, 1863.
53. Andrew Hartman, "Spiritualism in California." *Banner of Light*, March 21, 1863.

54. "Nothing but War." *Banner of Light*, January 10, 1863.
55. "The State of the Rebellion." *Banner of Light*, May 23, 1863.
56. "What Next?" *Banner of Light*, October 24, 1863.
57. "Peace and War." *Banner of Light*, June 6, 1863.
58. "The National Struggle." *Banner of Light*, October 12, 1863.
59. "The Present Crisis." *Banner of Light*, November 21, 1863.
60. "Proscription and Religious Faith in War." *Banner of Light*, June 27, 1863.
61. "Our Cause in Washington." *Banner of Light*, November 21, 1863.
62. U. Clark, *Plain Guide to Spiritualism: A Handbook for Skeptics, Inquirers, Clergymen, Believers, Lecturers.* Boston: William White & Company, 1863.
63. "Spiritualism Alias Jugglery." *Green-Mountain Freeman*, August 4, 1863.
64. "The State Benevolent Institutions at Jacksonville." *Illinois State Journal*, January 20, 1863.
65. "Popular Amusements." *New York Herald*, November 15, 1864.
66. O. Abbott, *The Davenport Brothers. Their History, Travels, and Manifestations*: Published for the author. New York: A. J. Davis & Co., 1864.
67. "Arrested." *Chicago Daily Tribune*, February 2, 1864.
68. "A Revelation." *Evening Star*, May 10, 1864.
69. "Spiritual Manifestations." *Evening Star*, February 26, 1864.
70. "Spiritual Manifestations." *Daily National Republican*, February 25, 1864.
71. "Maryland Institute." *The Sun*, March 18, 1864.
72. "Davenport Brothers." *The Sun*, March 14, 1864.
73. "Davenport Brothers." *The Sun*, March 21, 1864.
74. "Diabolism at the Cooper Institute." *New York Herald*, April 30, 1864.
75. "A New Era in Human Development." *New York Herald*, May 4, 1864.
76. "The Davenport Brothers." *Chicago Daily Tribune*, May 12, 1864.
77. "A Remarkable Exhibition in New York." *Memphis Daily Appeal*, May 26, 1864.
78. "Spiritualism Eclipsed." *The Smoky Hill and Republican Union*, June 4, 1864.
79. "Canterbury Hall." *Daily National Republican*, 1864.
80. "Amusements." *Evening Star*, July 5, 1864.
81. "Announcement." *Evening Star*, June 20, 1864.
82. "Amusements To-Night." *Evening Star*, July 8, 1864.
83. "Spiritual Manifestations by the Thorpe Brothers." *New York Herald*, August 10, 1864.
84. "Niblo's Saloon." *New York Herald*, October 6, 1864.
85. "An Evening With The Spirits." *Brooklyn Daily Eagle*, November 11, 1864.
86. "The Eddy Family." *New York Herald*, November 17, 1864.
87. "Popular Amusements." *New York Herald*, November 15, 1864.

Chapter Four

1. "Spiritual Convention." *Chicago Tribune*, August 15, 1864.
2. M. A. Lause, *Free Spirits: Spiritualism, Republicanism, and Radicalism in the Civil War Era.* Champaign: University of Illinois Press, 2016.
3. "Spiritual Convention." *Chicago Tribune*, August 15, 1864.
4. E. P. W. Packard and S.N.B. Olsen, *The Prisoners' Hidden Life.* Chicago: J.N. Clarke, 1871.
5. "Spiritual Convention." *Chicago Tribune*, August 15, 1864.
6. "Spiritual Convention." *Chicago Tribune*, August 12, 1864.
7. "Spiritual Convention." *Chicago Tribune*, August 15, 1864.
8. "Spiritual Convention." *Chicago Tribune*, August 15, 1864.
9. "Spiritual Convention." *Chicago Tribune*, August 15, 1864.
10. "Spiritual Convention." *Chicago Tribune*, August 17, 1864.
11. "Spiritualism." *The Sun*, April 2, 1864.
12. T. G. Forster, *Unanswerable Logic.* Boston: Colby & Rich, 1887.
13. "Spiritualism." *The Sun*, March, 26, 1864.
14. S. H. Paist and H. T. Childs. *A Narrative of the Experiences of Horace Abraham Ackley, M.D.* Philadelphia,

Printed for the author by Lippincott & Co., 1861.

15. "Spiritualism." *The Sun*, March, 26, 1864.

16. E. H. Britten, *Modern American Spiritualism*. New York: The author, 1870.

17. "Washington Spiritual Conference." *Evening Star*, April 16, 1864.

18. "Sunday Evening Spiritual Meeting." *Evening Star*, March 5, 1864.

19. D. Morris, *Boston in the Golden Age of Spiritualism: Séances, Mediums & Immortality*. Charleston, SC: The History Press, 2014.

20. "Spiritualism in Washington." *Evening Star*, February 1, 1864.

21. "Scandalous Table Talk." *Smoky Hill and Republican Union*, June 11, 1864.

22. "Spiritualism and Insanity." *Daily Alta California*, February 14, 1864.

23. Henry Gibbons, "Modern Spiritism." *Pacific Medical and Surgical Journal* 9 (16)(1875).

24. R. Buckland, *The Spirit Book: The Encyclopedia of Clairvoyance, Channeling, and Spirit Communication*. Canton Township, MI: Visible Ink Press, 2005.

25. E. H. Britten and M. Wilkinson. *Autobiography of Emma Hardinge Britten*. London: J. Heywood, 1900.

26. "Spiritualism." *Cleveland Morning Leader*, January 22, 1864.

27. "A Marvellous Incident." *The Manchester Journal*, January 19, 1864.

28. "Grand Exhibition." *Holmes County Farmer*, June 2, 1864.

29. "Police Court." *Cleveland Morning Leader*, April 16, 1864.

30. "Big Thing on the Spirits." *The Smoky Hill and Republican Union*, May 14, 1864.

31. "A Spiritual Humbug Exposed." *Cleveland Morning Leader*, August 31, 1864.

32. "General City News." *New York Times*, June 13, 1864.

33. A. A. Hopkins and H.R. Evans, *Magic: Stage Illusions and Scientific Diversions, Including Trick Photography*. New York: Munn & Company, 1901.

34. "Salle Diabolique." *New York Herald*, September 11, 1864.

35. Katharina Rein, "Mind Reading in Stage Magic: The "Second Sight" Illusion, Media, and Mediums." *Communication +1* 4 (2015).

36. Henry Ridgely Evans, "Recollections of Four Famous Fantasists." *New Age Magazine* (8)(1908).

37. H. Hermon, *Hellerism. Second-sight Mystery. Supernatural Vision Or Second-Sight. What Is It? A Mystery: A Complete Manual for Teaching this Peculiar Art*. New York: Lee and Shepard, 1884.

38. "Spiritualism." *The Sun*, October 21, 1865.

39. "Spiritualism." *Sangamo Journal Illinois State Journal*, October 2, 1865.

40. "Amusements." *New York Herald*, August 20, 1865.

41. "Amusements." *Chicago Tribune*, December 30, 1865.

42. "Spiritualism on Trial." *Cleveland Leader*, August 14, 1865.

43. "Uncle Sam v. 'Mediums.'" *Brooklyn Daily Eagle*, August 12, 1865.

44. "Spiritualism Jugglery." *New York Times*, August 27, 1865.

45. "Spiritualism in Court." *Chicago Tribune*, August 24, 1865.

46. "The Spirits on Trial." *New York Herald*, August 23, 1865.

47. "Spiritualism Is Jugglery." *New York Herald*, August 24, 1865.

48. "Spiritualism and Magic." *Sangamo Journal Illinois State Journal*, August 30, 1865.

49. "Spiritualism Pronounced Jugglery by an Intelligent Jury." *New York Herald*, August 24, 1865.

50. "The Spirits on Trial at Buffalo." *The New York Rerformer*, August 26, 1865.

51. "Colchester Repudiated." *New York Herald*, August 25, 1865.

52. "Spiritualism." *New York Herald*, September 25, 1865.

53. "Spiritualism and Jugglery." *New York Times*, August 27, 1865.

54. "The Spiritual Medium Case." *The Sun*, September 25, 1865.

55. T. E. Pemberton, *Memoir of Edward Askew Sothern*. London: R. Bentley and Son, 1889.

56. "Sothern the Actor and the Spirits." *Brooklyn Daily Eagle*, December 30, 1865.

57. "The Table Tossing Delusion." *The Norfolk Post*, December 29, 1865.

58. "John McQueen and Spiritualism." *The Hillsdale Standard*, February 28, 1865.

59. "Spiritualism Exposed." *The Hillsdale Standard*, February 21, 1865.

60. "A 'Spiritual Medium' Humbug

Exposed." *Brooklyn Daily Eagle*, November 17, 1865.
61. "Exciting Scene in Liverpool." *Brooklyn Daily Eagle*, March 4, 1865.
62. "The Davenports." *The Evening Post*, September 29, 1865.
63. "Radiates." *Richmond Daily Dispatch*, December 14, 1865.
64. "P.T. Barnum on Humbug." *The Sun*, March 6, 1865.
65. "Barnum's American Museum." *New York Clipper*, February 25, 1865.
66. P. T. Barnum, *The Humbugs of the World*. New York: Carleton, 1866.
67. "Victimized Spirituality." *Dayton Daily Empire*, June 2, 1865.
68. "Mrs. Leonard." *Westfield Republican*, December 27, 1865.
69. "The Tragedy at Battle Creek." *Chicago Tribune*, December 28, 1865.
70. J. G. Krasnow, *Jacktown: History & Hard Times at Michigan's First State Prison*. Charleston, SC: The History Press, 2017.
71. "Sarah Haviland and Martha Grinder." *Religio Philosophical Journal* 1 (21)(1866).
72. "Tibbets in a New Character." *New York Herald*, February 7, 1865.
73. "The Tibbets Case." *New York Herald*, February 8, 1865.
74. "Miscellaneous News." *New York Herald*, February 9, 1865.
75. "Superstition." *Richmond Dispatch*, March 31, 1865.

Chapter Five

1. J. D. McCabe, *Life and Campaigns of General Robert E. Lee*. Atlanta: National Publishing Company, 1866.
2. "The National Calamity." *New York Times*, April 16 1865.
3. "Our National Loss." *Chicago Tribune*, April 20 1865.
4. "Terrible National Calamity." *Banner of Light*, April 22, 1865.
5. "Assassination of the President." *The Friend of Progress*, May, 1865.
6. "Not Around." *Daily Reformer*, December 23, 1862.
7. A. Ward, *The Complete Works of Artemus Ward*. New York: A. L. Burt Company, 1898.
8. James M. Scovel, *Lippincott's Monthly Magazine, Personal Recollections of Abraham Lincoln*. Philadelphia: J. B. Lippincott and Company, 1889.
9. "Some of the English Journals." *Brooklyn Eagle*, September 9, 1863.
10. R. J. Lenardon, M.P.O. Morford, and M. Sham, *A Companion to Classical Mythology*. London: Longman, 1997.
11. "Presidential Aspirations and Exhalations." *New York Herald*, September 12, 1863.
12. "Obituary." *New York Times*, June 26, 1877.
13. William Eleroy Curtis, *Abraham Lincoln*. Philadelphia: Lippincott, 1902.
14. R. D. Owen, *Footfalls on the Boundary of Another World*. Philadelphia: Lippincott, 1860.
15. R. D. Owen, *The Debatable Land Between This World and the Next: With Illustrative Narrations*. New York: G.W. Carleton & Company, 1871.
16. "Spiritualism at the White House." *New York Herald*, May 30, 1863.
17. "Spiritualism and Hobgoblins." *Indiana State Sentinel*, May 13, 1863.
18. "A Spiritual Circle at the White House." *The Morgantown Monitor*, June 27, 1863.
19. "Spiritualism at the White House." *Morning Leader*, June 4, 1863.
20. C. M. Robinson, *Shark of the Confederacy: The Story of the CSS Alabama*. Annapolis, MD: Naval Institute Press, 1995.
21. "Spiritualism at the White House." *Morning Leader*, June 4, 1863.
22. "Will Mr. Lincoln Become a Dictator." *The Standard*, January 19, 1863.
23. "The Spiritualists Out of Harmony." *Brooklyn Eagle*, August 19, 1864.
24. "Message Department." *Banner of Light*, August 26, 1865.
25. "Spirit Message." *Banner of Light*, December 30, 1865.
26. M. Hull and W. F. Jamieson. *The Greatest Debate within a Half Century Upon Modern Spiritualism*. Chicago: Progressive Thinker Publishing House, 1904.
27. "Lecture on Abraham Lincoln, and a Poem." *Banner of Light*, May 6, 1865.
28. "Lyceum Hall Meetings." *Banner of Light*, July 1, 1865.
29. "Message Department." *Banner of Light*, August 26, 1865.

30. "Junius Brutus Booth." *Banner of Light*, October 7, 1865.
31. "Letter From Judge Edmonds." *Banner of Light*, December 22, 1866.
32. Insider, "John Wilkes Booth." *Brooklyn Daily Eagle*, February 8, 10, 1885.
33. "Abraham Lincoln." *Banner of Light*, March 16, 1867.
34. F. B. Carpenter, "Recollections of Abraham Lincoln." *Evansville Daily Journal*, February 9, 1866.
35. "Spirit Rappings." *Ebensburg Alleghanian*, September 12, 1867.
36. "From the Spirit Land." *The New York Times*, August 23, 1868.
37. "Spirits at the White House." *Atlanta Constitution*, September 13, 1868.
38. "Political Notes." *The New York Herald*, September 11, 1868.
39. "There Is a Story." *Richmond Dispatch*, September 9, 1868.
40. "There Is a Story." *The Daily News*, September 11, 1868.
41. "Message Department." *Banner of Light*, May 29, 1869.
42. "Spooks That Speak." *Brooklyn Eagle*, September 19, 1870.
43. "The Mumler Photographs." *New York Times*, May 23, 1869.
44. William H. Mumler, "The Personal Experiences of William H. Mumler in Spirit-Photography." *Banner of Light*, January 30, 1875.
45. "It Would Seem." *Vermont Phoenix*, April 19, 1872.
46. "A Curious Story About Mrs. Lincoln Reiterated." *New York Times*, February 24, 1872.
47. "Abraham Lincoln." *Banner of Light*, April 27, 1872.
48. "The Murderer of Lincoln." *Banner of Light*, August 24, 1872.
49. "Tad Lincoln." *Banner of Light*, July 27, 1872.
50. Jason Emerson, "The Madness of Mary Lincoln." *American Heritage*, 57(3) (2006).
51. M. E. Neely and R.G. McMurtry. *The Insanity File: The Case of Mary Todd Lincoln*. Carbondale, IL: Southern Illinois University Press, 1993.
52. "Mrs. Lincoln." *Missouri Weekly Patriot* August 5, 1875.
53. Abby Sheaffer, "Entranced: St. Charles' Secret Spiritualist History." *Kane County Chronicle*, October 26, 2012.
54. "Mrs. Lincoln." *Missouri Weekly Patriot* August 5, 1875.
55. "The Assertion." *Evening Star*, February 4, 1873.
56. "Strange Work for the Spirits." *New York Times*, February 10, 1873.
57. *Historical and Biographical Annals of Columbia and Montour Counties, Pennsylvania*, vol. 1. Chicago: J. H. Beers & Company, 1915.
58. Samuel Kase, "A Sensation." *St. Louis Republican*, September 10, 1876.
59. John Benedict Buescher, *The President's Medium*. Forest Grove, OR: International Association for the Preservation of Spiritualist and Occult Periodicals, 2015.
60. J. B. Conklin, "The Life of a Medium." *Nichols' Monthly: A Magazine of Social Science, and Progressive Literature*, June 1856.
61. John Benedict Buescher, *The President's Medium*. Forest Grove, OR: International Association for the Preservation of Spiritualist and Occult Periodicals, 2015.
62. "Spiritualists Encamped." *The Sun*, July 21, 1879.
63. N. C. Maynard, *Was Abraham Lincoln a Spiritualist?: Or, Curious Revelations from the Life of a Trance Medium*. Philadelphia: R. C. Hartranft, 1891
64. "Mrs. Nettie Colburn Maynard." *Banner of Light*, April 11, 1891.
65. "Was Abraham Lincoln a Spiritualist." *Banner of Light*, April 11, 1891.
66. "The Emancipation Proclamation—Mrs. Maynard Disavows." *Banner of Light*, May 16, 1891.
67. "Additional from Mrs. Nettie C. Maynard." *Banner of Light*, May 28, 1891.
68. M. P. Turner, "More Light on the Maynard Episode." *Banner of Light*, May 30, 1891.
69. R. C. Hartranft, "Letter to the Editor." *Banner of Light*, September 10, 1891.
70. "In Re Abraham Lincoln and Spiritualism." *Banner of Light*, December 12, 1891.
71. Hudson Tuttle, "Was Lincoln A Spiritualist?" *Banner of Light*, November 21, 1891.
72. N. C. Maynard, "Was Abraham Lincoln A Spiritualist?" *Banner of Light*, May 28, 1892.
73. "Transition of Mrs. Nettie C. Maynard." *Banner of Light*, July 9, 1892.
74. John F. Whitney, "Was Abraham

Lincoln A Spiritualist?" *Banner of Light*, October 8, 1892.
75. M. Bloomfield, *Bloomfield's Illustrated Historical Guide*. St. Augustine, FL: M. Bloomfield, 1885.
76. John F. Whitney, *Abraham Lincoln Papers, John F. Whitney to Abraham Lincoln*, 1861.
77. R. Redd, *St. Augustine and the Civil War*. Charleston, SC: The History Press, 2014.
78. "Wisconsin." *Banner of Light*, November 28, 1891.
79. "Consult Prof. A.B. Severance." *Light of Truth*, 20(15) (1897):11.
80. A. B. Severance, "Psychometric Delineation of a Lock of Hair." *Facts*, 3(2) (1884).
81. "Ex-Minister Robert T. Lincoln." *The Sun*, November 1, 1893.
82. W. H. Burr, "District of Columbia." *Banner of Light*, November 4, 1893.

Chapter Six

1. American News Company, *The American Booksellers' Guide*. New York: American News Company, 1871.
2. "Literature of Spiritualism." *The Spiritual Magazine*. London: F. Pitman, 1871.
3. "Seeing Is Believing." *Lippincott's Monthly Magazine*. Philadelphia: J. B. Lippincott and Company, 1880.
4. General Conference of Seventh-Day Adventists. *Advent Review and Sabbath Herald*. 1857.
5. A. Braude, "News from the Spirit World: A Checklist of American Spiritualist Periodicals, 1847–1900." In *Proceedings of the American Antiquarian Society*. Worcester, MA: American Antiquarian Society, 1990.
6. David K. Nartonis, "The Rise of 19th-Century American Spiritualism, 1854–1873." *Journal for the Scientific Study of Religion*, 49(2) (2010):361–373.
7. U. Clark, *Plain Guide to Spiritualism: A Handbook for Skeptics, Inquirers, Clergymen, Believers, Lecturers*. Boston: William White & Company, 1863.
8. F. L. Mott, *A History of American Magazines, 1850–1865*. Cambridge, MA: Harvard University Press, 1938.
9. "Something Worth the Age." *Herald of Progress*, 4(52) (1864).
10. Mary A. Livermore, "Where There's a Will There's a Way." *Herald of Progress*, 4(33) (1863).
11. "Progress of the War." *Herald of Progress*, 2(12) (1861).
12. Andrew Jackson Davis, "Medical Whispers." *Herald of Progress*, 3(19) (1862).
13. "Victory for One." *Herald of Progress*, 4(40) (1863).
14. "Heaven and Earth." *Herald of Progress*, 2(31) (1861).
15. "Whisperings to Correspondents." *Herald of Progress*, 3(45) (1862).
16. "Material Organization." *Herald of Progress*, 2(52)(1862).
17. "Escape From a Hospital." *Herald of Progress*, 3(46) (1863).
18. "A Young Soldier Drawn by His Mother's Anxiety." *Herald of Progress*, 3(34) (1862).
19. "Whisperings to Correspondents." *Herald of Progress*, 3(50) (1863).
20. "War Prophecies." *Herald of Progress* 4(30) (1863).
21. E. V. Wilson, *The Truths of Spiritualism*. Chicago, IL: Hazlitt and Reed, 1879.
22. "Miracles Performed in 1864!" *Herald of Progress*, 4(52) (1864).
23. D. Morris, *Boston in the Golden Age of Spiritualism: Séances, Mediums & Immortality*. Charleston, SC: The History Press, 2014.
24. D. Morris, *Boston in the Golden Age of Spiritualism: Séances, Mediums & Immortality*. Charleston, SC: The History Press, 2014.
25. J. W. Day, *Biography of Mrs. J. H. Conant*. Boston: William White and Company, 1873.

Chapter Seven

1. "Message Department." *Banner of Light*, May 16, 1863.
2. *Search for Soldiers*. https://www.nps.gov/civilwar/search-soldiers.htm, National Park Service [accessed January 14, 2019].
3. *Fold3*. Fold3, 2019 [accessed January 14, 2019].
4. J. H. Conant, "Robert Morriston." *Banner of Light*, June 8, 1861.
5. W. J. Cooper, *We Have the War Upon Us: The Onset of the Civil War, November*

1860-April 1861. New York: Knopf Doubleday Publishing Group, 2012.

6. T. H. Williams, *P. G. T. Beauregard: Napoleon in Gray*. Baton Rouge, LA: LSU Press, 1995.

7. Abner Doubleday, *Reminiscences of Forts Sumter and Moultrie in 1860-'61*. New York: Harper & Brothers, 1876.

8. J. H. Conant, "Theodore Guild." *Banner of Light*, May 23, 1863.

9. William E. Ormsby, "Compiled Service Records of Volunteer Union Soldiers Who Served in Organizations from the State of Massachusetts." RG94-CMSR-MA-2CAV-Bx0160_MISC. Washington, D.C.: The National Archives, 1863.

10. Timothy Swenson, *Charles S. Eigenbrodt: Alvarado Civil War Hero*. 2005.

11. Joan Waugh, "New England Cavalier." In *The Shenandoah Valley Campaign of 1864*, edited by Gary W. Gallagher, 314–316. Chapel Hill: University of North Carolina Press, 2006.

12. William E. Ormsby, "Compiled Service Records of Volunteer Union Soldiers Who Served in Organizations from the State of Massachusetts." RG94-CMSR-MA-2CAV-Bx0135. Washington, D.C.: The National Archives, 1863.

13. Ormsby Court Martial. In *William E. Ormbey (Ormsby) Company E, 2nd Massachusetts*: Records of the Adjutant General's Office, 1780–1917. 1864.

14. J. McLean, *California Sabers: The 2nd Massachusetts Cavalry in the Civil War*. Bloomington, IN: Indiana University Press, 2000.

15. J. H. Conant, "William E. Ormsby." *Banner of Light*, May 28, 1864.

16. Board of Trustees of the Antietam National Cemetery, Maryland. *A Descriptive List of the Burial Places of the Remains of Confederate Soldiers*. Hagerstown, MD: "Free Press" print, 1868.

17. J. H. Conant, "Colonel Alexander Harris." *Banner of Light*, November 15, 1862.

18. J. H. Conant, "Lieutenant Jacob Buckingham." *Banner of Light*, November 15, 1862.

19. J. H. Conant, "Joseph Whittier." *Banner of Light*, December 26, 1863.

20. *Search for Soldiers*. https://www.nps.gov/civilwar/search-soldiers.htm, National Park Service [accessed January 14 2019].

21. Joseph H. Whittier, "Compiled Service Records of Volunteer Union Soldiers Who Served in Organizations from the State of Massachusetts." RG94-CMSR-MA-34INF-Bx2842. Washington, D.C.: The National Archives, 1862.

22. J. H. Conant, "Joseph Whittier." *Banner of Light*, December 26, 1863.

23. J. H. Conant, "Lieutenant Hillyard." *Banner of Light*, February 7, 1863.

24. J. H. Conant, "Levi H. Griswold." *Banner of Light*, February 21, 1863.

25. J. H. Conant, "Thomas Ormsby." *Banner of Light*, May 28, 1864.

26. J. H. Conant, "Sidney T. Graves." *Banner of Light*, February 21, 1863.

27. J. H. Conant, "Lieutenant William Conway." *Banner of Light*, May 16, 1863.

28. J. H. Conant, "Thomas Christian." *Banner of Light*, October 24, 1863.

29. J. H. Conant, "William H. Smith." *Banner of Light*, February 20, 1864.

30. William H. Smith, "Compiled Service Records of Volunteer Union Soldiers Who Served in Organizations from the State of Massachusetts." RG94-CMSR-MA-35INF-Bx2895_MISC. Washington, D.C.: The National Archives, 1863.

31. A. C. Ellis, *The Massachusetts Andrew Sharpshooters: A Civil War History and Roster*. Jefferson, NC: McFarland, 2012.

32. J. H. Conant, "Jerry Deering." *Banner of Light*, June 11 1864.

33. J. H. Conant, "Jim Paige." *Banner of Light*, July 9, 1864.

34. J. H. Conant, "Richard S. Andrews." *Banner of Light*, September 17, 1864.

35. J. H. Conant, "Robert Reidelberg." *Banner of Light*, May 13, 1865.

36. J. H. Conant, "William Chamberlain." *Banner of Light*, August 31, 1861.

37. J. H. Conant, "Joseph Stillings." *Banner of Lght*, March 1, 1862.

38. J. H. Conant, "Nathaniel Jackman." *Banner of Light*, July 19, 1862.

39. J. H. Conant, "Jack Woodbury." *Banner of Light*, September 7, 1861.

40. J. H. Conant, "Robert Collins." *Banner of Light*, November 30, 1861.

41. J. H. Conant, "Charlie Hiland." *Banner of Light*, May 10, 1862.

42. J. H. Conant, "Joseph L. Sawyer." *Banner of Light*, November 29, 1862.
43. J. H. Conant, "James L. Smyth." *Banner of Light*, April 30, 1864.
44. J. H. Conant, "Thomas Woodbridge." *Banner of Light*, July 16, 1864.
45. J. H. Conant, "Henry T. Sanderson." *Banner of Light*, October 18, 1862.
46. J. H. Conant, "Richard Aldrich." *Banner of Light*, October 25, 1862.
47. J. H. Conant, "Henry A. Kingsbury." *Banner of Light*, November 1, 1862.
48. J. H. Conant, "Benjamin Creggan." *Banner of Light*, January 31, 1863.
49. J. H. Conant, "Billy Thornton." *Banner of Light*, April 11, 1863.
50. J. H. Conant, "James Monroe Granby." *Banner of Light*, May 2, 1863.
51. J. H. Conant. "Peter Connety." *Banner of Light*, May 30, 1863.
52. Michael Kelly, "Index to Compiled Service Records of Volunteer Union Soldiers Who Served in Organizations from the State of New York." RG94 NARA M551 Roll 0076. Washington, D.C.: The National Archives, 1965.
53. J. H. Conant, "Michael Kelly." *Banner of Light*, June 27, 1863.
54. J. H. Conant, "Abram Torrey." *Banner of Light*, July 25, 1863.
55. J. R. March, *Dictionary of Classical Mythology*. London: Oxbow Books, 2014.
56. J. H. Conant, "Moses Adams." *Banner of Light*, October 24, 1863.
57. J. H. Conant, "William Connors." *Banner of Light*, June 10, 1865.
58. J. H. Conant, "Colonel Thomas Weld." *Banner of Light*, September 5, 1863.
59. J. H. Conant, "Colonel Moses Delano." *Banner of Light*, October 17, 1863.
60. J. H. Conant, "John Grant." *Banner of Light*, January 30, 1864.
61. J. H. Conant, "Horace Jenning." *Banner of Light*, February 6, 1864.
62. J. H. Conant, "Joe Brown." *Banner of Light*, March 26, 1864.
63. J. H. Conant, "Lieut. Hamilton Burgess." *Banner of Light*, May 7, 1864.
64. J. H. Conant, "Captain Paul Higgins." *Banner of Light*, June 18, 1864.
65. J. H. Conant, "Charles Williams." *Banner of Light*, August 20, 1864.
66. J. H. Conant, "Charles A. Graves." *Banner of Light*, April 8, 1865.

Chapter Eight

1. L. F. Emilio, *History of the Fifty-Fourth Regiment of Massachusetts Volunteer Infantry, 1863–1865*. Boston: Boston Book Company, 1894.
2. William M. Briggs, "Compiled Military Service Records of Volunteer Union Soldiers Who Served with the United States Colored Troops: 54th Massachusetts Infantry Regiment (Colored)." RG94 NARA M1898. Washington, D.C.: The National Archives, 1863.
3. J. H. Conant, "William Briggs." *Banner of Light*, December 5, 1863.
4. William M. Briggs, "Compiled Military Service Records of Volunteer Union Soldiers Who Served with the United States Colored Troops: 54th Massachusetts Infantry Regiment (Colored)." RG94 NARA M1898. Washington, D.C.: The National Archives.
5. J. H. Conant, "James Peer." *Banner of Light*, October 31, 1863.
6. J. H. Conant, "William Sowie." *Banner of Light*, February 27, 1864.
7. J. H. Conant, "Archibald Lewis." *Banner of Light*, April 30, 1864.
8. J. H. Conant, "William Culnuigh." *Banner of Light*, May 28, 1864.
9. L. F. Emilio, *History of the Fifty-Fourth Regiment of Massachusetts Volunteer Infantry, 1863–1865*. Boston: Boston Book Company, 1894.
10. J. H. Conant, "William Andrews." *Banner of Light*, November 14, 1863.
11. J. H. Conant, "William Sampson." *Banner of Light*, November 19, 1864.
12. J. H. Conant, "Alice Burnap." *Banner of Light*, February 21, 1863.
13. J. H. Conant, "Col Thomas Jones." Banner of Light, January 3, 1863.
14. J. H. Conant, "Philip Mason." *Banner of Light*, August 15, 1863.
15. J. H. Conant, "Steven T. Dustin." *Banner of Light*, March 21, 1863.
16. J. H. Conant, "Hugh Fitzwilliam." *Banner of Light*, July 1, 1865.
17. J. H. Conant, "Julius Graham." *Banner of Light*, October 14, 1865.
18. J. H. Conant, "George L. Josselyn." *Banner of Light*, June 25, 1864.
19. J. H. Conant, "Prince." *Banner of Light*, October 22, 1864.
20. Michael Smith, "Index to Compiled Service Records of Volunteer Union Sol-

diers Who Served in Organizations From the State of Massachusetts." RG94 NARA M544. Roll 0037. Washington, D.C.: The National Archives, 1965.

21. J. H. Conant, "Michael Smith." *Banner of Light*, February 11, 1865.

22. J. H. Conant, "Patrick Walsh." *Banner of Light*, May 20, 1865.

23. J. H. Conant, "John O'Brien. " *Banner of Light*, January 7, 1865.

24. John O'Brien, "Index to Compiled Service Records of Volunteer Union Soldiers Who Served in Organizations From the State of Massachusetts," RG 94 NARA M544. Roll 0030. Washington, D.C.: The National Archives, 1865.

25. J. H. Conant, "John O'Brien." *Banner of Light*, August 12, 1865.

26. J. H. Conant, "Patrick Burns." *Banner of Light*, December 9, 1865.

27. J. H. Conant, "Michael Devine." *Banner of Light*, April 22, 1865.

28. J. H. Conant, "Dennis Casey." *Banner of Lght*, September 30, 1865.

29. J. H. Conant, "John Murphy." *Banner of Light*, April 29, 1865.

30. J. H. Conant, "Patrick O'Connell." *Banner of Light*, July 29, 1865.

31. J. H. Conant, "Dave Carney." *Banner of Light*, September 30, 1865.

32. Hudson Tuttle, "Catholicism and Spiritualism: The Opposing Religious Systems of the World." *Banner of Light*, August 12, 1865.

33. Hudson Tuttle, *Scenes in the Spirit World: or, Life in the Spheres*. New York: Partridge and Brittan Publishers, 1855.

34. H. L. Peeke, *A Standard History of Erie County, Ohio*. Chicago: Lewis Publishing Company, 1916.

35. Hudson Tuttle, *Career of Religious Ideas: Their Ultimate: The Religion of Science*. London: J. Burns, 1872.

36. Hudson Tuttle, "Catholicism and Spiritualism: The Opposing Religious Systems of the World." *Banner of Light*, August 12, 1865.

37. J. H. Conant, "Michael Connelly." *Banner of Light*, March 4, 1865.

38. New York Adjutant General's Office, *Annual Report of the Adjutant-General of the State of New York for the Year 1901*, vol. 3: Albany, NY: James B. Lyon, state printers, 1902.

39. J. H. Conant, "Michael Connelly." *Banner of Light*, March 4, 1865.

40. J. H. Conant, "The Soldier and the Suicide." *Banner of Light*, September 7, 1861.

41. J. H. Conant, "Philip Ropes." *Banner of Light*, November 7, 1863.

42. J. H. Conant, "Rebecca Thompson." *Banner of Light*, May 30, 1863.

43. J. H. Conant, "Ada Elliot."*Banner of Light*, March 26, 1864.

44. J. H. Conant, "Eddie Stevens." *Banner of Light*, April 2, 1864.

45. J. H. Conant, "Georgia Dodge." *Banner of Light*, July 2, 1864.

46. J. H. Conant, "Johanna Sheenan." *Banner of Light*, September 24, 1864.

Bibliography

Abbott, O. *The Davenport Brothers. Their History, Travels, and Manifestations.* Published for the author. New York: A. J. Davis & Co., 1864.
"Abraham Lincoln." *Banner of Light,* March 16, 1867.
"Abraham Lincoln." *Banner of Light,* April 27, 1872.
"Additional from Mrs. Nettie C. Maynard." *Banner of Light,* May 28, 1891.
Adjutant General's Office, Massachusetts. *Massachusetts Soldiers, Sailors, and Marines in the Civil War.* Norwood, MA: Norwood Press, 1933.
"Advertisment for Mr. A.B. Whiting." *Baltimore Sun,* January 29, 1858.
"Advertisment Mr. Laning." *Baltimore Sun,* February 6, 1858.
"Advertisment Spiritualism." *Baltimore Sun,* February 12, 1858.
"Advertisments." *The Spiritual Age,* January 1, 1859.
"Affairs in France." *The New York Times,* March 13, 1863.
American News Company. *The American Booksellers' Guide.* New York: American News Company, 1871.
"Amusements." *Chicago Tribune,* December 30, 1865.
"Amusements." *Evening Star,* July 5, 1864.
"Amusements." *New York Herald,* August 20, 1865.
"Amusements To-Night." *Evening Star,* July 8, 1864.
Andrew, A.P. *Statistics for the United States, 1867–1909, Compiled by A. Piatt Andrew.* Washington, D.C.: U.S. Government Printing Office, 1910.
"Announcement." *Evening Star,* June 20, 1864.
"Another Convert to Spiritualism." *Richmond Daily Dispatch,* April 17, 1857.
"Another Victim." *Baltimore Sun,* May 29, 1860.
"Arrested." *Chicago Daily Tribune,* February 2, 1864.
"Assassination of the President." *The Friend of Progress,* May 1865.
"The Assertion." *Evening Star,* February 4, 1873.
"Astrology." *New York Herald,* November 13, 1861.
Barnum, P.T. *The Humbugs of the World.* New York: Carleton, 1866.
"Barnum's American Museum." *New York Clipper,* February 25, 1865.
Barrett, H.D. *Life Work of Mrs. Cora L.V. Richmond.* Chicago: Hack & Anderson, 1895.
Bartlett, G.C. *The Salem Seer: Reminiscences of Charles H. Foster.* New York: United States Book Company, 1891.
Beauregard, P.G.T. "The Battles of 1861." *Richmond Daily Dispatch,* February 3, 1862.
"The Beauties of Spiritualism." *The Jeffersonian,* November 14, 1861.
Bennett, Bridget. *Transatlantic Spiritualism and Nineteenth-Century American Literature.* New York: Palgrave Macmillan, 2007.
"Big Thing on the Spirits." *The Smoky Hill and Republican Union,* May 14, 1864.
Bloomfield, M. *Bloomfield's Illustrated Historical Guide.* St. Augustine, FL: M. Bloomfield, 1885.
Board of Trustees of the Antietam National Cemetery, Maryland. *A Descriptive List of*

the Burial Places of the Remains of Confederate Soldiers. Hagerstown, MD: "Free Press" print, 1868.
Braude, A. "News from the Spirit World: A Checklist of American Spiritualist Periodicals, 1847–1900." *Proceedings of the American Antiquarian Society.* Worcester, MA: American Antiquarian Society, 1990.
Briggs, William M. "Compiled Military Service Records of Volunteer Union Soldiers Who Served with the United States Colored Troops: 54th Massachusetts Infantry Regiment (Colored)." RG94 NARA M1898. Washington, D.C.: The National Archives, 1863.
Britten, E.H. *Modern American Spiritualism: A Twenty Years' Record of the Communion Between Earth and the World of Spirits.* New York: The author, 1870.
Britten, E.H., and M. Wilkinson. *Autobiography of Emma Hardinge Britten.* London: J. Heywood, 1900.
Buckland, R. *The Spirit Book: The Encyclopedia of Clairvoyance, Channeling, and Spirit Communication.* Canton Township, MI: Visible Ink Press, 2005.
Buescher, John Benedict. *The Other Side of Salvation: Spiritualism and the Nineteenth-century Religious Experience.* Boston: Skinner House Books, 2004.
Buescher, John Benedict. *The President's Medium.* Forest Grove, OR: International Association for the Preservation of Spiritualist and Occult Periodicals, 2015.
Burns, W.E. *Witch Hunts in Europe and America: An Encyclopedia.* Westport, CT: Greenwood Press, 2003.
Burr, W.H. "District of Columbia." *Banner of Light,* November 4, 1893.
"Canterbury Hall." *Daily National Republican,* July 7, 1864.
Capron, E.W. *Modern Spiritualism: Its Facts and Fanaticisms, Its Consistencies and Contradictions. With an Appendix.* Boston: Bela Marsh, 1855.
Carpenter, F.B. "Recollections of Abraham Lincoln." *Evansville Daily Journal,* February 9, 1866.
Carroll, B.E. *Spiritualism in Antebellum America.* Bloomington: Indiana University Press, 1997.
Carroll, H.K., and United States Census Office. *Report on Statistics of Churches in the United States at the Eleventh Census, 1890.* Washington, D.C.: U.S. Government Printing Office, 1894.
"A Celebrated Spiritualist." *The Sun* November 1, 1858.
"The Cherry Colored Cat Outdone." *The Sun,* October 11, 1858.
Clark, U. *Plain Guide to Spiritualism: A Handbook for Skeptics, Inquirers, Clergymen, Believers, Lecturers.* Boston: William White & Company, 1863.
"Colchester Repudiated." *New York Herald,* August 25, 1865.
Conant, J.H. "Abram Torrey." *Banner of Light,* July 25, 1863.
Conant, J.H. "Ada Elliot." *Banner of Light,* March 26, 1864.
Conant, J.H. "Alice Burnap." *Banner of Light,* February 21, 1863.
Conant, J.H. "Archibald Lewis." *Banner of Light,* April 30, 1864.
Conant, J.H. "Benjamin Creggan." *Banner of Light,* January 31, 1863.
Conant, J.H. "Billy Thornton." *Banner of Light,* April 11, 1863.
Conant, J.H. "Captain Paul Higgins." *Banner of Light,* June 18, 1864.
Conant, J.H. "Charles A. Graves." *Banner of Light,* April 8, 1865.
Conant, J.H. "Charles Williams." *Banner of Light,* August 20, 1864.
Conant, J.H. "Charlie Hiland." *Banner of Light,* May 10, 1862.
Conant, J.H. "Col Thomas Jones." *Banner of Light,* January 3, 1863.
Conant, J.H. "Colonel Alexander Harris." *Banner of Light,* November 15, 1862.
Conant, J.H. "Colonel Moses Delano." *Banner of Light,* October 17, 1863.
Conant, J.H. "Colonel Thomas Weld." *Banner of Light,* September 5, 1863.
Conant, J.H. "Dave Carney." *Banner of Light,* September 30, 1865.
Conant, J.H. "Dennis Casey." *Banner of Light,* September 30, 1865.
Conant, J.H. "Eddie Stevens." *Banner of Light,* April 2, 1864.
Conant, J.H. "George L. Josselyn." *Banner of Light,* June 25, 1864.
Conant, J.H. "Georgia Dodge." *Banner of Light,* July 2, 1864.
Conant, J.H. "Henry A. Kingsbury." *Banner of Light,* November 1, 1862.

Conant, J.H. "Henry T. Sanderson." *Banner of Light,* October 18, 1862.
Conant, J.H. "Horace Jenning." *Banner of Light,* February 6, 1864.
Conant, J.H. "Hugh Fitzwilliam." *Banner of Light,* July 1, 1865.
Conant, J.H. "Jack Woodbury." *Banner of Light,* September 7, 1861.
Conant, J.H. "James L. Smyth." *Banner of Light,* April 30, 1864.
Conant, J.H. "James Monroe Granby." *Banner of Light,* May 2, 1863.
Conant, J.H. "James Peer." *Banner of Light,* October 31, 1863.
Conant, J.H. "Jerry Deering." *Banner of Light,* June 11, 1864.
Conant, J.H. "Jim Paige." *Banner of Light,* July 9, 1864.
Conant, J.H. "Joe Brown." *Banner of Light,* March 26, 1864.
Conant, J.H. "Johanna Sheenan." *Banner of Light,* September 24, 1864.
Conant, J.H. "John Grant." *Banner of Light,* January 30, 1864.
Conant, J.H. "John Murphy." *Baner of Light,* April 29, 1865.
Conant, J.H. "John O'Brien " *Banner of Light,* January 7, 1865.
Conant, J.H. "John O'Brien." *Banner of Light,* August 12, 1865.
Conant, J.H. "Joseph L. Sawyer." *Banner of Light,* November 29, 1862.
Conant, J.H. "Joseph Stillings." *Banner of Light,* March 1, 1862.
Conant, J.H. "Joseph Whittier." *Banner of Light,* December 26, 1863.
Conant, J.H. "Julius Graham." *Banner of Light,* October 14, 1865.
Conant, J.H. "Levi H. Griswold." *Banner of Light,* February 21, 1863.
Conant, J.H. "Lieut. Hamilton Burgess." *Banner of Light,* May 7, 1864.
Conant, J.H. "Lieutenant Hillyard." *Banner of Light,* February 7, 1863.
Conant, J.H. "Lieutenant Jacob Buckingham." *Banner of Light,* November 15, 1862.
Conant, J.H. "Lieutenant William Conway." *Banner of Light,* May 16, 1863.
Conant, J.H. "Michael Connelly." *Banner of Light,* March 4, 1865.
Conant, J.H. "Michael Devine." *Banner of Light,* April 22, 1865.
Conant, J.H. "Michael Kelly." *Banner of Light,* June 27, 1863.
Conant, J.H. "Michael Smith." *Banner of Light,* February 11, 1865.
Conant, J.H. "Moses Adams." *Banner of Light,* October 24, 1863.
Conant, J.H.. "Nathaniel Jackman." *Banner of Light,* July 19, 1862
Conant, J.H. "Patrick Burns." *Banner of Light,* December 9, 1865.
Conant, J.H. "Patrick O'Connell." *Banner of Light,* July 29, 1865.
Conant, J.H. "Patrick Walsh." *Banner of Light,* May 20, 1865.
Conant, J.H. "Peter Connety." *Banner of Light,* May 30, 1863.
Conant, J.H. "Philip Mason." *Banner of Light,* August 15, 1863.
Conant, J.H. "Philip Ropes." *Banner of Light,* November 7, 1863.
Conant, J.H. "Prince." *Banner of Light,* October 22, 1864.
Conant, J.H. "Rebecca Thompson." *Banner of Light,* May 30, 1863.
Conant, J.H. "Richard Aldrich." *Banner of Light,* October 25, 1862.
Conant, J.H. "Richard S. Andrews." *Banner of Light,* September 17, 1864.
Conant, J.H. "Robert Collins." *Banner of Light,* November 30, 1861.
Conant, J.H. "Robert Morriston." *Banner of Light,* June 8, 1861.
Conant, J.H. "Robert Reidelberg." *Banner of Light,* May 13, 1865.
Conant, J.H. "Sidney T. Graves." *Banner of Light,* February 21, 1863.
Conant, J.H. "The Soldier and the Suicide." *Banner of Light,* September 7, 1861.
Conant, J.H. "Steven T. Dustin." *Banner of Light,* March 21, 1863.
Conant, J.H. "Theodore Guild." *Banner of Light,* May 23, 1863.
Conant, J.H. "Thomas Christian." *Banner of Light,* October 24, 1863.
Conant, J.H. "Thomas Ormsby." *Banner of Light,* May 28, 1864.
Conant, J.H. "Thomas Woodbridge." *Banner of Light,* July 16, 1864.
Conant, J.H. "William Andrews." *Banner of Light,* November 14, 1863.
Conant, J.H. "William Briggs." *Banner of Light,* December 5, 1863.
Conant, J.H. "William Chamberlain." *Banner of Light,* August 31, 1861.
Conant, J.H. "William Connors." *Banner of Light,* June 10, 1865.
Conant, J.H. "William Culnuigh." *Banner of Light,* May 28, 1864.
Conant, J.H. "William E. Ormsby." *Banner of Light,* May 28, 1864.

Conant, J.H. "William H. Smith." *Banner of Light*, February 20, 1864.
Conant, J.H. "William Sampson." *Banner of Light*, November 19, 1864.
Conant, J.H. "William Sowie." *Banner of Light*, February 27, 1864.
"Concerning Chaplains." *National Republican*, December 28, 1861.
"Confession of a Table Mover." *The Geneva Gazette*, December 24, 1858.
"Confessions of a Medium." *The Atlantic Monthly*, December 1860, 699–714.
Conklin, J.B. "The Life of a Medium." *Nichols' Monthly: A Magazine of Social Science, and Progressive Literature*, June 1856.
"Consult Prof. A.B. Severance." *Light of Truth* 20(15) (1897):11.
Cooper, W.J. *We Have the War Upon Us: The Onset of the Civil War, November 1860–April 1861*. New York: Knopf Doubleday, 2012.
Cornell, W.M. *The Life and Public Career of Hon. Horace Greeley*. Boston: Lee & Shepard, 1872.
"A Curious Story About Mrs. Lincoln Reiterated." *New York Times*, February 24, 1872.
Curtis, William Eleroy. *Abraham Lincoln*. Philadelphia: Lippincott, 1902.
"The Danger to the South." *The Richmond Daily Dispatch*, June 27, 1861.
"The Davenport Brothers." *Chicago Daily Tribune*, May 12, 1864.
"Davenport Brothers." *The Sun*, March 14, 1864.
"Davenport Brothers." *The Sun*, March 21, 1864.
"The Davenports." *The Evening Post*, September 29, 1865.
Davis, A.J. *Answers to Ever-Recurring Questions from the People. A Sequel to* The Penetralia. New York: A. J. Davis & Company, 1862.
Davis, A.J. *The Penetralia; Being Harmonial Answers to Important Questions, Fourth Edition*. Boston: Bela Marsh, 1858.
Davis, A.J., and W. Fishbough. *The Principles of Nature, Her Divine Revelations, and a Voice to Mankind*. Boston: Colby & Rich, Banner Publishing House, 1847.
Davis, Andrew Jackson. "Medical Whispers." *Herald of Progress*, 3(19) (1862).
Day, J.W. *Biography of Mrs. J. H. Conant*. Boston: William White and Company, 1873.
"D.D. Hume and Napoleon III." *Banner of Light*, July 2, 1857.
Dewey, D.M. *History of the Strange Sounds or Rappings Heard in Rochester and Western New-York*. Rochester, NY: D. M. Dewey, 1850.
"Diabolism at the Cooper Institute." *New York Herald*, April 30, 1864.
"Dispepsia and Fits." *Nebraska Advertiser*, October 11, 1862.
Doubleday, Abner. *Reminiscences of Forts Sumter and Moultrie in 1860–'61*. New York: Harper & Brothers, 1876.
Dudley, Stephen. "Wonders at Koons' Spirit Room." *Spiritual Telegraph*, December 30, 1854.
"The Eddy Family." *New York Herald*, November 17, 1864.
Edmonds, John W., and George T. Dexter. *Spiritualism*, 3rd ed., vol. 2. New York City: Partridge & Brittan, 1855.
Edmonds, John W., and George T. Dexter. *Spiritualism*, 4th ed. New York: Partridge and Brittan, 1853.
Ellis, A.C. *The Massachusetts Andrew Sharpshooters: A Civil War History and Roster*. Jefferson, NC: McFarland, 2012.
"The Emancipation Proclamation—Mrs. Maynard Disavows." *Banner of Light*, May 16, 1891.
Emerson, Jason. "The Madness of Mary Lincoln." *American Heritage* 57(3) (2006).
Emilio, L.F. *History of the Fifty-Fourth Regiment of Massachusetts Volunteer Infantry, 1863–1865*. Boston: Boston Book Company, 1894.
"The End of Spiritualism." *Brooklyn Daily Eagle*, January 28, 1859.
"Escape from a Hospital." *Herald of Progress*, 3(46) (1863).
Evans, Henry Ridgely. "Recollections of Four Famous Fantasists." *New Age Magazine* (8) (1908).
"An Evening with a Spiritual Medium." *Brooklyn Daily Eagle*, April 1, 1862.
"An Evening with the Spirits." *Brooklyn Daily Eagle*, November 11, 1864.
Everett, J., and J. Koons. *A Book for Skeptics*. Columbus, OH: Osgood & Blake, printers, 1853.

"Ex-Minister Robert T. Lincoln." *The Sun,* November 1, 1893.
"Exciting Scene in Liverpool." *Brooklyn Daily Eagle,* March 4, 1865.
Faust, D.G. *This Republic of Suffering: Death and the American Civil War.* New York: Vintage Books, 2009.
Ferris, William H. "A Review of Modern Spiritualism." *Ladies' Repository,* January 1856.
"Fire-Incendiarism." *Meigs County Telegraph,* December 28, 1852.
"The Fish Family." *Northern New York Journal,* January 19, 1853.
Fogarty, R.S. *All Things New: American Communes and Utopian Movements, 1860–1914.* Lanham, MD: Lexington Books, 2003.
Fold3. Fold3, 2019 [accessed January 14, 2019].
Forster, T.G. *Unanswerable Logic.* Boston: Colby & Rich, 1887.
"From Gen. McClellan's Army." *New York Times,* May 8, 1862.
"From the Spirit Land." *The New York Times,* August 23, 1868.
"General City News." *New York Times,* June 13, 1864.
General Conference of Seventh-Day Adventists. *Advent Review and Sabbath Herald,* 1857.
Gibbons, Henry. "Modern Spiritism." *Pacific Medical and Surgical Journal* 9(16) (1875).
"Grand Exhibition." *Holmes County Farmer,* June 2, 1864.
Grasso, Christopher, *Skepticism and American Faith: From the Revolution to the Civil War.* New York: Oxford University Press, 2018.
Gutierrez, Cathy. *Plato's Ghost: Spiritualism in the American Renaissance.* New York: Oxford University Press, 2009.
Hare, R. *Experimental Investigation of the Spirit Manifestations, Demonstrating the Existence of Spirits and Their Communion with Mortals.* New York: Partridge & Brittan, 1856.
Hartman, Andrew. "Spiritualism in California." *Banner of Light,* March 21, 1863.
Hartranft, R.C. "Letter to the Editor." *Banner of Light,* September 10, 1891.
Hatch, Cora L.V. *Discourses on Religion, Morals, Philosophy and Metaphysics,* vol. 1, 2nd ed. New York: B.F. Hatch, 1858.
"Heaven and Earth." *Herald of Progress,* 2(31) (1861).
"The Herald of Progress." *The New Republic.* July 5, 1862.
Hermon, H. *Hellerism. Second-Sight Mystery. Supernatural Vision or Second-Sight. What Is It? A Mystery: A Complete Manual for Teaching This Peculiar Art.* New York: Lee and Shepard, 1884.
Historical and Biographical Annals of Columbia and Montour Counties, Pennsylvania, vol. 1. Chicago: J.H. Beers & Company, 1915.
Home, D.D. *D. D. Home: His Life and Mission.* London: Trubner & Company, 1888.
Home, D.D. *Incidents in My Life,* 5th ed. New York City: A.J. Davis and Company, 1864.
Hopkins, A.A., and H.R. Evans. *Magic: Stage Illusions and Scientific Diversions, Including Trick Photography.* New York: Munn & Company, 1901.
"An Hour with the Spirits." *New York Daily Tribune,* June 5, 1850.
Howitt, W. *The History of the Supernatural.* Philadelphia, J.B. Lippincott & Co., 1863.
Hull, M., and W.F. Jamieson. *The Greatest Debate within a Half Century Upon Modern Spiritualism.* Chicago: Progressive Thinker Publishing House, 1904.
"Hume, The Medium." *The Spiritual Age,* November 13, 1858.
"Hume, The Medium and Rufus Elmer." *Banner of Light,* December 4, 1858.
Hyatt, Isaiah. "Modern Inspiration, at Mountain Cove." *Spiritual Telegraph,* October 16, 1852.
"Hydro-Electric Cure." *Evening Argus,* June 19, 1862.
"In Re Abraham Lincoln and Spiritualism." *Banner of Light,* December 12, 1891.
"Infatuation, Fantacism, Delusion, Humbug." *New York Herald,* May 26, 1851.
Ingersoll, L.D. *The Life of Horace Greeley: Founder of the* New York Tribune, *with Extended Notices of Many of His Contemporary Statesmen and Journalists.* Chicago: Union Publishing Company, 1873.
Insider. "John Wilkes Booth." *Brooklyn Daily Eagle,* February 8, 1885.
"Interesting Interview Between Judge Edmonds and a Reporter." *Sunbury American,* December 3, 1853.

"It Is Said." *Wood County Reporter,* January 18, 1862.
"It Would Seem." *Vermont Phoenix,* April 19, 1872.
"John McQueen and Spiritualism." *The Hillsdale Standard,* February 28, 1865.
"Judge Edmonds and the Spirits, Visit of Our Reporter." *New York Herald,* October 30, 1853.
"Judge Edmonds on Spiritualism." *New York Times,* October 20, 1853.
"Junius Brutus Booth." *Banner of Light,* October 7, 1865.
"Just Published." *The Sun,* May 10, 1860.
"Just So." *Penn-Yan Democrat,* May 16, 1862.
Kase, Samuel. "A Sensation." *St. Louis Republican,* September 10, 1876.
Kelly, Michael. "Index to Compiled Service Records of Volunteer Union Soldiers Who Served in Organizations from the State of New York." RG94 NARA M551 Roll 0076. Washington, D.C.: The National Archives, 1965.
Koons, J. *The Spirits in Athens County,* ed. S.B. Brittan, vol. 3, *The Spiritual Telegraph.* New York City: Partridge & Brittan, 1853.
Krasnow, J.G. *Jacktown: History & Hard Times at Michigan's First State Prison.* Charleston, SC: The History Press, 2017.
Lande, R. Gregory. *Psychological Consequences of the American Civil War.* Jefferson, NC: McFarland, 2017.
Lause, M.A. *Free Spirits: Spiritualism, Republicanism, and Radicalism in the Civil War Era.* Champaign: University of Illinois Press, 2016.
"Lecture by Miss M. Johnson." *Brooklyn Daily Eagle,* January 10, 1860.
"Lecture on Abraham Lincoln, and a Poem." *Banner of Light,* May 6, 1865.
Lenardon, R.J., M.P.O. Morford, and M. Sham. *A Companion to Classical Mythology.* London: Longman, 1997.
"Letter from Brother Peebles." *The Herald of Progress,* March 22, 1862.
"Letter from Judge Edmonds." *Banner of Light,* December 22, 1866.
"Letter of Judge Edmonds on Spiritual Manifestations." *New York Herald,* August 6, 1853.
"Literature and Logic of 'The Interior.'" *The National Magazine* 1 (1852):353.
"Literature of Spiritualsm." *The Spiritual Magazine.* London: F. Pitman, 1871.
Livermore, Mary A. "Where There's a Will There's a Way." *Herald of Progress,* 4(33) (1863).
"Lyceum Hall Meetings." *Banner of Light,* July 1, 1865.
"Madame Victorine Hollard Advertisement." *Cass County Republican,* November 7, 1861.
"Magic and Mystery." *Marysville Daily Appeal,* February 11, 1860.
March, J.R. *Dictionary of Classical Mythology.* London: Oxbow Books, 2014.
"A Marvellous Incident." *The Manchester Journal,* January 19, 1864.
"Maryland Institute." *The Sun,* March 18, 1864.
"Material Organization." *Herald of Progress,* 2(52) (1862).
Maynard, N.C. "Was Abraham Lincoln a Spiritualist?" *Banner of Light,* May 28, 1892.
Maynard, N.C. *Was Abraham Lincoln a Spiritualist?: Or, Curious Revelations from the Life of a Trance Medium.* Philadelphia: R.C. Hartranft, 1891.
McCabe, J.D. *Life and Campaigns of General Robert E. Lee.* Atlanta: National Publishing Company, 1866.
McLean, J. *California Sabers: The 2nd Massachusetts Cavalry in the Civil War.* Bloomington: Indiana University Press, 2000.
"Mediums and Believers." *The Herald of Progress,* February 4, 1860.
"Message Department." *Banner of Light,* May 16, 1863.
"Message Department." *Banner of Light,* August 26, 1865.
"Message Department." *Banner of Light,* May 29, 1869.
"Miracles Performed in 1864!" *Herald of Progress,* 4(52) (1864).
"Miscellaneous News." *New York Herald,* February 9, 1865.
"Mobocracy in Michigan." *Chicago Tribune,* January 31, 1861.
"Modern Spiritualism." *The New York Herald,* March 7, 1858.
"More About the Spirits." *New York Daily Tribune,* January 29, 1851.
Morris, D. *Boston in the Golden Age of Spiritualism: Séances, Mediums & Immortality.* Charleston, SC: The History Press, 2014.

Mott, F.L. *A History of American Magazines, 1850–1865.* Cambridge, MA: Harvard University Press, 1938.
"Mrs. Anderson." *Chicago Tribune,* June 17, 1862.
"Mrs. Cora L.V. Hatch." *New York Herald,* April 13, 1862.
"Mrs. Cora L.V. Hatch at Brainard's Hall." *Cleveland Morning Leader,* July 15, 1862.
"Mrs. Cora L.V. Hatch in a Trance." *New York Times,* January 8, 1859.
"Mrs. Cora V.L. Hatch." *Evening Star,* April 15, 1857.
"Mrs. Leonard." *Westfield Republican,* December 27, 1865.
"Mrs. Lincoln." *Missouri Weekly Patriot,* August 5, 1875.
"Mrs. Nettie Colburn Maynard." *Baner of Light,* April 11, 1891.
Mumler, William H. "The Personal Experiences of William H. Mumler in Spirit-Photography." *Banner of Light,* January 30, 1875.
"The Mumler Photographs." *New York Times,* May 23, 1869.
"The Murderer of Lincoln." *Banner of Light,* August 24, 1872.
"The Mysterious Mr. Home." *Evening Star,* July 5, 1908.
Nartonis, David K. 2010. "The Rise of 19th-Century American Spiritualism, 1854–1873." *Journal for the Scientific Study of Religion* 49(2) (2010):361–373.
"The National Calamity." *New York Times,* April 16, 1865.
"The National Struggle." *Banner of Light,* October 12, 1863.
Neely, M.E., and R.G. McMurtry. *The Insanity File: The Case of Mary Todd Lincoln.* Carbondale, IL: Southern Illinois University Press, 1993.
"A New Colony." *Bradford Reporter,* January 10, 1861.
"A New Development." *The Troy Weekly Times,* July 31, 1858.
"A New Era in Human Development." *New York Herald,* May 4, 1864.
"The New Fashion in Spiritualism." *New York Times,* February 27, 1921.
"New Light on the Campaign." *Daily Intelligencer,* May 16, 1862.
New York Adjutant General's Office. *Annual Report of the Adjutant-General of the State of New York for the Year 1901,* vol. 3: Albany, NY: James B. Lyon, state printers, 1902.
"Niblo's Saloon." *New York Herald,* October 6, 1864.
Nichols, T.L. *Supramundane Facts in the Life of Rev. Jesse Babcock Ferguson.* London: F. Pitman, 1865.
"No Fighting." *Indiana State Sentinel,* June 26, 1861.
"Not Around." *Daily Reformer,* December 23, 1862.
"Nothing but War." *Banner of Light,* January 10, 1863.
"Obituary." *New York Times,* June 26, 1877.
"Obituary—Ex-Judge Edmonds." *New York Times,* April 7, 1874.
O'Brien, John. "Index to Compiled Service Records of Volunteer Union Soldiers Who Served in Organizations From the State of Massachusetts." RG 94 NARA M544. Roll 0030. Washington, D.C.: The National Archives, 1865.
Ormsby, William. "Compiled Service Records of Volunteer Union Soldiers Who Served in Organizations from the State of Massachusetts." RG94-CMSR-MA-2CAV-Bx0160_MISC. Washington, D.C.: The National Archives, 1863.
Ormsby, William E. "Compiled Service Records of Volunteer Union Soldiers Who Served in Organizations from the State of Massachusetts." RG94-CMSR-MA-2CAV-Bx0135. Washington, D.C.: The National Archives, 1863.
Ormsby Court Martial. In *William E. Ormbey (Ormsby) Company E, 2nd Massachusetts.* Records of the Adjutant General's Office, 1780–1917. 1864.
"Our Cause in Washington." *Banner of Light,* November 21, 1863.
"Our National Loss." *Chicago Tribune,* April 20, 1865.
Owen, R.D. *The Debatable Land Between This World and the Next: With Illustrative Narrations.* New York: G.W. Carleton & Company, 1871.
Owen, R.D. *Footfalls on the Boundary of Another World.* Philadelphia: Lippincott, 1860.
Packard, E.P.W., and S.N.B. Olsen. *The Prisoners' Hidden Life.* Chicago: J.N. Clarke, 1871.
Paist, S.H., and H.T. Childs. *A Narrative of the Experiences of Horace Abraham Ackley, M.D.* Philadelphia, PA: J.B. Lippincott & Co., 1861.
"Patriotic Woman." *Green Mountain Freeman,* May 1, 1861.

"Peace and War." *Banner of Light,* June 6, 1863.
Peeke, H.L. *A Standard History of Erie County, Ohio.* Chicago: Lewis Publishing Company, 1916.
Pemberton, T.E. *Memoir of Edward Askew Sothern.* London: R. Bentley and Son, 1889.
"The People and the Fast Day." *Richmond Daily Dispatch,* August 11, 1863.
Podmore, F. *Modern Spiritualism: A History and a Criticism.* London: Methuen & Company, 1902.
"Police Court." *Cleveland Morning Leader,* April 16, 1864.
"Political Notes." *The New York Herald,* September 11, 1868.
"Popular Amusements." *New York Herald,* November 15, 1864.
"Position and Progress of Spiritualism." *New York Herald,* March 5, 1854.
"Poughkeppsie Seer and His Revelations." *Fraser's Magazine for Town and Country.* London: James Fraser, February 1848.
"Powerful Manifestations of Spirits." *The Richmond Palladium,* February 23, 1855.
"The Present Crisis." *Banner of Light,* November 21, 1863.
"President Mahan on Modern Spiritualism." *Evening Star,* February 25, 1857.
"Presidential Aspirations and Exhalations." *New York Herald,* September 12, 1863.
"Prof. Grimes." *Penn-Yan Democrat,* May 30, 1862.
"Progress of the War." *Herald of Progress,* 2(12) (1861).
"Proscription and Religious Faith in War." *Banner of Light,* June 27, 1863.
"P.T. Barnum on Humbug." *The Sun,* March 6, 1865.
"Radiates." *Richmond Daily Dispatch,* December 14, 1865.
Rains, G.J., P.S. Michie, and H.M. Schiller. *Confederate Torpedoes.* Jefferson, NC: McFarland, 2011.
"Records of the Fifty-Fourth Massachusetts Infantry Regiment (Colored), 1863–1865." NARA M1659, RG94. Washington, D.C.: The National Archives, 2011.
Redd, R. *St. Augustine and the Civil War.* Charleston, SC: The History Press, 2014.
Rein, Katharina. "Mind Reading in Stage Magic: The "Second Sight" Illusion, Media, and Mediums." *Communication +1* 4 (2015).
"A Remarkable Exhibition in New York." *Memphis Daily Appeal,* May 26, 1864.
"Renunciation of Spiritualism." *The Sun,* February 10, 1862.
"A Revelation." *Evening Star,* May 10, 1864.
Robinson, C.M. *Shark of the Confederacy: The Story of the CSS Alabama.* Annapolis, MD: Naval Institute Press, 1995.
"A Sad Story." *The Caledonian,* November 7, 1862.
"A Sad Story." *The Sun,* November 1, 1862.
"Salle Diabolique." *New York Herald,* September 11, 1864.
"Sarah Haviland and Martha Grinder." *Religio Philosophical Journal* 1(21) (1866).
"Scandalous Table Talk." *Smoky Hill and Republican Union,* June 11, 1864.
Scovel, James M. *Lippincott's Monthly Magazine, Personal Recollections of Abraham Lincoln.* Philadelphia: J.B. Lippincott and Company, 1889.
Search for Soldiers. https://www.nps.gov/civilwar/search-soldiers.htm, National Park Service [accessed January 14, 2019].
"Seeing Is Believing." *Lippincott's Monthly Magazine.* Philadelphia: J.B. Lippincott and Company, 1880.
"Sentiments of a Southern Wife." *The Richmond Daily Dispatch,* June 15, 1861.
Severance, A.B. "Psychometric Delineation of a Lock of Hair." *Facts,* 3(2) (1884).
Sheaffer, Abby. "Entranced: St. Charles' Secret Spiritualist History." *Kane County Chronicle,* October 26, 2012.
"Should Spiritualists Go to War?" *Herald of Progress,* May 18, 1861.
"Skeptic." *The Free South,* July 11, 1863.
Sketch of Robert Hare. Popular Science Monthly, ed. William Jay Youmans, vol. 42. New York: D. Appleton, 1893.
Smith, J.R.W. *Speeches Concerning Politics and Government During the Civil War Period,* 1864.
Smith, Michael. "Index to Compiled Service Records of Volunteer Union Soldiers Who

Served in Organizations From the State of Massachusetts." RG94 NARA M544. Roll 0037. Washington, D.C.: The National Academy, 1965.
Smith, William H. "Compiled Service Records of Volunteer Union Soldiers Who Served in Organizations from the State of Massachusetts." RG94-CMSR-MA-35INF-Bx2895_MISC. Washington, D.C.: The National Academy, 1863.
"Some of the English Journals." *Brooklyn Eagle*, September 9, 1863.
"Something Worth the Age." *Herald of Progress*, 4(52) (1864).
"Sothern the Actor and the Spirits." *Brooklyn Daily Eagle*, December 30, 1865.
Spear, J.M. and S.C. Hewitt. *Messages from the Superior State*. Boston: Bela Marsh, 1853.
"Spirit Message." *Banner of Light*, December 30, 1865.
"Spirit Rappings." *Ebensburg Alleghanian*, September 12, 1867.
"Spirit-Rooms at the West." *The Spiritual Telegraph*, March 26, 1859.
"Spirits at the White House." *Atlanta Constitution*, September 13, 1868.
"The Spirits on Trial." *New York Herald*, August 23, 1865.
"The Spirits on Trial at Buffalo." *The New York Reformer*, August 26, 1865.
"The Spiritual Age." *The Spiritual Age*, January 2, 1858.
"A Spiritual Circle at the White House." *The Morgantown Monitor*, June 27, 1863.
"Spiritual Convention." *Chicago Tribune*, August 11, 1864.
"Spiritual Convention." *Chicago Tribune*, August 12, 1864.
"Spiritual Convention." *Chicago Tribune*, August 17, 1864.
"A Spiritual Humbug Exposed." *Cleveland Morning Leader*, August 31, 1864.
"Spiritual Languages." *Brooklyn Daily Eagle*, July 20, 1859.
"Spiritual Machine." *Scientific American* 21 (1855):162.
"Spiritual Magnetism." *The Star of the North*, April 19, 1855.
"Spiritual Manifestations." *Daily National Republican*, February 25, 1864.
"Spiritual Manifestations." *Daily Nashville Patriot*, January 24, 1861.
"Spiritual Manifestations." *Evening Star*, February 26, 1864.
"Spiritual Manifestations." *Richmond Palladium*, March 2, 1855.
"Spiritual Manifestations by the Thorpe Brothers." *New York Herald*, August 10, 1864.
"The Spiritual Medium Case." *The Sun*, September 22, 1865.
"A 'Spiritual Medium' Humbug Exposed." *Brooklyn Daily Eagle*, November 17, 1865.
"Spiritual Phenomena." *Sangamo Journal*, May 22, 1861.
"The Spiritual Rappings." *The Spirit of the Times*, June 25, 1850.
"Spiritualism." *Cleveland Morning Leader*, January 22, 1864.
"Spiritualism." *The Evansville Daily Journal*, January 25, 1861.
"Spiritualism." *New York Herald*, September 25, 1865.
"Spiritualism." *Sangamo Journal Illinois State Journal*, October 2, 1865.
"Spiritualism." *The Sun*, June 3, 1857.
"Spiritualism." *The Sun*, December 17, 1862.
"Spiritualism." *The Sun*, January 22, 1864.
"Spiritualism." *The Sun*, April 2, 1864.
"Spiritualism." *The Sun*, October 21, 1865.
"Spiritualism Alias Jugglery." *Green-Mountain Freeman*, August 4, 1863.
"Spiritualism and Hobgoblins." *Indiana State Sentinel*, May 13, 1863.
"Spiritualism and Insanity." *Daily Alta California*, February 14, 1864.
"Spiritualism and Jugglery." *New York Times*, August 27, 1865.
"Spiritualism and Magic." *Sangamo Journal Illinois State Journal*, August 30, 1865.
"Spiritualism at the White House." *Morning Leader*, June 4, 1863.
"Spiritualism at the White House." *New York Herald*, May 30, 1863.
"Spiritualism Eclipsed." *The Smoky Hill and Republican Union*, June 4, 1864.
"Spiritualism Exposed." *The Hillsdale Standard*, February 21, 1865.
"Spiritualism in Biography—John Murry Spear." *The Spiritual Magazine*, 8(5) (1864):344–351.
"Spiritualism in Bloomington, IL." *Banner of Light*, December 12, 1863.
"Spiritualism in Camp Dennison." *Cincinnati Daily Press*, November 18, 1861.
"Spiritualism in Court." *Brooklyn Daily Eagle*, March 16, 1855.

"Spiritualism in Court." *Chicago Tribune*, August 24, 1865.
"Spiritualism in Grand Rapids, MI." *Banner of Light*, December 12, 1863.
"Spiritualism in Washington." *Evening Star*, February 1, 1864.
"Spiritualism Is Jugglery." *New York Herald*, August 24, 1865.
"Spiritualism Jugglery." *New York Times*, August 27, 1865.
"Spiritualism on Trial." *Cleveland Leader*, August 14, 1865.
"Spiritualism Pronounced Jugglery by an Intelligent Jury." *New York Herald*, August 24, 1865.
"Spiritualist Lecture." *Cleveland Morning Leader*, December 20, 1862.
"Spiritualists Encamped." *The Sun*, July 21, 1879.
"The Spiritualists Out of Harmony." *Brooklyn Eagle*, August 19, 1864.
"Spirituality and Mathematics." *Wheeling Daily Intelligencer*, January 11, 1858.
"Spooks That Speak." *Brooklyn Eagle*, September 19, 1870.
"The State Benevolent Institutions at Jacksonville." *Illinois State Journal*, January 20, 1863.
"The State of the Rebellion." *Banner of Light*, May 23, 1863.
"Strange Work for the Spirits." *New York Times*, February 10, 1873.
"Suicide Caused by Spiritualism." *The Sun*, February 9, 1861.
"Sunday Evening Spiritual Meeting." *Evening Star*, March 5, 1864.
"Superstition." *Richmond Dispatch*, March 31, 1865.
Swenson, Timothy. *Charles S. Eigenbrodt: Alvarado Civil War Hero*. Author, 2005.
"The Table Tossing Delusion." *The Norfolk Post*, December 29, 1865.
"Tad Lincoln." *Banner of Light*, July 27, 1872.
Taylor, B. *Confessions of a Medium, Prose Writings of Bayard Taylor*. New York City: G.P. Putnam, 1862.
"Terrible National Calamity." *Banner of Light*, April 22, 1865.
"There Is a Story." *The Daily News*, September 11, 1868.
"There Is a Story." *Richmond Dispatch*, September 9, 1868.
"The Tibbets Case." *New York Herald*, February 8, 1865.
"Tibbets in a New Character." *New York Herald*, February 7, 1865.
"To Printers." *The Mountain Cove Journal and Spiritual Harbinger*, October 20, 1853.
"To the Public." *Indiana State Sentinel*, September 1, 1862.
"The Tragedy at Battle Creek." *Chicago Tribune*, December 28, 1865.
"Transition of Mrs. Nettie C. Maynard." *Banner of Light*, July 9, 1892.
Turner, M.P. "More Light on the Maynard Episode." *Banner of Light*, May 30, 1891.
Tuttle, H. *Career of Religious Ideas: Their Ultimate: The Religion of Science*. London: J. Burns, 1872.
Tuttle, H. *Scenes in the Spirit World: or, Life in the Spheres*. New York: Partridge and Brittan, 1855.
Tuttle, Hudson. "Catholicism and Spiritualism: The Opposing Religious Systems of the World." *Banner of Light*, August 12, 1865.
Tuttle, Hudson. "Was Lincoln a Spiritualist?" *Banner of Light*, November 21, 1891.
Twitchell, Joseph. "Spiritual Manifestations." *Daily Alta California*, December 28, 1852.
"Uncle Sam v. 'Mediums.'" *Brooklyn Daily Eagle*, August 12, 1865.
Underhill, A.L. *The Missing Link in Modern Spiritualism*. New York: Thomas R. Knox & Company, 1885.
United States Army. "Massachusetts Infantry Regiment, 35th. 1884." *History of the Thirty-Fifth Regiment Massachusetts Volunteers, 1862–1865: With a Roster*. Boston: Mills, Knight & Company, 1885.
"Victimized Spirituality." *Dayton Daily Empire*, June 2, 1865.
"Victory for One." *Herald of Progress*, 4(40) (1863).
"Visit to the Koons Family." *Plymouth Banner*, March 15, 1855.
"A Wag Beats Spiritualism." *Penn-Yan Democrat*, January 17, 1862.
"War Meeting in Brooklyn." *New York Herald*, September 4, 1862.
"War Prophecies." *Herald of Progress*, 4(30) (1863).
Ward, A. *The Complete Works of Artemus Ward*. New York: A.L. Burt Company, 1898.
"Was Abraham Lincoln a Spiritualist." *Banner of Light*, April 11, 1891.

"Washington Spiritual Conference." *Evening Star,* April 16, 1864.
Waugh, Joan. "New England Cavalier." In *The Shenandoah Valley Campaign of 1864,* ed. Gary W. Gallagher, 314–316. Chapel Hill: University of North Carolina Press, 2006.
"We Copy the Following Good Story." *The North Carolinian,* February 10, 1855.
Wells, R.B.D. *A New Illustrated Hand-book of Phrenology, Physiology and Physiognomy.* London: H. Vickers, 1860.
"What Next?" *Banner of Light,* October 24, 1863.
"Whisperings to Correspondents." *Herald of Progress,* 3(45) (1862).
"Whisperings to Correspondents." *Herald of Progress,* 3(50) (1863).
"The White House." *Sweetwater Forerunner,* September 10, 1868.
Whitney, John F. *Abraham Lincoln Papers, John F. Whitney to Abraham Lincoln.* 1861. Washington, D.C.: Library of Congress [accessed October 20, 2018].
Whitney, John F. "Was Abraham Lincoln a Spiritualist?" *Banner of Light,* October 8, 1892.
Whittier, Joseph H. "Compiled Service Records of Volunteer Union Soldiers Who Served in Organizations from the State of Massachusetts." RG94-CMSR-MA-34INF-Bx2842. Washington, D.C.: The National Archives, 1862.
Wilbur, H.W., and W.B. Hand. *Illustrated History of the Town of Hammonton; with an Account of Its Soil, Climate and Industries.* Hammonton, NJ: The Mirror Steam Printing House, 1889.
"Will Mr. Lincoln Become a Dictator." *The Standard,* January 19, 1863.
Williams, T.H. *P. G. T. Beauregard: Napoleon in Gray.* Baton Rouge, LA: LSU Press, 1995.
Wilson, E.V. *The Truths of Spiritualism.* Chicago: Hazlitt and Reed, 1879.
"Wiltsie." *The Ottawa Free Trader,* January 31, 1863.
"Wisconsin." *Banner of Light,* November 28, 1891.
"A Wonderful Child." *The Daily Exchange,* March 21, 1861.
"Wonders of the Nineteenth Century." *The National Era,* August 8, 1850.
"A Word with the Spiritualists." *Watertown Republican,* July 26, 1861.
Wright, Ben, and Zachery W. Dresser, eds. *Apocalypse and the Millennium in the American Civil War Era.* Baton Rouge: Louisiana State University Press, 2013.
"A Young Soldier Drawn by His Mother's Anxiety." *Herald of Progress,* 3(34) (1862).

Index

Numbers in **bold italics** indicate pages with illustrations

Ackley, Horace Abraham 70
Adams, Moses 163
Age of Progress 35
Alabama 141, 150–53, 157, 160, 166
CSS *Alabama* 97
Aldrich, Richard 160
American Booksellers' Guide 124
Anderson, John H. 80
Andrew, John A. 167
Andrew Sharpshooters 154
Andrews, Richard S. 155
Andrews, William 170, 173
Anguish, Andrew 30
animal magnetism 3, 31, 41, 71, 130
Ann Arbor 44, 89
Apostolic Movement 14–15
Atlantic Monthly 40

Baker, Daniel J. 88
Baltimore 31, 39, 49, 60, 70, 78, 126
Banner of Light: history ***131***; séances 135
Barnum, Phineas T. ***86***–87
Barnum's American Museum 86
Battle of Antietam 140, 149–56; dead soldiers ***156***; Dunker Church ***153***
Battle of Bull Run, First 1, 115, 140, 150, 156–59
Battle of Bull Run, Second 140, 156, 160–64
Battle of Chancellorsville 96, 175
Battle of Fort Pillow 177–78
Battle of Fredericksburg 140
Battle of Gaines Mill 182
Battle of Gettysburg 130, 140, 164–66
Battle of Richmond 140
Battle of Roanoke Island 174
Battle of Sharpsburg 129
Battle of Shiloh 140

battlefield atrocities ***138***
battlefield trophies 1, ***2***, 158
Beebe, Lottie 37
Bellevue Place 109
Benedict, E.A. 13–15
Benson, George 110
Berry, William 131–33, 135, 137
Booth, John Wilkes 92, ***93***, 99–100, 104, 108
Brainard's Hall 76
Briggs, William 170
Britten, Emma Floyd Hardinge 72, ***73***, 74
Brooklyn Daily Eagle 50, 101
Brown, Jacob 49
Brown, Joe 165
Buckingham, Lt. Jacob 149
Burnap, Alice 174
Burnap, Oliver 174
Burns, Patrick 180
Burtis, Lewis 80

California 16, 41, 47, 66, 69, 72, 74–75, 144–45
Camp Douglas 70
Cappy, Laura 55
Capron, Eliab 8
Carney, Dave 182
Casey, Dennis 181
Catholicism 137, 178–84
Chamberlain, William 156
Chase, Warren 53
Christian, Thomas 153
Church, William T. 54
Clafin, Tennessee 44
clairvoyant physician 45, 54
Clark, Uriah 56
Cleveland Leader 96
Colby, Luther 131–32, 135

217

Colchester, Charles 78–82, 110
Collins, Robert 158
Collyer, Robert H. 72
Conant, Frances: *Banner of Light* 131–32; early life *133*; *Message Department* 136–38, 140; séances 132, 135; spirit doctor 135
Conklin, John Benjamin 34, 44, 61, 74, 112, *113*, 120–21
Connelly, Michael 184
Connety, Peter 162
Connors, William 164
Conway, Lieutenant William 152
Cook, Josiah 79
Cook, Thomas 114
Cooke, Lucy A. 45
Creggan, Benjamin 161
Culnuigh, William 170, 172–73
Currier, Augusta A. 71

Davenport, Ira 58, 84
Davenport Brothers 58–63, 65, 76, 83–85; séance cabinet *59*
Davis, Andrew Jackson: books 33, 125; early life 31; *Herald of Progress* 34; lectures 32; medical advice 128; thoughts on Civil War 45
Dean, Albert 83
death: Catholics 173, 178; described 165; fever 159; grieving family *189*; painful 160, *161*, 173, 180; painless 129, 142, 154
Deering, Jerry 154
DeForce, Laura 44
Delano, Colonel Moses 164
Dennet, Oliver 24
desertion 144, 146–48, 154
Devil's Mark 50
Devine, Michael 180
Dexter, George T. 28–29
Dobbs, Abraham Smith 76
Dodge, Hiram 188
Dole, Deacon Abijah 67
Doten, Lizzie 67, 70, 99
Doubleday, Abner 143
drumhead court-martial *146*–47
Dudley, Stephen 35
Dustin, Steven T. 175
dysentery 128, 171
dyspepsia 36, 49

Eddy family 57, 64–*65*
Edmonds, Frank 100
Eigenbrodt, Charles 144–45
electromagnetic physician 34
Ellis, Laura V. 83
Elmer, Rufus 20

Emancipation Proclamation 95, 118–21, 167
equality, female 126, 187
execution, military 143

Fay, Henry Melville 76
Ferguson, Jesse Babcock 21
Ferrin, William 80
Ferris, William H. 30
Fetters, Abby 42
54th Regiment Massachusetts Volunteer Infantry: attacking Fort Wagner *169*; formation 167; Morris Island 168; spirits 142
Fisher, John 134
Fitzgibbons, William 64
Fitzwilliam, Hugh 175
Florence, Colonel Thomas 103
Florida 121, 141
Florida Invincibles 166
Flyn, Amos 30
Forster, Thomas Gales 70
Fort Donelson 23
Fort Moultrie 142–*43*
Fort Pillow 177–78
Fort Sumter 34, 45, 142
Fort Wagner 168–70, 172–73
Foster, Charles H. 50
Foster, Thomas 116
Fountain Grove Community 16
Fox, Leah 17
Fox sisters 7–9, 16–18, 20, 35, 41, 74, 78, 112, 124
Franklin, Benjamin 95
free love 46, 57, 67, 69, 125–26

gambling 55
Gibbons, Henry 72
Graham, Julius 177
Granby, James Monroe 162
Grant, John 165
Grant, Gen. Ulysses S. 92
Graves, Charles A. 166
Greeley, Horace 9, 16–18, 95
Griffing, Jane 44
Griswold, Levi H. 151
Guild, Theodore 144

Hannis, Hattie 88
Hardinge, Emma *see* Britten, Emma Floyd Hardinge
Hare, Robert 26–27
Harris, Col. Alexander 149
Harris, Thomas 14–16
Hartman, Andrew 54
Hartranft, Rufus C. 120

Index

Hatch, Cora *11*, 55
Haviland, Sarah 88
Heller, Robert 77
Hellerism 77
Herald of Progress 128, 131
Hermon, Harry 77
Herr Shockall 96
Hibbard, George B. 79–80
Higby, Charles 40
Higgins, Capt. Paul 166
Hiland, Charlie 158
Hillyard, Lt. Walter 150
Home, Daniel Dunglas 18, 21
Hooker, Gen. Joseph 96
Hope Chapel 63, 65
Howard, Caroline 109
Howard House Hotel 109
Hoxie, Joseph 51
Hoyt, Miss 46–47
Humbugs of the World 87
Hyatt, Isaiah S. 13, 16
Hydesville 5, 56
hydro-electric clinic 49

insanity: caused by Spiritualism 38, 40, 42, 51, 57, 72, 109; precipitated 72; risk 44

Jackman, Nathaniel 157
James Island 168
Jamieson, William F. 54
Jenning, Horace 165
Johnson, Miss 40
Jones, Stephen 67
Jones, Col. Thomas 174
Josselyn, George L. 177
jugglery 78–80

Kahn, Frank 80
Kansas 62
Kase, Samuel P. 110, 112–14
Kean, Thomas 80
Kelly, Michael 163
Kentucky Jerks 53
King, Johnny 58
Kingsbury, Henry A. 160
Koons, Jonathan 35–36

Laurie, Cranston 116
Lee, Gen. Robert E. 92, 130
Levingston, William 32
levitations 15, 21, 114
Lewis, Archibald 170, 172
Libby Prison 163
Lincoln: assassination 98; early spirit visit 98; meets Booth's Spirit 101; and the President's Medium 112; spirit 98, 101–03, 107, 118–19; spirit's conversion 102
Lincoln, Mary Todd: insanity 109; meeting with medium 107, 109, 121; séance 116; spirit photograph 106
Lincoln, Robert 122
Lincoln, Tad 108
Lincoln, Willie 104
Lindall, Mrs. 106–07
Lowell, Col. Charles Russell 144–47

machines: perpetual motion 24; spirit 87; spiritoscopes 26; spiritual 36
Mahan, Asa 37
Mason, Philip 175
Maynard, Nettie Colburn 49, 114, *117*, 119–21; *Was Abraham Lincoln a Spiritualist?* 120
McAlpin, Harvey 44
McClellan, Gen. George B. 52
McFarland, Andrew 57, 68
McQueen, John 83
Merritt, Lizzie 88
Message Department 136, 138
military ministers 56
Morris Island 168, 170–72
Morriston, Robert 142
Mosby, Maj. John 145
Mosby's Raiders 145, 147
Mountain Cove 13–16
Mumler, William 106
murder 6, 89, 141
Murphy, John 181

National Convention of American Spiritualists 66
Nevada 74
New Jersey 43, 88, 162–63
Newton, Alonzo 31
Niblo's Saloon 63
Nicolay, John G. 120–21

O'Brien, John 179
O'Connell, Patrick 182
odylic forces 38
Ormsby, William E. 144–48, 151–52
Owen, Robert Dale 94–95

Packard, Elizabeth 67–68
Packard, Theophilus 67
Paige, Jim 154
Paist, Samuel H. 70
Payne, George P. 38
Peebles, James Martin 48, 66
Peer, James 170–71
Peer, John 171

Peer, Sarah 171
phrenology 12–13, 183
Pierpont, John 71–72
Poe, Edgar Allan 99
Poughkeepsie Seer 31, 33

Reed, Charles 75–76
Reidelberg, Robert 155
Ropes, Philip 186
Rynders, Isaiah 11–12

St. Augustine 121
St. George sisters 62–63
Salem Seer 50
Salle Diabolique 77
Sampson, William 170, 172–73
San Francisco 16, 72, 144
Sanderson, Henry T. 160
Saratoga Hall 70–71, 78
Sawyer, Joseph L. 159
Scott, J.L. 13–16
séances: Booth's spirit 108; Frances Conant 132, 135; Lincoln's spirit 102; Mrs. Lincoln 116; parody 101; soldiers attending 140; White House 92, 96
second sight 77, 98, 130
Shaw, Robert G. 167
Sheridan, Gen. Philip 90
skeptics 8–9, 35, 38, 47, 53, 59–60, 64, 83, 87, 136
Smeed's Hall 71
Smith, Michael 178
Smith, William H. 154
Smithsonian Institution 95
Smyth, James L. 159
somnambulism 41, 73
Sothern, Edward Askew **82**–83
South Carolina 45, 53, 70, 104, 141, 149, 168, 170, 174
southern newspapers 53, 85
Sowie, William 170–72
Spear, John Murray 23
spirit cabinet 58–60, 63, 84–85
spirit messages: faking 101; monthly 139; published 150; soldiers 140; soldiers' regiments 142
spirit photography **105**
spirit trumpet 61–62
spirits: amorous 53; anguished 174; bad 30; benevolent 14; child 187–88; confederate 141; endorsing Lincoln 97; photograph 106; rappings 35; woman 180, 186, **188**
Spiritual Age 31
Spiritual and Moral Instructor 13, 15–16
Spiritual Magazine 82, 124

Spiritual Telegraph 16, 34–35, 37, 126
Spiritualism: advertisements 30–31, 47, 126; afterlife and religion 161, 180–82; afterlife and slavery 170; afterlife and suicide 184; afterlife blissful 29; afterlife explained 4, 24, 136, 139; afterlife regrets 159; afterlife reunion 2, 104, 109; Booth's punishment 101; critics 30, 33; equality 4; frequency 3; Lincoln's death 98; modern origins 4; philosophy 12, 33; publications 124
Stanton, Edwin 94, 97, 167
Stillings, Joseph 157
suicide 44, 184–86; mother 130; paired 44
Summer Land 129

table tipping: artifice 39; telekinetic 38
Taylor, Bayard 41
temperance 126
Texas 125
Thompson, Rebecca 186
Thornton, Billy 162
Thorpe Brothers 63–64, 78
Tibbets, Luther 89–90
Torrey, Abram 163
Townsend, Milo 45
transition: ethereal 13; evil 13; mother's 134; painless 129, 190; seamless 129; soldier's 129
trial: Baham 13; Colchester 78–82; insanity 68; Ormsby 147
Tuttle, Hudson 183
Twitchell, Joseph 15

Underhill, Abel 69

Van Vleck, F.W. 86
Vermont 45, 47, 161
Vinton, Francis 102

Waldron, Janette 30
Walsh, Patrick 179
Ward, Artemus 93–94
Weekman, Michael 5
Weld, Col. Thomas 164
White, William 132
Whiting, A.B. 30
Whitney, John Francis 121
Whittier, Joseph 150
Wilcoxson, Mary J. 104
Williams, Charles 166
Williams, Clark 36
Wilson, Ebenezer V. 130
Wiltsie, Nellie L. 53
Woodbridge, Thomas 159
Woodbury, Jack 157

www.ingramcontent.com/pod-product-compliance
Ingram Content Group UK Ltd.
Pitfield, Milton Keynes, MK11 3LW, UK
UKHW041953140426
5217IPUK00015B/780